BUILDING JEWISH ROOTS

Building Jewish Roots

The Israel Experience

FAYDRA SHAPIRO

McGill-Queen's University Press

Montreal & Kingston · London · Ithaca

305.235089
S52b

© McGill-Queen's University Press 2006
ISBN-13: 978-0-7735-3065-2   ISBN-10: 0-7735-3065-7

Legal deposit third quarter 2006
Bibliothèque nationale du Québec

Printed in Canada on acid-free paper

This book has been published with the help of a grant from the Canadian Federation for the Humanities and Social Sciences, through the Aid to Scholarly Publications Programme, using funds provided by the Social Sciences and Humanities Research Council of Canada.

McGill-Queen's University Press acknowledges the support of the Canada Council for the Arts for our publishing program. We also acknowledge the financial support of the Government of Canada through the Book Publishing Industry Development Program (BPIDP) for our publishing activities.

National Library of Canada Cataloguing in Publication

Shapiro, Faydra, 1970–
    Building Jewish roots : the Israel experience / Faydra Shapiro.
    Includes bibliographical references and index.
    ISBN-13: 978-0-7735-3065-2   ISBN-10: 0-7735-3065-7
    1. Jews, American – Education – Israel. 2. Jews, Canadian – Education – Israel. 3. Jewish youth – Education – Israel. 4. Jews – United States – Identity. 5. Jews – Canada – Identity. 6. Israel and the diasporal. I. Title.
    DS143.S446 2006   305.235089'924073   C2006-901142-7

Typeset in Sabon 10.5/13
by Infoscan Collette, Quebec City

For my parents, Michael Shapiro and Rosalie Shapiro,
who had the foresight to take us to Israel that first time.

אנו באנו ארצה לבנות ולהבנות בה
Anu banu artza livnot u'lehibanot bah
(We came to the land to build and be built by it)

Contents

Acknowledgments

Until I began writing these acknowledgments, the difference between sole-authorship and a collaborative effort seemed clear. It is only now, recognizing the assistance that I have received from different people, that I see how humbled the "sole" author should be. I feel extremely lucky to have such family, colleagues, and friends. Any insights and strengths of this book are the product of many hands, minds, and voices. Its weaknesses, at least, I can lay claim to being my own.

My thanks go out to the staff at McGill-Queen's, particularly to Kyla Madden for her patient suggestions, and to Don Akenson for his encouraging words to a graduate student many years ago. David Schwinghamer's copyediting improved the final version of the manuscript significantly. This project received funding from the Social Sciences and Humanities Research Council of Canada, and its publication was supported by the Canadian Federation of Humanities and Social Sciences, Aid to Scholarly Publications Programme. As such, I am indebted to the working Canadians whose tax dollars make such programs possible.

The first incarnation of this book was as a doctoral dissertation in the Department of Religious Studies at McMaster University. The work was guided by Ellen Badone's watchful eye, and I was often steadied by her confidence. My deep appreciation goes out to her, and to others who read, questioned, and supported the work at that stage – Louis Greenspan, Adele Reinhartz, Stuart Schoenfeld, and Billy Shaffir in Canada, and Harvey Goldberg and Steven Cohen in Israel. Paula Holmes and Lainie Tessier were there at every turn.

My heartfelt thanks also to colleagues and students in the Department of Religion and Culture at Wilfrid Laurier University. I am especially grateful to Ron Grimes for his constant encouragement and careful advice, and to Louise Gilmour and Shari Lash for their editorial assistance. Special thanks are owed to Paul Bramadat and to various anonymous reviewers for reading the manuscript. Their helpful comments only strengthened this effort.

This entire project would not have been possible without the exceptional assistance I received from people connected with Livnot U'Lehibanot itself. The Botzer, Evven-Esh, Shizgal, Nachmani, and Kahan families have been a long-term source of inspiration. I was honoured that so many Livnot participants from different programs gave of their personal time and stories to enable and enliven this research.

Finally, I am deeply grateful to my husband, Shaul Katzenstein, who has lived with this project, in various stages, as long as he has known me. The sacrifices that both he and our children have made for my work have been significant, and appreciated. Without the constant interruptions of a growing family, this book would have been completed sooner, but with much less love and laughter around it.

Glossary

ahavat ha'aretz: love of the land
aliyah: literally "ascent"; a term that denotes immigration to Israel
am yisrael: the nation of Israel; the Jewish people
Ashkenazi: Jews of central or eastern European descent

ba'al teshuvah (plural: ba'alei teshuvah): literally "master of repentance/
   return"; denotes a Jew who has assumed a more observant lifestyle
   than he or she was raised with
ben adam la Makom: literally "between a person and God"; refers to
   observances that involve only one's relationship with the divine
ben adam le chavero: literally "between a person and his fellow"; refers
   to observances that include interpersonal relationships
brachot: blessings

Chabadniks: Jews affiliated with Chabad Lubavitch, a large and
   influential branch of Hasidism
chadar ochel: a dining hall
challah: a special egg bread baked for *shabbat* and holidays
chevre: a group of friends
chevruta (pl. chevrutot): study partners
chutz la'aretz: literally "outside the land"; refers to anywhere outside
   of Israel

davening: praying
dvar Torah (pl. divrei Torah): literally "words of Torah"; refers to a
   commentary or oral teaching about a specific Torah passage

eretz yisrael: the land of Israel

haftorah: the additional weekly portion of the Bible, from prophets or
   the writings, read in synagogue on *shabbat*, following the Torah
   portion
halacha (halachic): Jewish law; conforming to Jewish law
haredi (pl. haredim): ultra-orthodox Jews
Hashem: literally "The Name"; a common term used to refer to God
hashkafic: from *Hashkafa* or philosophy, this term suggests something
   that is committed to a single philosophical outlook
Havdalah: a ritual marking the end of *shabbat*, on Saturday at nightfall
havurah: a small, informal prayer group

Kabbalat Shabbat: an additional prayer service to mark the beginning
   of *shabbat* on Friday evening after sundown
Kaddish: Aramaic prayer praising God, used to separate sections of the
   service and also recited by those in mourning
kashrut: dietary laws
Kiddush: *shabbat* or holiday blessings over wine
Kikar Meginim: "Defenders Square" in the Old City of Tzfat
kipah (pl. kipot): a ritual head covering commonly worn by men; also
   known as "skullcap" or "yarmulke"
kiruv rechokim: literally "bringing close those who are distant"; outreach
   by observant Jews to those who are less observant
kol hakavod: literally "all the honour"; used to congratulate someone
   on a job well done
lashon hara: literally "the evil tongue"; refers to pointless gossip or
   speech with malicious intention
kugel: a crusty baked pudding made of potatoes or noodles

Lecha Dodi: a prayer welcoming *shabbat*, described as a bride
Livnot U'Lehibanot: literally "to build and to be built"

maariv: an evening prayer service
madrich (plural: madrichim): a guide; can refer to a tour guide, counselor,
   leader
matzah: unleavened bread eaten during Passover
mechitza: the physical divider that separates men from women in an
   orthodox synagogue
medinat yisrael: the modern State of Israel founded in 1948

Midrash: a commentary on the Torah

mikvah: a pool of water used for ritual immersion

mitzvot: commandments or obligations

Mizrachi: literally "eastern"; used to refer to Jews from the Middle East and North Africa

Modeh Ani: a short prayer recited upon awakening

nigun: a wordless melody

nikayon: cleaning

oneg shabbat: literally "sabbath delight"; refers to a *shabbat* social gathering that includes snacks and *divrei Torah*

payot (Yiddish: payos): unshorn sidelocks of observant Jewish men

psukim: verses of the Torah

Rosh Chodesh: the new moon marking the start of the Hebrew month

seder: literally: "order"; the ritual meal on Passover

sefer Torah: handwritten Torah scroll used for public reading in the synagogue

Sepharadi: Jews with origins in the Iberian Peninsula; often used in a colloquial sense to refer to all non-*Ashkenazi* Jews, including *Mizrachi* Jews

sheitel: a wig; one common way for observant women to cover their hair in public

Shema: literally "hear"; the central Jewish prayer derived from Deuteronomy 6 that begins "Hear O Israel, the Lord is our God, the Lord is One"

shofar: A ram's horn, blown on Rosh Hashanah and at the conclusion of Yom Kippur

shomer negiah: the abstention of premarital physical intimacy between the sexes

shul: synagogue

siddur: a prayer book

Simchat Torah: a festival celebrating the end of the cycle of public Torah readings, and beginning the cycle anew

streimel: a circular fur hat worn by some Hassidic Jewish men

sukkah: temporary hut built for the festival of Sukkot, used for eating and sleeping

Sukkot: the seven-day fall festival commemorating the wandering of the Israelites in the wilderness for forty years following the Exodus from Egypt

taharat hamishpacha: laws governing physical intimacy between husband and wife

tanna (pl. tannaim): a teacher from the Mishnaic period

tfillin: two small black leather cubes containing parchment scrolls inscribed with biblical passages, bound to the arm and forehead with leather straps by men each weekday morning

tikkun olam: repair of the world

tiyul (pl. tiyulim): a hike

toranut: a rotation

tzitzit: fringes required on a four-cornered garment, also worn ritually

Vayikra: literally "and He called"; the biblical book of Leviticus

wadi: a dry riverbed that is filled with water for a short time during the winter rainy season

yediat ha'aretz: knowledge of the land

yeshiva: an institution for the advanced study of Jewish texts

BUILDING JEWISH ROOTS

I

Introduction

We stood together on a rooftop in northern Israel, watching a vast expanse of sky melt a fiery orange and red over the mountains. Small birds circled lazily over our heads. The gathering of North American Jews in their twenties swayed gently back and forth. The girls were dressed in skirts and sandals, standing off to the left side of the roof, while the young men in their white shirts and dark pants congregated to the right. It might have been a scene out of any religious Jewish youth group as we welcomed the Sabbath Bride with the traditional words that were written not far from that very place:

> Wake up! Wake up!
> For your light has come, rise up and shine;
> Awaken, awaken, utter a song,
> The glory of Hashem is revealed on you
> Come my beloved to greet the bride – the Sabbath presence, let us welcome![1]

But a closer look at the group reveals unexpected features for such a religious context – a pierced tongue here, a tattoo there, lesbians, psychic healers, budding careerists, dope smokers, graduate students, environmental activists, ex-Deadheads, and "all-American" kids among them. Many individuals struggled with the unfamiliar Hebrew words, while others gazed out silently, watching the sun set in all its radiant splendour. Some participants stood with their arms looped around the waists of friends, eyes moist with tears.

In 1992, I reluctantly returned to Israel after a month-long adventure in Egypt. I was twenty-two years old, and in need of a change of scene before starting graduate study. Toughened, dirty, and exhilarated by my own independence, I found myself suddenly reluctant to follow my original plan to spend three months on a work-study program, Livnot U'Lehibanot. After all, I remember thinking, what could I possibly have in common with the spoiled young Jews I expected to meet there? I wanted the challenges and thrill of travel, not some easy, pampered environment. Reminding myself that I was free to leave anytime, I decided to give the program a try, and hauled my bags up north to Tzfat. I had no idea what I was in for, or that I was about to have an experience that would continue to challenge me in the most fundamental ways for years to come.

When I came to Livnot, I was at most moderately interested in Judaism, having written an undergraduate essay on the twentieth-century successes of the Chassidic sect of *Chabad-Lubavitch* in North America.[2] While doing that research, I had stumbled upon the perplexing phenomenon of newly-religious Jews, which would become the topic of my Masters thesis a few years later. At the time, I simply could not relate to the desire some people had to become observant. While I had been raised in an active, conservative Jewish home, I had rejected Judaism as a teenager, declaring it irrelevant, unspiritual, and unsatisfying. I had few Jewish friends, little Jewish involvement, and a curiosity inspired only by my inability to make intellectual sense of others' commitments to Judaism.

I had, however, retained fond memories of a family trip to Israel. Returning seemed like a practical, logical option – neither too dull nor too risky a venture, and one that my parents supported. I chose to take part in Livnot, more specifically, because it was inexpensive, and of long enough duration to be more serious than simply touristic but short enough that I could return to school in September. The program's offer of a healthy balance of work, hiking, and study was appealing, and far surpassed the short-term alternatives for my age group in Israel. The option to study Hebrew bored me, *kibbutz* seemed like too much work, and *yeshiva* was simply out of the question for a self-defined heretic. Contrary to all my expectations, however, this particular Israel experience profoundly affected me.

It was just another unremarkably hot Israeli afternoon in 1992 when I sat in a tiny, damp, cavelike room to learn about death and mourning in Judaism. The teacher had an improbably long, unkempt beard, ritual fringes trailing from under his shirt, and the biggest *kipah* I had ever seen. Once I would have wondered what this guy could possibly teach me, the urban sophisticate. But after the class I remember standing with a girlfriend, tears in our eyes, embarrassed and stuttering, trying to articulate our developing feelings about Judaism. The depth, the richness, the immediacy of it all shocked us deeply. My attitudes were turned inside out that summer, when I felt I had found my true home in Israel. At Livnot, I nurtured a cautious but passionate curiosity about Judaism, surpassed what I thought were my physical and emotional limits, and shared intense personal relationships with the other group members. It was a time when all my assumptions and preconceptions about Jews, Judaism, and Israel were examined, questioned, and often found wanting. It was the time of my life.

This book examines the workings and significance of that program, Livnot U'Lehibanot, a three-month work-study experience in Israel for North American Jews in their twenties. I explore the Jewish message and methods of Livnot in order to assess its impact and significance for participants' Jewish lives. While Livnot is, as Jonathan Woocher suggested of another Jewish educational context, probably typical of nothing, it is indicative of a great deal.[3] Livnot is a prism through which numerous core facets of contemporary Jewish life in North America become visible, including Jewish education, assimilation, "personal" or "creative" spirituality, youth culture, and Jewish outreach (sometimes called "inreach").

THE SEARCH FOR A MEANINGFUL JEWISH IDENTITY IN THE TWENTIETH CENTURY

While assimilation and the ambivalent promises of integration into non-Jewish society are clearly not new experiences for Jews, responses to these challenges changed radically in the latter half of twentieth-century America following the Holocaust. While the goal of integration into American society by first and second generation immigrants was primary through the 1950s, Jewish survivalism was established as an important value. Once that integration seemed assured, however, concerns emerged that the homogenizing effect of anglo-conformity and the American melting pot ethos were eroding attachment to minority ethnic traditions and communities. As evidence of declining Jewish involvement mounted by the mid-1960s, the sense of threat to Jewish survival began to mount, coming to include fears of disappearance through assimilation and culture loss. In the same period, the emergence of the "black pride" movement in the 1960s lent a new legitimacy to more general causes of cultural survivalism, ethnic pride, and particularism. Moreover, during the Six-Day War of 1967, the perception that a desperately threatened Israel had been abandoned by the world committed American Jews in new ways to Israel and the survival of its people. It was during these late 1960s in particular that the major concern of American Jews was clearly transformed from integration into the dominant society to survival as an ethnically distinct group.

Since that time, an acute anxiety about assimilation, seen in increasing rates of intermarriage, combined with declining Jewish commitments, rates of synagogue affiliation, ritual participation, and Jewish education, has continued to grip the Jewish community. In a 1985 national sample of American Jews, a great majority of respondents agreed with the statement "The current rates of assimilation and intermarriage pose serious dangers to American Jewish survival."[4] At the institutional level, this anxiety is even more marked. Ensuring Jewish cultural continuity has come to be defined as the top priority of Jewish communal institutions in North America. Sociological studies of Jews in North America have mirrored this concern, and focused to a large degree on the situation of Jewish community life and trends in Jewish self-identification.

Overwhelmingly, the trope underlying Jewish accounts of North American Jewish life in the second half of the twentieth century is one of marked culture decline and loss. These fears increased dramatically following the release of the 1990 National Jewish Population Study, which showed a community with a much higher rate of intermarriage than expected. This survey spurred the Jewish community into action to deal with what came to be called a "crisis of continuity."

The Jewish community spends considerable resources on attempts to stem these perceived assimilationary trends. Educational and social programs, believed to contribute to the development of Jewish identity, are high priorities for North American Jewish institutions. This intense Jewish institutional concern with cultural continuity stands in marked contrast to the common perception that religious choices in the modern world have become private, individual issues.[5]

Programs promoted to maintain and strengthen Jewish identity and affiliation have included day schools, supplementary religious education, and the recreational and educational programs of Jewish community centres, youth movements, and summer camps. Another, more recently developed mechanism to encourage Jewish identity is the "Israel experience program," involving short-term travel, volunteer work, and/or study in Israel for young North American Jews. It was recently estimated that there are over 200 Israel programs, which include *kibbutz* work, archaeological digs, artistic trips, and Jewish studies programs. Spokespeople for Israel experience programs say that some

16,000 young American Jews travel to Israel each year.[6] Recognizing that no precise numbers are available, Steven Cohen estimates that about 7,000 North American Jewish youths annually participate in organized, educational Israel programs.[7]

Israel experience programs were envisioned by some as a simple, immediate panacea for the problems of decreasing Jewish affiliation and identification. While the following vision is wildly optimistic, the hope that it expresses is in no sense unique:

Imagine how the Jewish landscape would look if 30 percent of our youth were graduates of Israel trips ... The atmosphere would be colored by boys and girls filled with Jewish pride, ready to explore routes of affiliation and identification. They would have experienced a common bond and seek a community in which to continue to share their experience, promising increased participation in Jewish youth groups. We would also see a critical mass of young people returning with an agenda of concern for the welfare of Israel and the Jewish people, motivated by their new connections to the Jewish state.[8]

At the November 1998 general assembly meeting of the Council of Jewish Federations, a program called "Birthright Israel" was inaugurated, to begin in the year 2000.[9] Financed by the Israeli government, private donors, and the Council of Jewish Federations, the program commits to paying for the airfare to Israel and the first ten days of an Israel experience program for Jews aged fifteen to twenty-six. It is expected to cost 300 million dollars over five years. Michael Steinhardt, one of the initiators of the Birthright Israel program, described the almost ritual centrality that he hoped Israel programs would achieve in North American Jewish life: "It is our hope that the Birthright trip can develop into a tradition analogous to that of the Bar or Bat Mitzvah ... Our hope is that a trip to Israel will be another rite of passage of Jewish life."[10]

Businessmen and philanthropists Michael Steinhardt and Charles Bronfman are so deeply committed to this project that each is contributing five million dollars to the venture. Israel programs are clearly a central, well-supported, popular feature of young North American Jewish life, and many large North American cities have Israel program centres devoted to the recruitment of participants and dissemination of program information.

Anxiety about cultural assimilation and efforts to strengthen Jewish continuity describe the communal, institutional role of the Israel experience phenomenon. Far more illuminating is the personal side of the

Israel experience, and where it fits into peoples' late twentieth-century Jewish lives. For many individuals, post-1960s Jewish life has been characterized by a profound identity questioning and the search for a meaningful Judaism. Trends such as the *havurah* movement, Jewish renewal, and the *ba'al teshuvah* movement might all be viewed as part of this search.[11] While markedly different from each other, what these movements share is the desire to locate a Judaism that is felt to be spiritual, meaningful, and personally relevant. Where communal institutions have tended to emphasize survival and continuity, Jews themselves have been actively looking for more intimate communities, deeper participation, and a greater experiential aspect to their Judaism. In some ways, we might think of Livnot, as well as phenomena like the *havurah* movement, Jewish renewal, and the *ba'al teshuvah* movement, as part of a rejection of pure survivalist Judaism in favour of a "content-based" or "meaningful" Judaism. After all, communal survival must be worthwhile for a credible, compelling reason.

This search for a meaningful Judaism is, of course, part of a larger North American trend toward seeking a personal inner authenticity rather than locating one's identity in communal enterprises and group definitions. Observers of religious life have noted a post-1960s move away from organized institutional religion, and an increasingly powerful desire to create personal, spiritual life stories rather than inherit remembered narratives from generations past. The trend obviously affects not only Livnot participants, and not only Judaism in North America. Rather, as Wade Clark Roof explains, "the boundaries of popular religious communities are now being redrawn, encouraged by the quests of the large, post-World War II generations, and facilitated by the rise of an expanded spiritual marketplace."[12]

But self-fulfillment, personal authenticity, and choice are hardly traditional Jewish values. As criteria they contribute to the development of forms of Judaism that would have been unrecognizable to earlier generations. These are not necessarily dangerous developments. In fact, in many ways we might read the Livnot experience as bringing the individual and the group together, offering a vision of Judaism that might speak to the questing individual, but one that is grounded in a historical Jewish tradition and the Jewish community. As will be discussed below, Livnot participates in and encourages concepts of self-fulfillment, autonomy, and choice in the creation of personally meaningful Judaisms, making explicit use of the "marketplace" metaphor. At the same time, by carefully limiting the contents of that marketplace,

Livnot steers its audience toward buying communal, historical Jewish products, however attractively packaged. For the individual, there are abundant creative options for a post-Livnot Judaism. Livnot serves as the initial door through which those young people can become open to the possibility of a more meaningful Judaism, a possibility that was unavailable to them before they possessed an active interest or desire to search, let alone adequate Jewish tools or vocabulary for that search.

As no book can be all things to all readers, let me state at the outset what this book is not. While *Building Jewish Roots* describes the workings and effects of a Jewish educational experience, this is not a study of Jewish education per se. Certainly many of the specific pedagogical techniques used at Livnot are present in other forms of Jewish education across the denominational spectrum. Readers interested in Jewish education will, I believe, find in this book a detailed case study of informal education for young adults. Similarly, Jewish community activists will find an in-depth examination of how one long-standing Israel experience program works, and perhaps does not work. For an ethnic group that allocates a massive amount of communal resources to both education and Israel experience programs, the Livnot program is worthy of careful investigation.

Building Jewish Roots is aimed squarely at readers interested in the broader questions of contemporary North American religion. Too often, material that examines Jews as a case study is parochial, limiting its engagement to a very narrow field of Jewish community vision and rendering it of questionable value to larger concerns of religious studies, sociology, and anthropology.

This book speaks to many well-documented themes in contemporary North American religion, such as religious individualism, privatism, and postmodernism. But several aspects of this study differentiate it from other explorations of post-1960s religion in North America, such as Robert Bellah's *Habits of the Heart* (1985), Robert Wuthnow's *After Heaven* (1998), and Wade Clark Roof's *Spiritual Marketplace* (1999).

First, this book focuses on a single group. While a general survey is crucial to illuminate the broader phenomenon, I am convinced that at least some of the truth lies in the details. It is also significant that the case study of this work is Jewish. While I do not mean to suggest that the Jewish story is entirely different from that of mainstream Christian America, the specific Jewish experience and the realities of living as part of a minority religion nuance the picture in significant ways. Finally, related literature on the contemporary American religious landscape addresses the baby boom generation. In contrast, *Building Jewish Roots Built* speaks of the next generation, the children of baby boomers, investigating their own processes of religious and ethnic identity construction. It is a group for whom feminism and the metaphor of the religious "supermarket" are taken for granted. It is also a group whose members have far less knowledge of institutional religion than did their parents, as a result of how their parents chose to raise them.

Anyone surveying the religious scene over the last few decades will not be surprised to learn that, as Wade Clark Roof observes, "religious identities in contemporary society are fluid, multilayered, and to a considerable extent personally achieved."[13] Often with pejorative connotations, it is now commonplace to label much of North American religious life as eclectic, do-it-yourself, supermarket, salad-bar, à-la-carte, cafeteria, smorgasbord, pick and choose, individualistic, or postmodern. North American Judaism is, of course, no exception.

In a recent work, Barack Fishman proposes a model of "coalescence" to describe the way that American Jews integrate American and Jewish aspects of their lives. She carefully distinguishes coalescence from "adaptation." Adaptation, the author suggests, points to a continuing awareness of the distinct nature of those "American" and "Jewish" aspects being brought together, whereas coalescence implies a more radical merging of the two. As she explains, "In coalescing American values and Jewish values, many American Jews – including some who are very knowledgeable and actively involved in Jewish life – no longer separate or are even conscious of the separation between the origins of these two texts."[14]

Cohen and Eisen document similar trends in American Jewry. Examining moderately affiliated Jews, they point to the tendency toward a subjective, personal Judaism whose contours are more idiosyncratic than in previous generations. Much like Livnot participants, the Jews with whom they spoke "celebrate the autonomy of this choosing and do not worry about its authenticity."[15]

Like these studies, *Building Jewish Roots* acknowledges the mixed, hybrid, subjective nature of Jewish life in the contemporary world. In contrast to other studies, this work examines this very phenomenon of coalescence and the making of personal Judaisms, in action. It offers a dynamic picture of the process by which unaffiliated young adults with little Jewish education respond to and integrate a significant Jewish experience, and the ways that they construct their own Jewish identities in response. It documents a part of the process by which individuals journey from what Roof calls "I happen to be" religion[16] to "I choose to be" religion.

METHODOLOGY

This study employs qualitative, ethnographic, and interview methods in order to understand the Livnot U'Lehibanot participants' conceptions of themselves as Jews, their experiences in the program, and the long-term effects of those experiences on alumni. Briefly, ethnographic field-work involves the direct observation of human actions and events in their natural settings, rather than in an artificial, academic, or labora-tory environment. This method requires direct participation in others' daily lives, to gain an intimate, insider or "emic" point of view in addi-tion to a more distanced, analytic, or "etic" perspective. In order to increase analytic depth and to ascertain the validity of observer impres-sions, participant observation is often supplemented by such methods as interviews and document analysis. Ethnographic data is produced in the form of field notes, journals, and interview transcriptions. This kind of qualitative data can offer a holistic view of social phenomena and a more nuanced portrait of complex human situations than is provided by quantitative social research. Referring to such limitations, a number of social scientific studies of contemporary Judaism have pointed to an excessive reliance on quantitative analysis in this field, and called for greater use of qualitative methods.[17]

My fieldwork took place in several places and over several periods. In Israel, I engaged in participant-observation at Livnot and interviewed participants during much of the 1996 summer program, and through-out the entire program in fall 1997. I also interviewed past-participants in Israel, Toronto, New York, and San Francisco. In addition, I carried out many telephone interviews with Livnot alumni[18] across Canada and the United States. Interviews with past participants took place between fall 1997 and fall 1998.

A total of sixty-eight Livnot participants, past participants, and staff members were interviewed during the course of this research. Twenty-seven individuals were interviewed while they were taking part in Livnot, nine in 1996 and eighteen in 1997. Interviews were also carried out with eight staff members at Livnot, in 1996 and 1997. Of the twenty-seven participants that were interviewed during the program, twenty-three were interviewed twice, once close to the beginning and again toward the end of the program. Four key staff members were interviewed twice.

Forty-nine individuals were interviewed after they had completed the program. This number includes sixteen "follow up" interviews with participants who had been interviewed while they were at Livnot and an additional thirty-three people who had done the program in the six years prior to the interview. Thus, in sum, one hundred and eleven interviews took place with sixty-eight people. Of the thirty-three individuals who were interviewed only after they had completed the Livnot program, five resided in Canada, eight in Israel, nine in New York city, nine in the San Francisco Bay area, and two in other American cities (Chicago and Portland, Oregon). The nineteen "follow up" interviews involved participants living all over North America, from Euless, Texas, to Columbus, Ohio, Manhattan to Denver, and Vancouver to Santa Fe.

Thirty-eight of the participants interviewed were women, and twenty-two were men.[19] Sixteen individuals were interviewed between six months and a year after they had finished Livnot. Three people were interviewed less than two years after completing the program. A further six were interviewed less than three years following Livnot, and ten people were interviewed less than four years after doing the program. Three individuals were interviewed less than five years after Livnot, eight people were interviewed less than six years following the program, and three more were interviewed less than seven years after their Livnot experience. Whether conducted in person or by telephone, interviews lasted from forty-five minutes to three hours in length.

Livnot has changed since I did my research there. Buildings have been acquired and lost, staff members come and gone, new philanthropic partnerships made, and different kinds of programs developed. The three-month program of which I write no longer exists; in its place are options of both shorter and longer programs, as well as specialized versions of Livnot.

THE ENGAGED SCHOLAR

Clearly, it is significant for this research that before I came to the field in a research capacity, I had also taken part in the program both as a participant and, one year later, as a temporary staff member, acting as *madricha* or guide for other participants. While it is now commonly accepted that the ethnographer's partiality inescapably affects the collection, interpretation, and representation of data, the self is still perceived by some to be a research liability. Indeed, the view in anthropology has largely been to accept authorial positioning as an inescapable feature of ethnography and to admit its presence, rather than to consider how the ethnographer's self might actually serve our understanding of others in a valuable fashion.[20]

Since, during my Livnot fieldwork, I was both an academic engaged in ethnographic research and a member of the community under study, I had access to the confusing, exhilarating, bi-focal perspective of the "native" or "indigenous" anthropologist.[21] This perspective permitted me a privileged insight into the emotions and struggles of my respondents. I had myself shared in some of these struggles and emotions. Moreover, I was able to recognize that just as my own responses, complexities, and voice cannot be totally subsumed into a homogenizing generalization, so too Livnot participants and alumni possess individual, particular, and unique experiences.

During the research at Livnot itself, I was clearly, to some degree, an outsider. My ubiquitous tape recorder, late-night sessions at the computer, constant interviewing, and a degree of emotional detachment from the intense processes that participants were undergoing all marked me as different. Yet I was also an insider, called on for emotional support and sought out for feedback as someone who had been through the program before. I was granted privileged access to participants, past participants, staff members, and private meetings, as I was both a Livnot past participant and former staff member. Maintaining this double role of insider and outsider became complicated at times, occasionally leaving me unsure of my position. Staff members wondered aloud if perhaps my study of Judaism was simply a strategy to avoid practicing it. They were also concerned about my personal involvement with a non-Jewish partner and the message that relationship might send to participants. Staff members also requested my impressions of problematic participants and group dynamics whenever tensions developed. Participants questioned me closely on my feelings about and commitments to Judaism, grilled me about my personal life, and sometimes looked askance at my choices. I observed these people and the culture of Livnot from across a vast distance of theory, academic cynicism, and jargon. I also danced with them, wept with them, slept beside them, and was awed next to them by the experiences we shared.

In *The Vulnerable Observer*, Ruth Behar discusses the role of the self, emotion, personal experience, and autobiography in the production and consumption of anthropological knowledge. The conclusion to her final chapter is haunting. She writes, "Call it sentimental, call it Victorian and nineteenth century, but I say that anthropology that doesn't break your heart just isn't worth doing anymore."[22] The path of my own research, fieldwork, and writing has been littered with broken hearts and self-investigation. That this ethnographic work has been directly responsible for a renewal of my own levels of Jewish observance and involvement is something for which I am deeply grateful. At the same time, the fact that this project has never been "just" research adds a special burden. Talking with Livnot participants about their own Jewish identities and commitments prompted me to ask similar questions of myself. Anthropologist Jonathan Boyarin points out, "a degree of auto-cannibalism (self-absorption?) is inevitable for an academic writing about the problematics of 'his own' collective identity."[23] Being open to that vulnerability of which Behar writes, to the possibility of being moved, increased my ability to understand and empathize with the narratives of others who had experienced Livnot. It was truly anthropology worth doing.

OUTLINE

Following this introduction, chapter 2 explores the ethnographic context of Livnot U'Lehibanot. An in-depth look at life at Livnot – including the physical setting for the program, a typical day, hiking, and *shabbat* – this chapter provides the reader with a "thick description" that seeks to evoke the experience of Livnot in a way that makes the following analyses both compelling and plausible. At the end of chapter 2, the Jewish backgrounds of seven Livnot participants are profiled, including an exploration of their motives for attending Livnot, in an attempt to offer a nuanced and empathetic portrait of program participants. Finally, a few selected vignettes of life at Livnot are described for the reader. These are episodes which were significant for participants and which individual participants alluded to as cherished memories. Through these "snapshots," I hope to recreate for the reader some of the subtle, emotional moments that are crucial to participants' experiences at Livnot.

Chapter 3 opens a three-chapter analysis of Livnot's message, presentation, and goals in order to more closely examine the Jewish worldviews that participants learn and in which they participate. The chapter centres on the issue of land, analysing the construction of Israel offered by Livnot and the ways in which Israel is transformed for participants from a vague, unfamiliar space to a holy place. Chapter 4, focusing on the Jewish nation, examines the selective presentation of Jewish history and the Jewish people at Livnot, to show how the program constructs for participants a sense of familiarity and kinship with the Jewish people across history and space. Chapter 5 explores Judaism itself, and the ways in which the Jewish religious tradition is chosen by Livnot staff and selectively emphasized to appeal to an audience of young, liberal, North American Jews.

Chapter 6 explores the Jewish lives of past participants, following their experience of Livnot, with attention to both general trends and specific examples of the ways in which past participants create diverse and hybrid Jewish identities and commitments for themselves by drawing on the information and experiences they acquired at Livnot. It is here that the reader will encounter some of the critical views of the program. While the vast majority of responses that I encountered were positive, this is not meant to imply a unanimously positive experience of the program. Thus, chapter 6 also examines the ways in which Livnot controls dissent.

The final chapter discusses the role of Livnot in an attempt to go beyond Jewish community concerns about assimilation and emphasis on cultural continuity. I suggest that Livnot offers participants knowledge and experience that empowers them to make informed Jewish decisions. In this sense, Livnot provides participants with agency by enabling them to pick and choose from Jewish tradition in order to fashion their own creative, personal Jewish identities.

2

Life at Livnot

The core campus[1] of Livnot U'Lehibanot is located in Tzfat, in the Upper Galilee, a city of about 24,000 people. Perched atop Mount Canaan, the city is located inland and quite far north, not far from the Lebanese border. Tzfat is traditionally known as one of four Jewish holy cities in Israel, an honour shared with Jerusalem, Hebron, and Tiberias. Briefly mentioned in the Talmud, Tzfat was one of the summits upon which beacons were once lit to mark new months and the new year.[2] This small, ancient village achieved prominence during the Crusader period, when it was transformed into a regional centre. The king of Jerusalem, Fulk of Anjou (1131–43), built a fortress there in 1140 to guard the village because of its strategic location close to the Acre-Damascus trade route. The castle housed some 2,000 permanent soldiers and was the largest Crusader fortress built in Palestine. In 1168 the castle became Templar property, only to be destroyed in 1266 by the Mamelukes.

Under the Mameluke regime in the fourteenth century, Tzfat became the capital of the Galilee region. While the town developed into a centre of Muslim activity and culture in this period, it also swelled with Jews, a result of the Spanish expulsion. After Palestine became part of the Ottoman Empire in 1516, Jewish immigration increased from Turkey and European countries. Immigrants chose Tzfat because it was both the Jewish centre closest to Syria, and it was close to the graves of several sages from the Mishnaic period.[3] Unlike Jerusalem, which was economically weak in this period, Tzfat also possessed the advantage of being a location that was not revered by any another religious traditions. The town developed a strong economy based on weaving and dyeing, which was aided by its proximity to the harbours of Acre and Sidon for the import of wool and the export of finished products to Europe. The nearby water sources required for textile manufacturing also helped promote this industrial specialization. In 1535 an Italian Jew observed: "as in Italy, [where] improvements are being made and new plantations planted and the community is growing every day, so it is in this city. Anyone who saw Safed[4] ten years ago and sees her now must marvel. For Jews are coming plentifully all the time and the garment-making industry is increasing every day."[5]

By the middle of the sixteenth century, Tzfat had expanded into a major cultural and spiritual centre of world Jewry as the *Kabbalah*, the Jewish mystical tradition, underwent a period of particular creativity and development. Brought with the Spanish exiles, the *Kabbalah* was used to give cosmic significance to the human dramas of exile and the hope for redemption. The most fundamental text of the Jewish mystical tradition is the *Sefer Ha-Zohar* (The Book of Radiance), which is commonly believed by scholars to have been composed in late thirteenth-century Castile. Jewish tradition, however, attributes this text to R. Simeon bar Yochai, the second century teacher whose grave, tradition has it, is located at Meron, quite close to Tzfat. The proximity of this "mystical" grave site, in tandem with the economic considerations mentioned above, attracted some of the greatest Jewish minds of the time to Tzfat, including Joseph Caro, Solomon Alkabetz, Isaac Luria, and Moses Cordovero. Their scholarly presence helped to fuel Tzfat's population growth, and its development as a religious centre, and ultimately effected nothing less than a renaissance of Jewish mysticism. For it was in sixteenth-century Tzfat that the Lurianic formulation of *Kabbalah* took shape,[6] with its vital mystical developments and new conceptual directions for the process of creation, the problem of evil, and the nature of God, as well as exile and restoration.

This period of intense intellectual, spiritual, and commercial success was short-lived, however. By the end of the sixteenth century, European countries had begun to manufacture their own cloth, and Tzfat was unable to compete. This economic decline, compounded by epidemics and a series of earthquakes, caused great harm to the community. While the town was strengthened by eighteenth-century immigration from central Europe to Palestine, and immigration of Hassidim from Eastern Europe, this improvement did not last long. Another series of natural disasters and plagues crippled the town. Following the worst of the earthquakes, in 1837, Tzfat's population was reduced through death and relocation to only several hundred people by 1845.

In the first half of the twentieth century, the Arab population of Tzfat greatly increased, to the point that by the early 1940s Jews made up only 17 per cent of the population – 2,114 Jews out of a total population of 11,980. The Jewish areas of the town suffered greatly under Arab siege in the 1948 War of Independence. But despite Arab numerical advantage, Tzfat fell into Jewish hands when the Arab population fled. Today, Tzfat is an entirely Jewish town.

Since the establishment of the state of Israel in 1948, it has become clear that Tzfat is more than just physically remote from the rest of Israel. The largely religious and predominately *Sepharadi*[7] population of Tzfat possessed a worldview and a way of life that was quite distinct from that of the largely European and secularist immigrants who came to Israel during the period of the British Mandate. Also, Tzfat did not fall easily into the two major strains of settlement development in Israel, being neither urban (like Haifa, Jerusalem, or Tel Aviv) nor agricultural. There is no doubt that Tzfat is unique in Israel, often viewed by Israelis as old-fashioned, quaint, and unusual. For most of the Israelis outside Tzfat with whom I spoke, the idea of spending three entire months in Tzfat was inconceivable.

The ascent to Tzfat is spectacular. Isolated by its elevation of 2,720 feet, Tzfat is accessible by two main roads, one arriving from Acre on the Mediterranean coast and the other from near Tiberias. Approaching from the west, it appears that the town is hanging off the face of the mountain it sits on, its buildings barely clinging on. While the visitor is afforded no real view of Tzfat when arriving from Tiberias in the east, the climb itself is dramatic, beginning as one does from 680 feet below sea level. Dangerously steep and chillingly narrow, the road winds breathtakingly up the side of the mountain, offering sweeping views of the Sea of Galilee below. Public buses labour painfully through the approach, and it is precisely this arduous climb and geographical isolation which ensures that bus service is usually a local milk run. Efficient travel to most major cities from Tzfat requires a bus transfer in more accessible towns.

The newer part of Tzfat is a rather charmless array of concrete and apartment buildings. It is the old city of Tzfat that captures the imagination of travellers. The old city is small, made up of an intricate network of winding stone alleyways and stairs. There are no cars in the old city, except on parts of the main street. There are, however, access roads around the old city, and a large car park and tourist bus stop on the periphery. Because Tzfat is built on the west side of the mountain, one can walk across the town, or up and down the slope. It is easy to get lost there, to mistake one small passage for another, to become disoriented in the maze of similar stone and rubble. Owing to Mount Canaan's steep grade, there is no flat land for construction, leaving the town looking like a series of teetering, unstable rooftops and buildings built above or below each other. Tzfat's moderate summer weather, stunning mountain views, and quiet isolation have helped turn the town into a kind of short-term "getaway" resort for Israelis. At the same time, its extensive Jewish history, beautiful old synagogues, and diverse artists' galleries ensure that, however remote, Tzfat has an important place on the itineraries of many tour groups.

The vast majority of residents in the old city are devoutly religious, including a large Chassidic presence. Most of Tzfat's men dress in the general black and white look of the ultra-Orthodox, with small but telling variations among different sects. Women generally dress according to the modesty dictates of Jewish law and community standards, including long skirts, sleeves, and often stockings. It is a city of covered heads: for men, big round fur *streimels*, various shapes of black hats, and the occasional knitted *kipah* of the modern Orthodox; for women, wigs, large hats, or colourful flowing scarves which hide their hair from public view. The town has also developed into a flourishing colony of artists, many of whom are not religious. A large area of the old city is peppered with their galleries, showrooms, and shops for painting, sculpture, and pottery.

The old city is made up primarily of synagogues, homes, schools, *yeshivot*, and artists' galleries. Piles of loose garbage litter the streets in some areas, and a number of properties have been abandoned over time and left to ruin. The town is not at all well kept, and in many places it is distinctly dirty, rundown, and crumbling. The houses in Tzfat are old and often decrepit, some of them dating from the Ottoman period. With little in the way of real industry or extensive job opportunities, Tzfat is by no means affluent. Equally, the high number of ultra-Orthodox residents ensures the presence of many large families, which are often not well-to-do, dependent as they are on the government stipends that allow men to engage in full-time Torah study.

Close to the top of the town is Rechov Yerushalayim (Jerusalem Street), the old city's main thoroughfare. From the residential area below, one often arrives at Jerusalem Street short of breath, the result of trudging up several steep sets of stairs. Here one finds the most obvious traces of contemporary Israel. There are pizza shops, cafés and restaurants, the post office, grocery stores, banks, and a few small shops for clothing, books, and kitchen goods. On Rechov Yerushalayim, the town looks somewhat less homogeneous and medieval than it does in other places. Just above, at the highest point on the mountain, is the citadel, the ruins of the crusader castle. Surrounding the site is a large public park, one of the few blissfully green spaces in a town of otherwise unrelenting stone.

Kikar Meginim is a central square in the old city, from which several lanes run off in different directions. In the square itself sits a health food store, a souvenir and tourist art shop, the small workshop of a scribe, and an empty building that once housed a restaurant. The square boasts several benches and two public telephones which are always humming with activity. Its centrality and open space make it a popular place to congregate in a somewhat claustrophobic town where everything is built too close together. Heading downhill, a set of stairs leads past the Ashkenazi Ari synagogue, with its signs requesting modest dress and reminding tourists that photography is not permitted on *shabbat*. A flight of rough stone stairs finally deposits the visitor on Rechov Alkabetz, in front of a door surmounted by a somewhat incongruous, back-lit, blue and white sign which informs the reader in English that this is Livnot U'Lehibanot, To Build and To Be Built.

THE LIVNOT CAMPUS

The campus of Livnot U'Lehibanot consists of several buildings close together in a central area of the old city. Livnot occupies a thin strip that falls between two streets. At the top, that is, higher up the mountain, is Rechov Alkabetz, a central, pedestrian vein for the old city. At the lower edge of the campus is a rarely used narrow alley that runs from the car park on the edge of town into the core of Tzfat's complicated labyrinth of lanes and alleys. The actual number of Livnot buildings and the uses to which they are put have changed often over the years, depending on program needs, building schedules, and the tricky state of property claims in a city as ancient as Tzfat. While the campus is technically private property, there is nothing that actually separates it as an entity from the rest of the city. There are at least two buildings in the middle of the campus that do not belong to Livnot, but the owners of these properties are rarely in residence. Sometimes it can be difficult to tell precisely where a particular building begins and ends in Tzfat. As a result of the many earthquakes that have occurred in this region over the centuries, owners often buy a property only to discover several more rooms below it which had been buried over time. Livnot properties are no exception, and do not always consist of discrete buildings. To apply the word "campus" to Livnot seems too grand, too organized, too sterile for this somewhat ragged, homey collection of buildings.

After participants have spent a certain amount of time at Livnot, the campus comes to feel like a world unto itself. It is possible to go for days at a time without leaving this small area. Here the quiet, spiritual, pensive atmosphere of Tzfat gives way to something else entirely. For this part of the old city, Livnot, is inhabited by young North American men and women who come to stay for three months at a time. Often dashing around the campus in tight shorts and tank tops, shrieking at one another, slamming doors, laughing or chattering on the telephone, Livnot participants form a sharp contrast to the rest of Tzfat. Here the black and white, timeless aura of the old city gives way to a riotous technicolour range of orange t-shirts and bright green kerchiefs.

A tour of the campus would begin most naturally in the kitchen area since, as a large communal area, it is a spot where Livnot participants like to congregate. Entering through an unmarked door from Rechov Alkabetz, one comes into a hallway with a big open kitchen and serving window on the left. As the front door is often left open, it is not uncommon for tourists to come in from the street, thinking they have happened upon a public restaurant. The kitchen is large enough to accommodate cooking for groups, with a dairy side and meat side, in compliance with Orthodox dietary requirements. Industrial-sized pots and utensils are identified as either meat or dairy with a jagged, fading strip of red or blue spray paint. Clearly well used over the years, the pots are battered and burned, sporting mismatched lids and often lacking such amenities as handles. Plates, bowls, and cups are sensible plastic, dessicated from too much use. A graceful stone archway incongruously bisects part of the ceiling.

Beyond the immediate kitchen area is a dining space, called the *chadar ochel*, with several long tables surrounded by uncomfortable white-plastic chairs. The stone walls are decorated with maps of Israel and homemade posters of previous Livnot programs that include photographs of past participants. My own face looks down from some of these posters. As everywhere else at Livnot, the dining area floors are cold tile. The decor is sparse and utilitarian. A stairway leads upwards to the classroom, a large room with more long tables and plastic chairs. The only comforts are two tired, mouldy-smelling couches situated around the several bookshelves that make up Livnot's library. While the collection is restricted to books related to Judaism or Israel, it is diverse within those limits: everything from sacred texts to novels by Leon Uris, from works on the Holocaust to books about the holidays, from explorations of women in Judaism to guides to nature in Israel.

From the classroom, double doors lead out onto a spacious balcony, the rooftop of another building. The balcony is a cherished spot at all times of day, with its long panoramic view west, interrupted only by other mountains. However, it is particularly at sunset, when the sky explodes in a spectacular expanse of colours and hues, that people gasp and point open-mouthed at the beauty. Most big-city life has nothing to compare with such vistas.

Entering the lower part of the campus, down the stairs from Rechov Alkabetz, are several girls' rooms. These rooms resemble dark caves, built as they are into the bottom section of another building. The men's rooms are at the other end of the campus. Each room is romantically named after a natural site or region in Israel, such as Carmel, Tavor, Golan, Kinneret, and Gilboa. The reality is that rooms at Livnot are small and cramped, housing up to six men or six women in one room. Beds are sagging, tremendously-uncomfortable single cots jammed too close together.[8] Washroom facilities are spartan, with no shower stalls separating the user from the toilet, just the bare shower-head protruding from the wall in one corner and a drain in the floor. Storage space for clothes and personal items in the rooms is extremely limited, causing great consternation among female participants looking for room to hang dresses. As a rule, everything in Tzfat is prone to a great deal of dust, and the rooms at Livnot are no exception. While pleasantly cool in summer, the rooms are unheated and quite cold in the winter, requiring space heaters for comfort. Understandably, the first encounter with these conditions can be something of a shock for participants who often arrive from comfortable, upper–middle class North American homes.

In addition to these communal areas and rooms, the Livnot campus also has an office which hums with its own brand of chaos generated by two computers, several phone lines, a dilapidated photocopier, and a fax machine. The office is presided over by an extremely efficient secretary and is used by staff for everything from preparing classes on the computer to fundraising, from financial affairs to alumni contact.

Other buildings on campus include two private residences. One of these was formerly the program's kitchen and dining area and is now home to the coordinating couple.[9] The other home is that of Benjamin and Naomi Green, the founders and director of Livnot, along with their seven children. It was actually in their house that Livnot began in 1980.

A description of the Livnot campus requires several harsh adjectives: spartan, crumbling, comfortless, stony. And yet, at the same time, the campus is psychologically very comfortable and secure. Soon the physical discomforts come to seem normal for participants, or somehow praiseworthy. Everyone is happy to get back to Livnot after a long hike, a trip to the Jerusalem campus, or a free weekend. In no time at all, the campus comes to serve as home, a safe place of understanding, mutual support, and friendship where English is spoken and it's okay to wear tank tops. Once-taken-for-granted amenities like a microwave, bathtub, carpeting, television, or a room of one's own come to feel like luxuries.

TYPICAL DAYS

The regular daily schedule at Livnot can feel grueling at times. Wake-up is at 6:30 in the morning, and breakfast is at 6:45. Morning showers are unheard of at Livnot, and everyone arrives at breakfast in grubby work clothes. Israeli news in English is played on the radio at 7:00 a.m., followed by a commentary on the news and general announcements. Work begins at 7:30 a.m., and can involve several possible activities. Most of the manual labour at Livnot involves the reconstruction of buildings in Tzfat's old city. Such work usually means some combination of hauling rocks, clearing debris and garbage, chiselling, mixing cement in a wheelbarrow, mortaring, or other activities necessary for building or reconstruction. There are also a number of special projects that can be underway at any given time, and participants are sometimes divided into smaller groups to work at different sites. Groups might paint a mural on a school, repair headstones in a cemetery, operate a day camp for local children, or paint the houses of poor residents or new immigrants. The work is always physical, performed using extremely basic tools and aided by little in the way of training or safety protection. Most participants have had no manual labour experience, and find the work quite demanding, particularly at the beginning of the program. But work can also be a great deal of fun as an activity shared with a tightly knit group of people one's own age. This fact ensures that the actual labour is regularly punctuated by the singing of movie

tunes, impersonations, competitions, teasing, and the constant din of
conversation among participants about themselves and their lives, and
their opinions and thoughts about what they are learning at Livnot.
One staff member serves as a work coordinator, and his own disposition
affects the pace of work and its ratio to play. Midway through the
morning there is a fifteen-minute break with snacks of fresh fruit. Pre-
dictably, after several weeks of the program, the breaks and play sessions tend to get longer. Work ends at 11:30 a.m., in time for lunch,
which everyone eats together in the *chadar ochel* at the Livnot campus.

From noon until three o'clock, the *chevre*, as participants are called
at Livnot, enjoy a much needed free period, usually spent in some combination of reading, showering, napping, making telephone calls, writing letters home, and running errands in town. There is never quite
enough unstructured time to get everything done, and part of life at
Livnot is the constant feeling of being under tremendous time pressure.
Classes are given from 3 to 5 p.m. and from 5 to 7 p.m., with a short
break in between, and followed immediately by dinner. Classes, as I
describe below, are neither passive nor especially relaxing. Evening
activities vary, but always have some kind of educational goal. Everyone
is quite exhausted by that time, and it requires creative, interesting, and
non-demanding programming to keep people involved. Several evenings
each week are taken up with discussion groups, guest speakers, a charity
auction, role-playing, or movies that illustrate some theme from classes,
and which are followed by discussion. There are usually two free evenings each week, with participants getting some release from life at
Livnot by visiting cafés, watching a movie at Tzfat's community centre,
or simply relaxing. Tzfat has very little to offer young people in the
way of night life; there are just a couple of small bars, and the sole
dance club I remember from my own time at Livnot closed in the early
1990s. But simply getting away from campus and onto Jerusalem Street
for a slice of pizza is often sufficient to recharge batteries depleted by
the rigorous schedule.

While official programming usually ends by 11 p.m., intense late-
night conversation is *de rigueur* at Livnot. In the library, the *chadar
ochel*, in rooms, around town, or hanging out on the balcony, groups
of people cluster to talk about everything from personal experiences,
life plans, and Judaism, to lighter subjects like post-program travel and
the opposite sex. While some people do manage to get to bed at a
reasonable hour, finding oneself up talking until 1:30 in the morning is
not at all uncommon. These late-night discussions prove extremely

painful the next morning, at 6:30 wake-up, when it all begins again for these exhausted participants.

At Livnot, all cleaning and meal preparation is done on a rotational basis by participants. Each day, two or three people are on *toranut* (rotation), and are responsible for preparing the meals for that day. This task requires detailed planning of meals and ingredients the night before.[10] As Livnot runs on a very tight budget, available ingredients are extremely simple, and everyone is careful not to waste food. As a result, *chevre* on *toranut* are always checking for perishables that need to be used up and finding creative ways to reuse leftovers again and again. A day on *toranut* starts at 6 a.m. so that *chevre* can get a head start on breakfast and give a wake-up knock to each room. Instead of working at a building site, *toranut* entails a morning in the kitchen, and often a good part of the afternoon break, preparing lunch and dinner.

Standard Livnot breakfasts include Israeli cornflakes, which are tasteless but inexpensive, and some hot dish of eggs, oatmeal, or French toast. Lunch is the main meal of the day, and usually consists of one or two simple starch dishes and a vegetable salad. Dinner is often left-overs supplemented by a fresh salad. The quality of the food depends on a combination of participants' cooking experience, kitchen conditions, available ingredients, and the taste of each particular group. Meal quality can vary widely. Meat is served on *shabbat*, and even then it is restricted to chicken. Each group of participants has its own kinds of food issues, but complaints about too much starch and too little protein are especially common. At the same time, for many participants the diet at Livnot is the healthiest they have ever encountered. The absence of processed food in the regular diet and the lack of immediately available junk food can make a difficult adjustment for North American *chevre*. Trips into town to satisfy a burger or pizza craving are not uncommon. While dishes are simple and choices are few at each meal, there is always a lot of food available. Crates of fresh fruit and vegetables sit in the kitchen, available for snacking between meals. Recently, Livnot designated one refrigerator for *chevre* food, enabling people to buy and have on hand whatever treats and special ingredients they desire.

Like cooking, cleaning is also performed on a rotational basis. Each day, two people leave work at the mid-morning break and return to the campus to take care of the basic cleaning or *nikayon* of high-traffic communal areas. Like the morning's manual labour, cleaning in an institutional setting such as Livnot is heavy work compared to cleaning an apartment in America. The tools and methods of cleaning are different in Israel, and the lack of North American cleaning amenities causes some anxiety for participants. Rather than mopping, for example, soapy water is thrown on the floor, which is next scrubbed and the dirty water then dragged with a long-handled squeegee into a drain in the floor or out the door onto the street. The same process is followed with rinse water. Cleaning methods at Livnot are much more active and basic, requiring more involvement on the part of the cleaners than the more detached and sterile North American methods. Moreover, the buildings at Livnot get filthy in the way that only communal spaces with open doors and windows can get, particularly in the Middle East.

HIKES (*TIYULIM*)

The regular Livnot day is highly-structured, busy, and often extremely wearying. But while this schedule certainly makes up the majority of time spent at Livnot, there are other kinds of days, most notably hike days and *shabbat*, which offer participants very different experiences. Hiking is a central part of the Livnot program. Generally, there is one hike or *tiyul* each week, depending on the intervention of Jewish holidays, bad weather, and other scheduling issues. While hikes can include fun, "touristy" activities, like a screaming, wet, hilarious day spent inner-tubing down one of the Jordan tributaries, *tiyulim* are rarely so light or easy. Most hikes take participants to remote nature reserves in the Golan or Galilee regions that are rarely part of a normal tourist itinerary. The group travels by hired bus to get to the starting point for the hike. Although these hikes often appear to begin in the middle of nowhere, they are actually routed along parts of the extensive system of marked trails that criss-cross Israel. Participants carry a day's supply of water on their backs – usually three or four litres, depending on the season – and ingredients for a picnic lunch. The point, according to Livnot staff, is to "hike Jewishly," that is, not necessarily to hike quickly or cover lots of ground, but to be aware of and appreciate one's surroundings, both in nature and history. The hiking itself is physically challenging, but the group breaks often to enjoy the environment and its significance: sitting on a windy slope over an ancient city to learn of its first-century heroism, relaxing in the shade of a large tree to understand the Jewish significance of the carob, or stopping near abandoned mills to learn about the sixteenth-century textile industry. The hikes are a time of intense contact with nature, a chance to study raptors circling overheard, to eat grapes growing on a rock face, to play with chameleons.

Depending on the season, there might be an opportunity to swim under a chilling, crashing waterfall, surrounded by pink flowers. While some participants have hiked and camped in the wild before, most have not "roughed it" to this degree, and must adjust to experiences like urinating in the woods and, on longer hikes, sleeping outdoors without tents. One of the highlights of the program is a three-day hike, which represents an extraordinary test of determination and commitment. The hike route extends from the Sea of Galilee to the Mediterranean, through breathtaking mountains, nature reserves, Druze villages and, finally, the banana fields of the coast. Even the experienced hiker is exhausted and sore after three days of setting out at 5:30 a.m. and hiking for some twelve hours. Later in the program, the two-day Desert Hike offers *chevre* a different sort of physical, emotional, and spiritual challenge. Livnot places a high value on the hiking process and presents itself as a program that uniquely combines work, study, and hiking. These *tiyulim* come to form some of the most potent and cherished memories that participants take home from Livnot. While *tiyulim* are different from typical Livnot days, the hikes form a regular and vital part of the Livnot experience.

A DAY OF REST – SHABBAT

Another special day that differs from the ordinary schedule is *shabbat*, the celebration of the Jewish sabbath, which occurs each week from Friday evening until Saturday night. There are three rotating "kinds" of *shabbat* at Livnot: group, family, and free. Ideally, when nothing else interrupts the schedule, participants take part in these different kinds of *shabbat* on a three-week cycle.[11] A "free" *shabbat* is designed for *chevre* to spend a few days away from Livnot, sightseeing around the country, visiting family, or just relaxing on the beach, taking a break from the pressures of program life. For many participants who come to Israel immediately before the program and leave soon afterwards, these weekends provide the only real opportunity to tour the country and to see cities other than Tzfat and Jerusalem.

While important for participants' sanity and their ability to cope with both Livnot's arduous schedule and the isolation of Tzfat, these free *shabbatot* are neither controlled by, nor really part of the program itself. It is, rather, the group and family *shabbatot* that form the core of the actual Livnot *shabbat* experience. For almost all participants, traditional *shabbat* observance is a radically new experience. At Livnot, however, they find themselves dressed up, sitting at a long table with a group of other young Jews, lustily singing in a Hebrew they do not understand, banging on tables and smiling broadly. For the first time, perhaps, a woman might light the traditional Friday night candles, as she may or may not have seen her mother do. And everyone, regardless of how shy in public, dances heartily in a circle of men or women, their hands on each others shoulders, singing boisterously about King David. Group *shabbat* at Livnot is a loud, participatory, joyful experience and one that leaves a strong impression on participants and visitors alike.

The Thursday night before a group *shabbat* is taken up with advance food preparation, as cooking on *shabbat* is prohibited by Jewish law. Group cooking is one of the most supremely chaotic moments at Livnot. Participants sign up in groups to make particular dishes, which include challah, soup, chicken, starch dishes like potato kugel, and desserts. Food must be prepared for two meals, Friday night dinner and Saturday lunch. Because *shabbat* always includes many guests, there are even more people to cook for than on regular *toranut* duty. And because it is *shabbat*, certain luxury ingredients are available, like chocolate chips for cookies and lettuce in salads. Group cooking involves several groups of two or three people vying for ingredients, pots, utensils, and preparation space all at the same time. If you are too slow and miss out on grabbing a cutting board, your preparation is delayed, ensuring an even later night in the kitchen. The three ovens work straight through the evening and into the small hours of the night. Group cooking begins with everyone together, chatting, listening to music, tasting food, and laughing at the chaos, but tends to turn into a very long hard night of washing up and waiting for dishes to come out of the oven.

The next morning, Friday, is not a regular work day. Participants enjoy a slightly later wake-up, and the morning is spent intensively cleaning in groups assigned to tasks on a rotating basis. These jobs around the campus include scouring the kitchen, tidying the office, sweeping the roofs and paths, and cleaning rooms. Friday afternoon is left unscheduled, during which participants have time to shower and get ready for *shabbat*. Everybody meets in the *chadar ochel* for candle-lighting at an appointed time, just before sundown. For participants it is a pleasant shock each week, after so much time in torn jeans, and covered in paint, dirt, and sweat, to see one another shaved or made-up, with hair done, and wearing heels and stockings, button down shirts, and flowing dresses. Everyone appropriately "ooohs" and "ahhhs": this is something special.

When participants are gathered together in the dining hall, a staff member will give a short talk about *shabbat*, its meaning and significance, perhaps illustrated by a story which sets the mood. Someone breaks into a song, people start to clap along, and *shabbat* really begins – men and women separate to dance and sing at opposite ends of the room. One by one, most of the women and the odd man drift over to light candles placed out on a plate, with transliterations of the blessings placed nearby. The singing builds, the dances become more frenzied, laughter breaks out. Everyone takes part and there is no room for being shy or uncomfortable. After a time, the energy is cooled down by a staff member who announces that *Kabbalat Shabbat* will be held on the roof in ten minutes.

Kabbalat Shabbat is a very short, lyrical service highlighted by extensive singing, and that is traditionally prayed by Jews on Fridays between afternoon and evening prayers to welcome the sabbath. It is a relatively recent development, significantly created in Tzfat itself during the sixteenth century by Luria and his followers. Standing on the rooftop at Livnot, participants look west toward Mount Meron at sundown, watching the sun spread strokes of colour across the sky. Since most of the inhabitants of the old city are religious, the only sounds at this hour are birdsong and prayer from nearby groups. There are no cars, radios, or blaring televisions.[12] A collective sigh goes up: it has been a long week, and now it is time to relax and enjoy a different mode of existence. As is common in Orthodox practice, women and men are separated onto different sides of the balcony for the service, although no actual physical barrier is placed between them. The service is slowly sung aloud by a staff member[13] from start to finish, and those who read Hebrew can follow along in the prayerbooks that are distributed. This slow reading of each word at Livnot contrasts starkly with the common synagogue practice in which congregants mumble the prayers at breakneck speed, coming together again at the end of each section. Sheets with transliterations are handed out for the climax of the service, *Lecha Dodi*, so that everyone, even those who cannot read Hebrew, can participate. But many choose not to take an active part in the service, preferring instead to listen, to watch the sunset and daydream, or to pray in their own fashion.

Before dinner, everyone washes his or her hands in the traditional manner, but this ritual is performed to the loud chorus of clapping and an upbeat *nigun*, a repetitive, wordless tune.[14] *Kiddush* is made – the special *shabbat* blessing over wine – and everyone sits down to eat.

After a regular week of Livnot food, *shabbat* dinner is luxurious. The meal consists of several courses, and includes homemade *challah* and meat. Simple things like using napkins and nice clothing also contribute to creating a special, party-like atmosphere. There are rotating groups charged with serving and clean-up duties, allowing most participants to sit back and be served. Eating is punctuated with interludes of high-spirited singing, in which everyone can participate thanks to the Livnot songbooks that provide transliterations of the songs. Traditional *shabbat* songs are accompanied by increasingly carefree and enthusiastic rhythmic table pounding, making cups spill and tables bounce. A couple of participants and maybe a staff member give *divrei Torah*, a short talk on the weekly Torah portion, drawing attention to some point of interest or its relevance to program life. At the end of the meal, "Grace after Meals" is sung aloud, again using the songbook transliterations.

Friday night dinner can take several hours. Afterwards there is little to do, as participants are not permitted to go out on Friday nights, and there is almost nothing open in Tzfat on *shabbat* anyhow. Writing and turning on lights are also prohibited by Jewish law, so that participants cannot read or write letters home after dinner either. Usually there is an *oneg Shabbat* get-together held at the home of the coordinating family, with snacks, discussion, and singing. Often people will just relax on the roof and talk, or try to walk off some of the meal.

There are no officially planned activities at Livnot on Saturday until lunch, which is held around noon. Traditionally, Jews go to prayer services, and Tzfat's many synagogues are packed. While staff members normally attend one particular community synagogue, Livnot participants are neither required nor particularly encouraged to attend services themselves. Later in the program, some *chevre* might decide to check out a synagogue, but generally the morning is spent sleeping late. The rest of the day is spent in a combination of free time, eating well, and resting, with the occasional optional class offered. The citadel is a lovely green place to escape to, while the hardy might hike down to Wadi Amud below Tzfat. However *shabbat* is spent, it is, ideally, a relaxing, soul-restoring, joyful day. At nightfall, *Havdalah*, the short ceremony marking the end of *shabbat*, is celebrated together, on the roof when the weather is calm, with traditional songs, candlelight, spices to smell, and wine. As the candle is passed around for the traditional practice of seeing the light reflected on fingernails, participants are invited to pull some of the light into themselves, to try and keep some of the spirit of *shabbat* with them into the week. *Shabbat* ends with a combination of relief and wistfulness. After announcements everyone scatters quickly for a free evening, usually spent out in town after a restful but restricted day. As is the practice in Israel, Sunday is the beginning of the week, a regular work day for Livnot.

VIGNETTES

For its participants, Livnot is a deeply significant experience, full of profound moments, intimate relationships, and personal victories. It is these brief instants that form the most cherished memories that partici-pants carry with them from Livnot. At the same time, it is often these crucial moments, the very texture of the experience, that are most apt to get lost in an academic study. After all, if material does not possess clear analytical significance, it can be difficult to justify its inclusion. However, at least part of the goal of ethnography is to enable the reader to view an experience or culture from the participant's point of view and to encourage the development of empathy between readers and participants. Livnot, we must recall, does not affect participants solely through factors that can be critically analysed, but also because of intangible, emotional scenes like the ones below. In the brief snapshots that follow, I have tried to speak with immediacy, from within the moment, attempting to perceive events as might a Livnot participant, without forgetting that not all participants experience such events in the same way. These vignettes are shared, group experiences, as recorded in my field notes. The more individual, personal moments, both my own and those of participants, are left to the imagination of the reader. The individuals named are staff members.[15]

Panting with exertion in the cool pre-dawn desert, we straggle to the summit alone or in pairs. The rock allows a sweeping, spectac-ular view of desert below, as far as the eye can see. Miles of time-less rock and sand, isolated in a ringing silence that makes your ears ache. The rising sun begins to spread colour across an unin-terrupted sky. And there Daniel stands alone, strikingly handsome, strong and gentle. Everyone's hero. He is discretely off to the side, facing Jerusalem, wrapped in white prayer shawl, his arm bound in leather. The sun continues its journey, while Daniel prays quietly to God, and we all watch, awe-struck at the splendour of Jews back in their desert.

Driving back to Tzfat from Jerusalem once, late at night. We break at a rest-stop to get snacks and use the bathrooms. A busload of strange-looking Chassidim, the men in black with long sidecurls, pull up a few minutes later. Waiting around for who knows what, a group of them begin to quietly sing and dance a little. Suddenly, everyone jumps in. The group swells with other Chassidim and they pull in young men from Livnot. A women's circle gathers nearby. The singing gets louder and louder, the dancing more frenzied, the hand clapping more intense. Under the stars at a highway rest-stop, these strangers were brothers, and the world tilted with spontaneous Jewish joy.

Weary on a hike somewhere in the Golan Heights. Someone lets out an excited yelp – there are grapes growing on vines that hug the rock face! One woman clambers up, and passes down clusters of deep purple grapes, fat and moist. Someone else has opened the pomegranates found nearby. Sunlight filters through the trees as we sit on the ground to feast, eyes wide with pleasure. City kids from North America feeling strong, healthy, natural, eating from the trees from which our ancestors ate, sustained by the Land of Israel.

It is the second night on the three-day hike. We are sitting around a campfire, aching, tired and dirty, near the highway. Pounding on drums and other instruments, we finally get a chance to cut loose, let off steam and really complain. We sing "The Livnot Blues." Everyone has at least one verse to offer (My feet are kind of tired/ They feel like aching stumps/I've got several nasty blisters/And what are those swollen lumps? I've got the Livnot blues from my head down to my shoes, I got the Livnot blues.) But how blue can anyone really be, toasting marshmallows, laughing and singing with friends before going to sleep under the stars?

In the isolation of the Golan Heights after an arduous descent, we arrive at the ancient city of Gamla, whose inhabitants had martyred themselves for the Jewish people some 1,900 years ago. We sit on stone slabs at the ruins of the synagogue they would have used. Daniel reminds us that it is the month of Elul, when Jews world-over are hearing the shofar[16] blast to "get psyched" for the High Holidays. And that the same shofar might have summoned people in ancient times, like the inhabitants of Gamla to begin their battle for freedom. Eliyahu pulls out the long, twisted shofar he has been carrying throughout the hike, and sounds it clear and loud. The blast rings out, resounding off the hills. Jews again at Gamla, this time in freedom and without fear.

The final shabbat of the program has just ended. Everyone gathers together for *Havdalah*. Wine, spices and finally a lit, braided candle are passed around the circle. Ariela suggests that we all take some of the light from this shabbat into ourselves for the coming week, for all the different places we are going to be next shabbat. People move slowly, motioning the candlelight toward themselves, the tears beginning to run freely. What will next shabbat look like, without the chevre, without Tzfat, without any celebration?

PEOPLE AT LIVNOT − STAFF

It is impossible to talk meaningfully about Livnot without reference to its real lifeblood and focus: people. The Livnot staff includes a number of regular teachers, a work coordinator, a director of education, the coordinating couple, a hike leader, the director/founder of the program, and one or two national-service girls.[17] In contrast to the non-observant, largely unaffiliated participants, the vast majority of staff at Livnot are religious Orthodox Jews.[18] Women cover their hair with hats or kerchiefs, and wear long skirts and long sleeves, in accordance with Orthodox tradition. Men wear *kipot* (headcoverings) and *tzitzit* (fringes), although not all have them visible, and some are bearded while others are clean shaven.[19] For most participants, Livnot represents the first time they have ever spoken to an Orthodox Jew, much less developed a close relationship with one. Most of the staff are *ba'alei teshuvah*, that is, people from liberal or non-religious Jewish homes who chose religious observance as adults. Similarly, except for the national-service girls, almost all of the staff are originally from North America. Because staff, like participants, are in most cases from similarly non-observant and North American backgrounds, the staff are able to relate well to participants in their Jewish and American experience.

While each staff member has a specific, technical area of focus, all staff members play similar roles in participants' experience of Livnot. More than anything else, the staff talk extensively with *chevre*. In some respects, the main job of staff members is to be there, to be accessible and caring during what is often a difficult period of group living, far from home, in participants' first serious encounter with religious Judaism.

Participants are encouraged to feel free to ask staff members both intellectual and personal questions about anything Jewish. All the staff
exude a tremendous sense of sincerity, commitment, and caring, ensuring that relationships between staff and participants develop into very
intimate, cherished ties.

The coordinating couple for the programs in which these interviews
took place, Ron and Ariela,[20] live on campus, and serve a kind of sur-
rogate parental role for the program. They are always available and
are often sought after for in-depth conversation, help with addressing
life problems, the venting of daily frustrations, and dealing with Jewish
issues on personal or theoretical levels. At the time of my fieldwork,
Ron and Ariela had two young boys and were expecting their third
child. Their home had an open door policy, and often *chevre* could be
found there at all hours, eating peppermint brownies and seeking advice,
feedback, or just chatting. Another staff member, Uri, coordinates the
work program. Mornings hard at manual labour would often turn into
learning sessions as participants grilled Uri about everything from
Jewish views on birth control, to how his parents feel about his religious
commitments; from why he wears a long beard and *payot*, to what kind
of music he likes. The current hike leader and teacher, Daniel, is another
particularly charismatic and well-loved staff member. He and his wife
were the previous coordinating couple for many years, until they left
Tzfat to live on a *moshav* in the Golan Heights. His humility, humour,
wisdom, and integrity combine with a love of nature and deep spirituality to form a man whose praises Livnot participants cannot sing sufficiently highly. Without a doubt, the Livnot staff are some of the most
inspiring, caring, and truly good people I have ever had the honour of
knowing. And while program life is not without normal, occasional
tensions between members of staff and individual *chevre*, I believe that
the vast majority of participants would agree with my assessment.

PARTICIPANTS

On the other side of the human equation are Livnot's participants.
Livnot is designed for North American Jews in their twenties, and who
possess what is termed a "limited" Jewish background. Typically, participants grew up in Reform or nominally Conservative homes, celebrated major Jewish holidays with family dinners, had some Hebrew
or Sunday school education until their early teens, and would have
attended temple or synagogue services on the High Holidays with their

families. For many *chevre*, even this degree of Jewish involvement declined during their teenage years as a result of increasing competition from other interests, and developing independence. By the time they come to Livnot, most participants have been living away from their parents in order to work or attend college. For the overwhelming majority of participants, their Jewish involvement became weaker during this period of independent living than during childhood, and Judaism became extremely peripheral to their lives. Some participants come to Livnot without ever having been to a synagogue, while others come from families that attended synagogue more regularly. Participants with only one Jewish parent are not uncommon. In some rare cases, a participant might have attended a day school in the primary years.

Many participants described their previous Jewish experiences as negative and alienating. Other participants described more positive Jewish experiences in childhood, but as adults have come to feel their Judaism to be empty or meaningless. Some *chevre* have explored other religions to satisfy their spiritual interests, including neo-Paganism, Buddhism, and Christianity. Others have been involved with radical feminist, leftist, environmental, or gay politics. But the vast majority of people who come to Livnot are average, upper–middle class Jewish kids who participate fully in mainstream North American life. Most have been to university, many are in relationships, and as in any other group of people, some are thoughtful and serious, while others are more interested in having fun. However, owing to the nature of the program, Livnot tends to attract many serious participants who are interested in a program which stresses education. Moreover, it is obvious that participants must have at least some interest in Judaism to come to Israel and even to consider taking part in a program like Livnot. But at the same time, in order to be accepted into the program participants must possess a Jewish knowledge that is felt by staff to be sufficiently limited, or feel a level of ambivalence or hostility toward Judaism.[21]

PARTICIPANT PROFILE – LAURA EISEN

Laura is a twenty-seven-year-old receptionist and part-time waitress in the southern United States, with flaming, henna-red hair and an infectious, uproarious laugh. She grew up in the northeast, in a strongly Italian Catholic neighbourhood, desperately wanting to be the same as everyone around her: "Trying to fit in with the majority I rebelled against my Judaism. My mother always tried to get me 'into it.' She sent me to Jewish summer camps, Hebrew School, and as a teenager [to] a young Jewish group. I just didn't want to be Jewish."

At the same time as Laura wanted to be more like her peers and neighbours, her encounters with Jews and Judaism left her feeling alienated and alien:

> I wanted no part of it [Judaism]. I always felt like all the Jewish people I met were very different than me. And I never wanted to explore it. Anytime I went to Temple I felt different being there. I used to go to Church. I used to feel comfortable there. Spiritually, going to Temple would never do anything for me. It would just make me feel uncomfortable. So I went to Church and I felt at ease there. I wanted to celebrate Christmas, I didn't want to celebrate *Hannukah*.
>
> I never really hung out with anybody who was my age and Jewish. I never clicked with them ... My experiences with most Jewish people was that they were really kind of stuck up and snotty.

Laura has particularly bad memories of synagogue, which she felt was little more than a social event or a fashion show attended by hypocritical, even sanctimonious members: "You go to *shul* [synagogue] and everybody's dressed up and everybody's looking at each other's outfit, and you wonder why are you actually here. You say one thing and you do something else. You say you're so Jewish and this and that, but if you were like that, you'd accept everybody for who they are. And people don't do that."

She once went to investigate an Orthodox shul, and found to her disappointment that "the men were on one side praying, and the women were on the other side talking. Just gossiping. Where's the spirituality here? You're wearing your wig and you're wearing a long skirt and you're not tearing toilet paper,[22] but where's your spirituality? I walked into *shul*, nobody would talk to me. Nobody would talk to me. And that's what I've grown up with. That's why I didn't want to be part of anything. Because there's these people just going through the motions, I felt like."

As a child Laura had wanted to be part of the majority and not feel different from those around her. But her experience of moving to a town in the South made her decide that perhaps the majority was not really where she wanted to fit in anymore. Being tagged as an exotic minority in an overwhelmingly Christian environment had an impact on her perception of her own Jewish identity: "Talk about being a minority. I don't think they even knew what being Jewish was until I moved there. Let's just say, in [the southern town where I lived] they don't ask where you are from, they ask what church you belong to. I finally found out what it meant to live in the Bible Belt. With a pretty open mind I tried a couple of their churches and for the first time in my life, I didn't feel right going against the grain, so to say. I became very lonely and felt something was missing. It wasn't money or a companion, it was being with my fellow Jewish people."

Laura moved to a big city in the South, and began exploring the Jewish community there, becoming involved with the Jewish Community Centre and a social group for singles. She came to Israel and Livnot, she says, because "I wanted to get more into it and I figured this was a good point in my life. I was at a standstill as far as work and school and where I wanted to be in the future, and I'm not too settled in my ways. So I thought it would be a good time to come here and do a program like this. I want to know more about being Jewish, about my heritage."

Laura also explained, somewhat embarrassed, that she was "hoping to find something that's been missing in my heart since I've been a child."

PARTICIPANT PROFILE – HANNAH JACOBS

A funny, charismatic woman from the mid-western United States, Hannah naturally draws people close to her with the vibrant force of her personality and her acerbic tongue. She came to Israel to participate in Livnot at the age of twenty-three. While Hannah grew up quite involved in Reform Jewish life, she recalls that many features of her background were actually negative Jewish experiences, particularly Hebrew School and attending services at Temple:

From the young age of five, I was sent off to a place referred to as Sunday School. Every Sunday was especially traumatic because this place that we had to go to was not only boring but it just didn't make sense. As I got older, Hebrew School was introduced to me and I couldn't understand why my parents kept making me go to these educational lectures and lessons that made no impact on my

life, except that I couldn't sleep late and I couldn't join in any
after school activities … I do look back and realize that there was
room for some Jewish enlightenment, but not when it was being
pushed on me.

   My experience was that I hated going to Temple. It was boring
to sit there and be saying this bullshit. It was just bullshit in
English. And even now when I read the prayers in English it just
sounds so corny and so contrived. These aren't my words. And the
whole fashion show thing. For Sunday School, you had to wake
up early on a Sunday to learn about boring, boring stuff with an
old lady teacher. Hebrew School was after school, and you just
want to go home after school and not deal with it. Nothing really
was positive. There was just nothing positive about the experience.

Still, Hannah notes that "it wasn't that I didn't like being Jewish,
because I think I always was proud of being Jewish. I always had Jewish
pride." She retains positive memories of attending Jewish summer
camps, and finds that most of her good friends are Jews. Hannah's
grandparents are survivors of the Holocaust, and she has always had
a sense of the small size of the Jewish community, the dangers Jews
face, and the need for the culture to continue without losing its distinctive Jewishness. But while Hannah is adamant on the importance of
Jewishness, she is not sure about Judaism: "It just happens to be that
most of my close friends are Jewish. I am not really sure why, though.
As much as I know Judaism is important to me, I do not have a strong
grasp as to why, or what role it should play, and how important should
it really be in my life."

Hannah finished college six months before coming to Livnot. After
moving back to her parents' home she learned that her university degree
found her only a temporary clerical position. She was "between things,"
eager to get away from her family, and looking for something to do for
a while. She came to Israel and to Livnot largely by accident: "I didn't
come to get any Jewish whatever. I wasn't like, oh, I'm going to learn
about my Jewish past. It's like, this is a totally good priced trip and it's
three months and I have nothing to do … It wasn't until a week before
I came that Rebecca [the Livnot representative in New York] called me
and said 'You are aware that this is basically all learning.' I was like
'okay, sure' … But since I'm so open to anything, I was just so excited
to not be home for this length of time, it doesn't matter what I'm doing.
As long as I'm not at home and just doing something."

PARTICIPANT PROFILE – BRAD SILVER

A tall, athletic, soft-spoken twenty-three-year-old, Brad is one of the few Canadians at Livnot. He was raised by an Israeli Jewish mother and a non-Jewish father. When Brad and his siblings were young, the family received gifts for Christmas, though his father is not a practicing Christian. Since money was tight, Brad attended neither Hebrew School nor Jewish camps. Moreover, since his mother's family was in Israel, Brad grew up with almost no Jewish friends or Jewish influence in his life. He did not celebrate his *bar mitzvah*,²³ and in fact had never been to synagogue services before coming to Livnot. He notes that this lack of Jewish background has left him with no bad feelings toward Judaism, which differs from the experience of some participants. Rather, he simply has very little Jewish experience.

While his mother did not actively teach him about Judaism, Brad feels that her influence was critical in developing what Jewish identity he does possess: "She gave us Jewish views without saying 'it's Jewish.' And without saying this is how it is. It's just the way she raised us. I think she raised us Jewishly but without saying this is Judaism, this is the way you have to be. She just raised us a certain way. What's good and what's bad."

It was through reading Bible stories when he was young and asking his mother about them that Brad developed a feeling of connection with the historical Jewish community: "Those stories gave me an identity with the Jewish people, the Hebrews. I'd read these stories and know they were in my past. These are people who are in my history, that are part of me."

A critical turning point came when Brad went to Israel for two months at the age of twelve to visit his mother's family. This trip had an intense impact on him and on his self-understanding as a Jew: "I learned more about the people living now than I did the past, which I learned from books. The culture of my mother's family was in stark contrast to my father's, being very, very close – I will never forget the large *shabbat* dinners at my Grandmother's house in Jerusalem every Friday night and playing soccer with cousins and neighbours on the streets. Visiting ancient sites made the events and people I read about more real."

Although he actively wanted to return to Israel, Brad came to Livnot more on a whim than from any concrete motivation: "I don't know if it [deciding to come] was anything deep. This came about. A girl that had gone before told me it was an amazing program and I wanted to travel and get away, and be in Israel since I hadn't been here for so long. I didn't want to come to Israel and just vacation, I wanted to come here and do something."

PARTICIPANT PROFILE – WENDY TROPER

Wendy came to Livnot as a participant when she was twenty-three. A lithe, graceful young woman with dark eyes, she makes a living teaching aromatherapy, and supplements her income working as a store clerk. Her parents' difficult divorce, which occurred when Wendy was quite young, had a dramatic effect on her Jewish future. It was her father who had been the more Jewishly active parent, and his subsequent move away from the family left Wendy with a confusing Jewish environment:

> My father and mother participated within the Jewish community in opposite ways, which inevitably affected my participation and created ambivalence. My mother almost never participated within the community or attended services at her Reformed[24] temple, and in contrast my father was very active with the Conservative Synagogue and encouraged me to attend with him. My parents' divorce impacted my Jewish life greatly ... My siblings and I switched temples and participated in a Reformed style with an unfamiliar congregation and Rabbi ... I felt upset mainly because religion was the only constant in my life and now the struggle was expanding.

Even without her mother's active support, Wendy persisted in a desire to attend Hebrew School and celebrate her *bat mitzvah* and eventually Confirmation. But inevitably this lack of parental involvement affected her participation and interest in Jewish activities. Although Wendy became a member of B'nai Brith Girls in high school, she explains sadly that "I was the only one who came from a broken home. I struggled with my mother's lack of support and I found myself jealous and angry for not being like everyone else. Therefore I felt I could not participate and dropped out later that year."

These negative feelings associated with Judaism that resulted from her difficult family situation caused Wendy to try to cut her ties to Judaism when she went away to college: "When I was eighteen I left home and went to college. I felt like I wasn't even Jewish. I didn't want to bring all that crap with me to college. But you kind of do. Even though you don't want to bring it with you, it's still there."

As an adult with an interest in meditation, mysticism, and nature, she sought spiritual sustenance in religious traditions and philosophies other than Judaism. Along the way, Wendy also developed a feminist consciousness and acute sensitivity to women's issues, labelling herself an "independent womyn" on her application form. She also became involved in a serious relationship with a man who is not Jewish. Wendy did continue to celebrate major Jewish holidays with family and friends, and was even at one point marginally involved with a Jewish career networking and social group. But she did not find her experiences with this group positive, as she explained: "I didn't like it because they had this stereotypical American Jewish snobbery ... I really didn't feel like I fit in."

Participation on an Israel experience program was suggested to Wendy by her therapist as a way to demonstrate her adult independence from her mother in a structured and supportive environment. Wendy also hoped that participation in Livnot would enable her to deal with some of her unresolved issues around Judaism in response to her "realization that I was unsure of my Jewish identity as an adult and angry for all of the struggle I underwent as a youth."

PARTICIPANT PROFILE – FERN ROSENFELD

Fern is a vivacious, inquisitive, and professional young woman. At the age of twenty-seven, she came to Israel to take part in the Livnot program. Her Jewish background is far more extensive than that of most Livnot participants. When Fern was growing up, her family attended a multi-denominational, nominally Orthodox synagogue for the holidays. They celebrated *shabbat* with candlelighting, *Kiddush*, and a family dinner on Friday nights. When she was very young, they sometimes went to *shul* on *shabbat* mornings, and her family kept some level of *kashrut* in the home. Fern attended Hebrew school until grade seven, which culminated in the celebration of her *bat mitzvah* at the age of twelve. From that point on, however, her Jewish education and experiences was, as she put it, "a trickle." Indeed, since going away to college, Fern says, "Judaism has not played a major role in my life." While she still attended synagogue on the High Holidays with her family, she had little other Jewish involvement and mostly dated men who were not Jewish.

It was only after college, when she had started her professional life, and became conscious of herself developing into an adult and taking responsibility for her own life, that Fern realized she had not yet developed an adult relationship to Judaism:

> My Jewish education pretty much stopped in high school and then I just kind of did what my family always did growing up. But the older I got the further and further and further away I felt from – not from being Jewish, because I always felt a strong identity as a Jew – but the traditions and rituals I was practicing, I felt no connection to them. Because I'd been celebrating certain holidays my whole life. But the more conscious I became of choices and becoming an adult, the more I realized that I didn't know why really I was doing what I was doing.
>
> I do Jewish things because I have always done them. For example, I go to synagogue with my family on holidays because, as my grandmother has said, "we're just supposed to." I adhere to my parents' rules of keeping kosher in our house because, as my mom has said, "that's just what we do" ... In essence, I do not know why I do the things I do, and as an adult woman this is no longer acceptable to me. The time has come for me to take responsibility for my Judaism ... to decide for myself what it means for me to be a Jew.
>
> As a twenty-seven-year-old woman, I feel that it's time I take a look at how do I want to live my life, at least now, based on a conscious decision to explore that. Not based on a childish kind of reaction to the way I was brought up.

This understanding did not actively inspire Fern to seek out an Israel experience program. It was only when a past participant from Livnot joined her workplace and shared his experiences with her that Fern even considered joining an Israel program. Although she knew that Livnot is aimed at people with less Jewish background than she possesses, Fern regarded the program as a unique opportunity to go "back to the basics in a non-threatening religious environment."

PARTICIPANT PROFILE – MARNI HILLMAN

Marni came to the Livnot program when she was twenty-five. A spiritual, thoughtful young woman with a wide grin, she works in a professional position. Her family was very involved in Jewish community work, but did not have an equally active religious life: "My mother is what I call 'culturally' Jewish, even though her parents are third generation atheists. That she should marry another Jewish person is the extent of her Jewish identity. My father is also 'culturally' Jewish and has devoted his professional life to serving the Jewish community."

Marni attended Hebrew school until her *bat mitzvah* at the age of thirteen. She also went to Jewish summer camp for many years, an experience which left her with fond memories. Since then, however, Marni has had no Jewish education and very little in the way of Jewish involvement: "From the age of thirteen to the present, my practice of Judaism has consisted of attending Temple during *Rosh Hashana* and *Yom Kippur* and celebrating *Hanukkah* and Passover in the home. Until recently, I went through the motions of these holidays blindly and out of tradition. I did not grasp their deeper meaning and roots, nor did I want to, until now."

Growing up, Marni explained, the greatest value instilled in her was a tolerance for diversity and a love for all people, regardless of race, religion, or culture. Her family taught her to embrace and be open to learning from difference. Thus she was shocked when her parents expressed their deep concern about her long-term relationship with a practicing Catholic. Marni found herself unable to understand why, suddenly, she was expected to only marry someone Jewish. While very interested in spirituality and religion, Marni did not feel a need to limit her spiritual quest and search for philosophical insight to Judaism.

As part of her professional life, Marni became involved in a success team, which brought members together to discuss their goals and dreams, in both career areas and personal life. Through this group, she became aware that to a certain degree she was dissatisfied with her career, and decided to take some time off work to explore other aspects of her personality and her interests. Marni claims that she came to Livnot to remove herself from her regular environment, as well as to fuel her spiritual and religious growth.

PARTICIPANT PROFILE – WARREN GOLDMAN

Warren is a sensitive, gentle, handsome man with a professional job in the northeastern United States. At the age of twenty-seven he took part in Livnot. His background was, as he terms it, "conservatively labelled, non-observant." Warren's family celebrated the High Holidays together

and held a *seder*, or ritual meal, at Passover. They also attended synagogue for the major holidays. Warren's deepest point of Jewish connection, however, came from watching his more traditional grandmother.
"I knew I was Jewish because I remember going to my grandmother's
house. She was from Poland and she used to light *shabbat* candles and
stuff like that." Warren's experiences of Hebrew school, on the other
hand, did not serve as a positive model of Jewish learning or Jewish
identification: "As a child I was relegated to Hebrew school three days
a week after school and on Sundays. I suppose the predominant feeling
during those years was alienation. I felt like a Martian. I had no idea
why I had to go to this place, and had absolutely no interest in learning
what was being taught."

His *bar mitzvah* followed soon after, and was "a terrific success, at
least to all those who attended ... [but] I distinctly remember coming
to the last line of my Half Torah[25] not knowing how I got there and
having no sense of what had just happened.

"There was no meaning behind what I was doing. I started to make
the quote-unquote adult choice at fourteen that I didn't want this. It
had nothing to do with me. I rebelled against it and fought against
going to services with my family ever since, really."

Being Jewish in a town with very few other Jews was a difficult
experience. In high school Warren was made fun of and ridiculed for
being Jewish. It was a combination of these childhood experiences of
alienation from the religion and encounters with anti-Semitism that
pushed Warren to isolate himself as much as possible from Judaism: "I
spent the next ten years attempting to wield my power of 'adult' choice
rebelling against any form of Judaism. I certainly did not want to spend
any time or energy associating myself with a way of life that I did not
believe in or understand, and most of all, with one that was connected
with a lot of pain, confusion and conflict."

It was only after college, when he entered a period of introspection
about his life and started to question what gave him meaning, that
Warren thought about reconsidering Judaism: "I guess it started after
I graduated from college, this whole idea of starting to look into myself.
Who am I, what is important in my life, what are my priorities. At first
it had nothing to do with Judaism. Then a few years into it I started
to realize that's actually a part of my roots. So I started questioning.
People would ask me 'what about this holiday, what about that holiday?'
I had no idea what it meant for me to be Jewish."

It was this desire to take a second look at Judaism that brought
Warren to Livnot, to pursue Jewish learning, and to fulfill his growing

desire to "claim what has always been mine to have: a connection with my religion."

The self-professed goal of Livnot is quite general: to provide a positive Jewish experience to Jews of limited Jewish backgrounds. Livnot understands itself as a program designed to introduce people who are alienated from Judaism and who possess little Jewish knowledge, to "traditional" Judaism. This goal is both a cognitive and an affective one, seeking simultaneously to teach participants about Judaism and to make them feel more positively disposed toward their religion. In the words of education director Eliyahu Levy, "Education is only one of our goals. The wider goals are basically to turn people on to their Jewishness." However, Livnot does not ascribe superiority to affective goals or limit itself to an experiential approach. Rather, the program consciously attempts to offer both intellectual and emotional development, to provide both information and positive experiences. As Eliyahu noted: "I don't know how well we do it. But we try for a blending, an integration of heart and mind. We wouldn't be comfortable with a merely affective approach to things. We don't want to just give them a whole series of 'wow' experiences. We want their heads to work too. We want them to think about things ... We want mind and heart together, without one having predominance over the other ... We don't want people to merely have moving experiences, or merely be addressed on their intellectual level. Rather we want them to have both."

Perhaps the single most significant feature that distinguishes Livnot's approach from that of other religious organizations providing outreach to disaffiliated Jews is Livnot's emphasis on Jewish education rather than seeking a "conversion" to religious observance. While program staff certainly hope to change participants' attitudes toward Judaism, they do not actively encourage participants to take on an Orthodox lifestyle. In a discussion of how Livnot perceives success and failure, staff member Ron explained to me that "if somebody walks away [from the program] with a slightly better impression of Judaism, that it's not so stupid, it's not so archaic, that's fine. That's a success."

The traditional Jewish concept of *kiruv rechokim* or "drawing close those that are distant" is grounded in a belief that non-observant Jews are somehow removed from the Torah and commandments, and need to be brought closer to them.[26] In most *kiruv* or outreach work, the goal is not simply to educate less-observant Jews about the demands of *halacha*, but rather to make those Jews both more informed and more inclined to observe those demands. In fact, Jewish sources actively discourage education about particular laws in the absence of a reasonable possibility that the individual will observe them. Education about the requirements of *halacha* is understood to increase the responsibility of the individual, transforming his action from unintentional to willful.

Like Ron, program staff were unanimous in expressing the view that Livnot does not engage in the type of outreach aimed at making people observant of Torah and the commandments:

> Livnot doesn't believe in *kiruv*. The way I understand that is that *kiruv* means you're explaining something in a specific way in order to cause them to be religious and live an observant life. And this [Livnot] is educating from religious people and presenting it with excitement and by showing them a model. But it's not necessarily in order to bring them to a certain point. In other words, if people come back [to North America] and they're more involved in the Jewish community and they're more knowledgeable about Judaism, and Judaism is important to them, then definitely that is a goal that we've accomplished.

The essential distinction made at Livnot between *kiruv* and non-*kiruv* is based on the nature of one's ultimate goal. Livnot maintains that its program is not *kiruv*, because participants are openly permitted and encouraged to make their own choices about the form their Judaism will take.[27] When one of the staff members, Daniel, was asked about this, he was adamant in his response: "It's not *kiruv*. No way. Because, in my opinion, the staff doesn't want the *chevre* to do anything. In *kiruv*, in general, even if you don't say so, you want the people to become religious, do *mitzvot* [commandments], make *aliyah* [emigrate to Israel], not intermarry. Here, I think, we make our own choices. In general, the *chevre* are given the experience and they do with it what they want. If people decide to choose a different path, that's accepted."

Only a radical reformulation of the concept of *kiruv* could allow such a label to be applied to the goals and philosophy of Livnot. Viewing Livnot as an experience that moves Judaism closer to the centre of the individual's priorities, concerns, and psyche, Eliyahu Levy noted:

> In the past, we've been very wary of the word [*kiruv*] because of its associations. It's indelibly associated with the Orthodox world,

and even more specifically, certain segments of the *haredi* [ultra-Orthodox] world, and sometimes associated with dissimulation about your ultimate goals and objectives, beard shaving and things like that. Therefore, it's kind of become anathema in certain segments of the liberal Jewish world, because it automatically means a deligitimization [of liberal Judaism], because they have to be drawn close. But if we understand it in the sense of drawing close – this is the way I usually describe what Livnot tries to do – you take people for whom Jewish issues, Jewish life, Jewish consciousness, is in some way at the periphery of their personalities or of their beings. It's there somewhere. But it's somewhere on the periphery. Maybe it's already started waking up and gravitating to the centre. We try to, for the entire program, move it to the centre. That's *kiruv*, that's moving closer, but it's moving closer with a model that's very different than the model of what *kiruv* is in the *yeshiva* world.[28]

Many of Livnot's core emphases are actually at odds with outreach efforts that seek to make Jews more religious. As will be discussed at length below, an emphasis on the voluntary nature of religious observance, metaphors of the Jewish supermarket, and concepts suggesting Judaism has seventy faces encourage the picking and choosing of traditional elements and a multiplicity of acceptable forms of being Jewish. These ideas are fundamentally incompatible with traditional *kiruv*, which is grounded in a more monolithic and normative understanding of Jewish tradition, and one toward which disaffiliated Jews must be drawn. Livnot clearly owes more to styles of Jewish education that were shaped by the Enlightenment than it does to ideals of *kiruv* or to traditional models of religious learning.

Livnot is the only formal Jewish education that most participants have undertaken since Hebrew school. For many North American Jews of liberal denominations, childhood experiences of Hebrew school form the primary model of Jewish education that endures throughout the rest of their lives. Often terminated with relief at *bar* or *bat mitzvah*, supplementary Jewish schooling is not always a fondly remembered experience. As David Schoem observes in his detailed ethnographic study of Shalom School, a Hebrew afternoon school, the negative experiences of students and parental ambivalence pervade this popular North American system of cultural and religious education. Schoem quotes one parent in this regard: "You know, on occasion, Eddie has told me he hates Hebrew school, and I say 'Edward, that's wonderful. You're carrying on a Jewish tradition. Because when I went to Hebrew school, I hated it too. Because all good Jews hate Hebrew school.'"[29]

Another parent in Schoem's study explained that "Hebrew school is not really for liking; you just have to go."[30] And while Reimer did locate an intriguing example of supplementary Jewish education that was "successful" – in an effort to demonstrate that the negative attitudes on display in studies like Schoem's are not inevitable – it is the relative rarity of Reimer's case study that makes it so interesting. Even in the introduction to Reimer's study, Jonathan Woocher notes that "tales of long hours spent in painfully boring 'Hebrew School' classes abound."[31] Finally, in *The Vanishing American Jew*, Alan Dershowitz offers a scathing judgment against the efficacy of Jewish after-school education as it is currently practiced in North America for ensuring Jewish cultural continuity: "Why not Jewish learning? For anyone who has attended after-school Hebrew classes, the answer is obvious. For the most part, these classes today are boring and poorly taught. They simply aren't fun. More important, it isn't good education. No upwardly mobile American Jew would ever accept the quality of today's *Jewish* education in *secular* elementary, high school or college classes to which they send their children ... we continue to tolerate mediocrity in the Jewish schools to which we send our children."[32]

Schoem's descriptions of bored, apathetic students would have resonated deeply with those Livnot participants who received a supplementary Jewish education. Attending Hebrew school is regularly cited by prospective participants on application forms as their most negative Jewish experience. A typical Livnot recollection of childhood Jewish education was voiced by Josh: "When I was in Hebrew school I spent most of the time in the office. Because I'd already been through six hours of school, why'd I have to sit through two more hours of school? And then the Jews I was with weren't so happy about it either. It was an overall feeling that we didn't want to be there. It was like we were made to be there."

Similarly, as Hannah who was profiled above stated, she deeply resented the fact that "for Sunday School, you had to wake up early on a Sunday to learn about boring, boring stuff with an old lady teacher. Hebrew school was after school, and you just want to go home after school and not deal with it. Nothing really was positive. There was just nothing positive about the experience."

Moreover, like many North American Jews, the vast majority of Livnot participants who did receive Jewish schooling in childhood did not continue any form of Jewish education after their *bar* or *bat mitzvah*. The relegation of Judaism to a space secondary to "real" school, lack of resources, poor teaching, and parental ambivalence transmit an obvious message to young Jews about the importance and value of Jewish learning. Thus, most participants come to Livnot both negatively disposed toward Jewish education and poorly educated about Judaism.

Such negative childhood experiences of Hebrew school often affect participants' formative attitudes toward Judaism. Discussing the perception of Judaism that the students at Shalom School were acquiring, Schoem notes that "for many of them Shalom School was the primary, if not singular, Jewish experience in their lives, and they disliked it. As one teacher warned: 'If they hate it [Shalom School], they cannot feel strongly about being a Jew.'"[33]

As at the Shalom School, the various modes of presentation used at Livnot for transmitting information about Israel, Jews, and Judaism colour the way in which that information is received. The Livnot experience, for many participants, contrasts sharply with their memories of Hebrew school and early Jewish education. Methods of teaching such as hiking, the development of empathy between staff and participants, and Livnot's philosophy of religious non-coercion, themselves transmit messages about the Jewish content that is communicated. The following chapters offer an analysis of both medium and message at Livnot, focusing on both the roots of Israel, Jews, and Judaism that Livnot constructs for participants, and the routes that Livnot travels, that is, the methods it uses to introduce participants to these roots.[34]

3

Routes to Israel

The experience of Livnot U'Lehibanot has a radical, transformative effect on participants' understanding and relationship to Israel. For 66 per cent of the participants that I interviewed while they were taking part in the Livnot program, it was their first visit to Israel. Of those who had been to Israel before, most had spent their prior visit travelling the country with a tour group or youth program. As Tamara said of her earlier trip, "It was basically 200 kids in four buses. But we could have been anywhere. That was my six-week trip to Israel." Most participants, both those who had been to Israel before, and those who had not, professed little knowledge of Israel and few feelings of affinity toward the country prior to taking part in Livnot.[1] Many individuals described a feeling of transformation in terms of their relationship to Israel, and felt this was a direct result of having experienced the country through Livnot. Some voices can illustrate the common themes among participants:

I had really no opinion about Israel before. I didn't even know where it was on the map before I came to Livnot. I had to look on the map ... I just thought the whole place was like a war zone, actually. WARREN

I definitely notice a change [in how I feel about Israel] because I love it here ... The land here is beautiful. The views, the sunsets ... I used to feel, like Israel, whatever. Israel, Florida, Mexico, whatever. Definitely nothing special. Nothing special would happen when I talked about Israel, and now there is ... When I go home

I'll want to know what's happening in Israel now. I feel a connection to Israel. HANNAH

I came to Israel three years ago, and that's when my feelings for Israel really started to develop. Before I was here I really had no connection to the land, or no connection to Israel. It was just another place. It wasn't just another place, but it was just another place. Once I got here three years ago, I felt a connection to Israel, but it was not too strong. But now this time, I feel it has been strengthened an unbelievable amount. It was partly the three-day hike, because we went across the whole country ... I feel very strongly about it. I don't know how to explain it. Israel's my home. America's not my home. I just live there. SHAUN

Before I would do things related to Israel because I felt like I was supposed to. Now I would do things for Israel because I have this intense love inside and because I want to. That can sum up what Livnot has done for my relationship with Israel. FERN

When I got here I was anti-*aliyah* [immigration to Israel]. Especially because we had bad experiences in the beginning with the bombing.[2] Trying to communicate was very frustrating. Everyone was rude. At first, Livnot even, we went to the airport and we were expecting this program. Finally we found the person we were looking for at the airport. It was kind of unorganized ... we were like, "Whoa, what are we getting into?" I was like, "Okay, I could never live here. I went to the food store, I was like, I could never live here." I miss America, the real stuff. Tel Aviv is like a "wanna-be" America but a bad version, you know? I don't understand, but in the last couple weeks, I could live here. Now, faced with leaving, I'm so not ready to leave ... I can't leave yet. I'm so not ready to leave. I'm torn. I can't make *aliyah* because I'm too close to my family. But I want to make sure I can come back here a lot. I love it now. NANCY

Only three weeks after the beginning of the fall 1997 program, when asked in a class to free associate one word with *eretz yisrael* (the Land of Israel), participants offered the following: "overwhelming," "secure," "spiritual," "finally," "beautiful," "empowering," "freedom," "peaceful," "home," "alive," "inspiring," "uplifting," "ancient." The single negative contribution was "foreign."[3] This high degree of positive feeling toward Israel seems to contrast sharply with the fact that many of these participants had come to Livnot almost randomly or by accident. Many Livnot participants arrive seeking little more than a change from the "routine" at home, often at times when they are either between jobs, dissatisfied in jobs that they had planned as temporary, taking a year off from school, unemployed recent graduates, or college students on summer holidays. Many come to Israel simply for a change of pace, at a convenient time in their lives. Israel is not always a carefully chosen destination, but is sometimes picked by participants because of parental pressure and financial support, the availability of Jewish community scholarships, and the presence of safe, structured programs like Livnot.

Steven, a university student from the Midwestern United States, really dreamed of going to Italy, but was urged by his mother to try Israel: "I didn't want to come in the first place. It wasn't my idea. It was my mom's idea. She wanted me to see Israel. It wasn't a thing that I wanted to do."

Similarly, Barb, an energetic young professional from Canada, had been planning a trip to India. She ended up in Israel when she found to her chagrin that none of her friends could travel to India with her when she wanted to go. Barb's parents strongly encouraged her to visit Israel, which she had never really considered before: "I was going to go to India when I graduated from university. I was taking a year and nobody wanted to travel at that point or had the money to go for a whole year, so I decided fine I'm going on my own. What the hell, everybody goes to India. And my parents were like 'You've never been to Israel' ... I never had a desire to go to Israel, I guess until I was ready to do it. So I contemplated their suggestion. It took me a couple of months and I thought, 'Why not? Let's give it a shot.' So I decided to go to Israel."

Like some others, Laura had no particularly compelling urge to go to Israel. Rather, she sought a change from a life that she felt was somewhat stalled, and thought that the Livnot program afforded her a good opportunity to try something different and exciting by going to Israel: "I figured this was a good point in my life. I was at a standstill as far as work and school and where I wanted to be in the future, and I'm not too settled in my ways. So I thought it would be a good time to come here and do a program like this."

Participants who travel to Israel to take part in Livnot are part of the ever-growing tide of international tourism. As a result of increased leisure time, knowledge about other countries, disposable income, and improved transportation, this voluntary, temporary global movement of people seeking everything from education to recreation is an inescapable part of contemporary life. Whether motivated by the desire for a diversion from life in North America or by the seeking of new, possibly Jewish experiences, participants come to Israel as tourists, responding, like many other tourists, to both push and pull factors in their travel.

Even though Livnot offers a case of Jews travelling to the historical spiritual centre of Judaism, it is impossible to classify their travel as a pilgrimage in any traditional sense of the word. A basic condition of pilgrimage is the idea of travel to a "holy place" or "sacred centre." While Israel might be perceived by participants as being somehow different from other countries by virtue of its Jewish character, even those participants who had been to Israel before were often ambivalent or lacking in any significant feeling of personal connection to Israel. For most participants, prior to Livnot, Israel is neither a particularly meaningful nor symbolic destination. More "distant space" than "holy place," Israel represents a country toward which, before the program, participants tend to feel more abstract pride than religious reverence.

This tendency mirrors the findings of sociologist Steven Cohen in his research on the role of Israel in the Jewish identity of American Jews.[4] Cohen argues that while support for Israel is a focal point of public Jewish life in America, and that although pro-Israelism is part of the American Jewish understanding of what it means to be a Jew, these attitudes are often very superficial, particularly among Jews with moderate to low levels of affiliation. While an analysis of public, American Jewish life might give the impression that Israel plays a central role in contemporary Jewish identity, Cohen asserts that for most American Jews Israel remains largely peripheral in the private, religious sphere. This country whose existence is perceived to be of vital importance and whose image is hotly defended publicly in the Jewish community, does not function as a sacred centre for many North American Jews.

Thus, Livnot participants leave North America for Israel as tourists, not as pilgrims. Like many tourists, however, Livnot participants do not see themselves as such and are eager to differentiate themselves and their experiences from tourists and the touristic domain. The belief that "a place is not good for tourists if it is too touristic" sums up this paradoxical, touristic search for authentic, non-touristic experience.[5] Livnot participants express similar themes, perceiving their experiences to be "authentic" rather than "touristic" as a result of the program. It was a pleasant surprise for Wendy to find that she did not feel like a tourist in Israel, but rather believed that she had found a new home: "I feel very nurtured [in Israel]. I feel like it is almost this motherly nurturing. It's this innate sense of belonging. It's also very scary to just confront it, because if I feel this innate sense of belonging, aren't I supposed to be here and live here? ... It's scary to feel this innate sense of home. I don't feel like a tourist. I never did. This is home. Here I am."

Similarly, a twenty-three-year-old Canadian named Diane felt that she had taken part in activities that are unavailable to tourists and had developed a kind of connection to Israel that tourists could not acquire: "I'm able to say, 'Wow, I lived in Israel for three months.' And it's not just that I did the tourist thing. I actually walked on the land. We walked across the breadth of Israel. That's amazing! I have such a deep connection to Israel ... Israel is not just this foreign place off in the middle of the desert somewhere. It actually has character. It has a part of me, in Israel."

While it seems logical to classify the travel mode of Livnot participants as "tourism," rather than "pilgrimage," this tourism is clearly of a distinct type. Livnot is no vacation – the hard work and spartan surroundings clearly make it impossible to think of this as leisure tourism. Instead, coming to Livnot is a kind of travel that holds within it an openness to the possibility of being moved, of being changed. As indicated above, participants' attachment to Israel before the program is neither deep, meaningful, nor personal. Rather, much of their relationship to Israel reflects a sense of puzzlement about the attachment to Israel that they understand they are supposed to have. Before coming to Livnot, participants do know that Israel is somehow supposed to be special to them, supposed to be different from other countries. They know that Israel is important to other Jews, their parents, and the organized Jewish community. But while they might have a vague sense of pride in the abstract success of Israel as a Jewish state, Livnot participants coming to Israel have very little feeling about the country otherwise.

Livnot participants begin their travels as tourists, mostly seeking some diversion from the routine of everyday life or searching vaguely for new experiences, and arrive at a place that holds little in the way of personal or religious meaning. Their mode of travel comes to change, however, as a result of a transformed relationship to their destination. By experiencing Israel at close range through the particular lens of Livnot, participants gradually come to perceive the land as a sacred centre, a meaningful or even holy place. By the end of their stay, participants have become "potential pilgrims," making Israel into what some scholars have called an elective, sacred centre.[6] "Such a centre may be completely extraneous to his culture of origin, the history of his society or his biography. But it may also be a traditional centre to which he, his forbears or his 'people' had been attached in the past, but become alienated from."[7]

Thus, through the experience of Israel that Livnot constructs and presents, however idealistic or staged it might be, participants develop a personal, emotional feeling of connection to Israel, and come to invest the land with a kind of sacredness or religious centrality. Israel does not start out as a religious centre for these Jews, nor is it a country brimming with sacredness to which they travel. Owing to their weak Jewish backgrounds, participants do not invest Israel with such meaning. However, as participants experience Israel with Livnot U'Lehibanot, the country gains that sacred status of destination, of being a uniquely special, Jewish place to which they can return in the future. Learning about Israel through Livnot transforms tourists into potential pilgrims. And it is precisely this kind of deeply meaningful, engaged relationship with Israel that Livnot seeks to develop, as Eliyahu Levy explained:

What I would hope that they would come to feel is the indispensability of a living relationship with Israel as part of their Jewish lives. That means that three months in Livnot is not the only time they'll ever be here. That they'll somehow be drawn back. Maybe time and again. Maybe for long periods of time, or for shorter periods of time. That there will always be a feeling of connection, of longing, of tension … But that Israel isn't a one-time kind of thing. "Wow, I had my Israel experience." I think that an Israel experience that you can pack away in dusty volumes and pictures you put on your shelf and pull down occasionally and feel nostalgic, that's not the ideal. The ideal is people who feel "I really want to be back."

Through the lens offered by Livnot U'Lehibanot, participants experience Israel and come to assign the religious meaning and personal relevance to the country that transform it from vague space into holy place. The role of the program in altering participants' relationship to Israel makes it necessary to carefully interrogate the construction of Israel at Livnot. Through a portrait of Israel that is primarily rural, mythic, ancestral, depoliticized and unified, Livnot seeks to develop a relationship between participants and Israel that is radically different from any relationship they could possess with another country.

THE ROLE OF LOCATION

A basic factor to consider in Livnot's picture of Israel is that of location, the actual places in Israel where program participants spend their time. The great majority of the program takes place on the Livnot campus in the Old City of Tzfat, a setting that is distinctly anachronistic in relation to the rest of contemporary Israel. Tzfat often serves as a destination for urban Israelis seeking a taste of something romantic, quiet, and old-fashioned. The town is cute, quaint, mystical, and enjoyed precisely because of the qualities that most distinguish it from the rest of Israel. Participants praised similar characteristics of Tzfat. As Diane explained: "Tzfat is beautiful. I just love it. It's so nice to walk down these alleyways. There's no cars to worry about, you can walk right down the middle. Especially on *shabbat* everybody is so into the community. It's really nice to see that. It's really like an old-fashioned town with old-fashioned ideals."

Participants' tendencies to compare the rest of Israel against their primary location of Tzfat means that participants often return from free weekends of travelling other parts of the country breathing a sigh of relief. As a result of unrealistic expectations, many of the places that *chevre* visit on their free weekends in Israel are perceived to be disappointing, dirty, or unnerving. I heard many shocked, negative stories from participants about cities like Tel Aviv, Akko, and Tiberias.

Some participants arrive in Israel before the program begins, providing an opportunity to travel before taking part in Livnot. Their first impressions of Israel are not always positive and many participants arrive at Livnot relieved to escape from wherever they have been touring. Rose, a schoolteacher from a small city in the southern United States, spoke of the initial surprise she experienced during her first week in Israel: "People always talk about how beautiful and incredible Israel is. When I first got here, I was like, this place reminds me of some of the really old not so nice neighbourhoods around my area [at home]. I was just like, God, it is just terrible. That was my first impression. After the first week – we travelled the first week I was here, I came a week early – I was just like, I don't know if I want to stay. I was really debating going home ... It was just, this place is incredibly dirty and I don't know about this. It totally was not what I expected."

It was only later, through Livnot, she explained, that she got to see the Israel she had heard so much about and almost forgotten: the beautiful Israel, the Israel of milk and honey, of olives, pomegranates, and dates: "I definitely feel more for the land. When I first got here I kept wondering why do people call this place so beautiful? It's just not so beautiful. The way people described it to me was totally not what I saw when I got here. I was like, what is so beautiful about this place? Now if people ask me, I'm like, it's just *beautiful* ... I just walk along and think 'this is Israel. This is *mine*. This belongs to me and it's part of me and it's part of who I am.' Israel has *become* beautiful."

The only other city in Israel that participants encounter as part of the official Livnot program is the Old City of Jerusalem. Like Tzfat, the Old City of Jerusalem is hardly representative of contemporary Israel. Moreover, the Livnot tour of the Old City is restricted to the Western Wall and to the Western Wall tunnels, accessed through the Jewish quarter. If participants want to experience the rest of the Old City, the souk and the sights of the Muslim, Armenian, or Christian quarters, they must do so during their free time. Other than a trip to the military cemetery of Har Herzl, the new city of Jerusalem, was ignored.[8] Livnot is interested solely in Jewish, religiously significant Israel.

PHYSICAL ROUTES IN THE LAND

Beyond the quaint, religious old cities of Tzfat and Jerusalem, the other Israel that Livnot offers is rural. Spent for the most part in Tzfat, the Livnot program is broken up only by weekly, day-long nature hikes. Through hiking in scenic, isolated nature reserves or remote parts of the Galilee and Golan Heights, Livnot constructs a picture of Israel that is predominately rural, and endowed with tremendous natural beauty.

Hiking is an extremely popular social and educational activity among Israelis. Many people hike in Israel, and it is enjoyed in youth movements, annual school outings, or family excursions. The Zionist practice of hiking the land has its roots in German youth movement culture, and groups like the *Wandervogel* and the German Jewish youth association *Blau Weiss*, which encouraged such activity as a way to experience nature and as an expression of high respect for physicality. The practice of hiking was imitated by the early Zionist movement, and was envisioned as a way of transforming the traditional Jewish ideal of "love of Zion" from abstract feeling into concrete practice. Hiking has, in Zionist praxis, traditionally been perceived as a way of strengthening one's love for the land (*ahavat ha'aretz*), through the development of an experiential knowledge of the land (*yediat ha'aretz*).[9] However common, these hikes or *tiyulim* are not an uncontested element of Israeli life. As a result of the inevitable safety hazards and accidents that have occurred on school hikes, some Israeli parents view the price of this knowledge of the land as being too high. Hiking, rooted in the culture of modern, secular *Ashkenazi* (European) Jews, has been supported by educators as a practice in the questionable effort to "help" *Mizrachi* (North African and Middle Eastern) Jews to "modernize" and develop an appreciation for nature and physicality comparable to that which *Ashkenazim* feel themselves to possess. Hiking the land has also been used for political ends, in protests organized by the Society for the Preservation of Nature against land appropriation for military purposes.[10] Equally, hiking has been used by supporters of Israeli settlements in the West Bank and Gaza Strip as a method of symbolizing land possession.[11]

Weekly *tiyulim* at Livnot offer participants an opportunity to learn about the Land of Israel through intensive immersion in it; walking the Land, eating from its vegetation, and swimming in its rivers. These hikes focus on learning about nature, and experiencing Israel through its birds, trees, and animals – themes that resonate deeply among environmentally conscious, North American youth.[12] Just as extensive time in Tzfat offers a small-town portrait of Israel, so too does hiking offer an Israel that is primarily rural, and one whose essence and meaning can be located in its physical landscape.

The act of walking itself is a way of marking territory and designating ownership, belonging, and connection.[13] At Livnot, participants are encouraged to interpret their *tiyulim* in this fashion. They attend a class specifically on the hiking ethic – entitled "In the Footsteps of Avraham, Through the Eyes of Moshe" – in which a number of traditional Jewish sources are discussed, including the Talmudic teaching that "If one walks the length and breadth of a parcel of land which he has purchased, he thereby takes formal possession of it."[14] Through participants' extensive hiking of Israel, the land becomes perceived as "theirs." No longer simply an abstract concept, nor just another location far from home,

Israel is transformed into a place that belongs to participants by virtue of their Jewishness and the presence of their footsteps.

Israel is also presented as a country that has been marked with the presence of Jews throughout history, and is ready to be similarly marked by the presence of Livnot participants. In a discussion of a text that states that "Anyone who walks four cubits in the Land of Israel is assured a portion in the World to Come,"[15] participants were taught by Eliyahu Levy that, as Rabbi Yochanan said, "when you walk four cubits in the Land of Israel, you have basically marked off your personal space. You have, in some kind of abstract sense, written with your feet 'Kilroy was here.' You know, that famous ancient graffiti? 'Kilroy was here in the Land of Israel.' You can't read it. You look at the stones, and you can't see that it says 'Kilroy was here' on the stones. But it does ... Jewishly speaking, by walking the land, one establishes one's presence in the Land."

AN ANCESTRAL AND MYTHICAL LAND

Through Livnot, Israel is presented to participants as the land of Jewish history and ancestors. The prophetess Devorah of the book of Judges, the first-century martyrs at Gamla, the biblical patriarchs Abraham, Isaac, and Jacob, and the second-century revolutionary Bar Kochba are all figures that populate the Israel of Livnot *tiyulim*. This portrait of the nation is one that studiously ignores the Israel of urban blight, development-town poverty, and materialist longings for American consumer products. Rather, Livnot offers participants the land of the Bible and historic legends, the setting for the dramatic heroes and tragic defeats of the Jewish past. This creation of a link between Israel and participants' ancestors is regularly reinforced on hikes that stop at sites deemed to possess historical significance. On a night outing during a two-day hike in the desert, for example, the hike-leader Daniel explained to the group that

> In this place, in this *wadi* behind us, where we're camping, according to most of the people who've really looked into it, this is where we wandered when we came out from Egypt and were walking toward the Land of Israel, and we went to the other side of the Jordan. We actually walked through this *wadi*. And if it wasn't this *wadi*, it was definitely this area ... That's a very

powerful thing to say we are back in the place where our
ancestors were. That's a very special thing. This is really what
makes the desert a Jewish thing, is we wandered in the desert for
forty years. In my opinion, I think that has an imprint on our
people. In other words, every one of us, even if we were born in
the city and raised in the city and went to university in the city,
every time a Jew goes to the desert, and certainly every time a Jew
goes to the desert in the same place where their ancestors walked
three thousand five hundred years ago, something happens.[16]

As the "land of our ancestors," rather than a typical modern nation-
state that possesses some of the same problems that plague other countries, it is the physical land of Israel, with its plants and animals, that
is rendered uniquely meaningful to participants. This construction of
Israel affected Tamara, who is from California and committed to organic
farming and environmentalism: "I'm intrigued by learning about the
trees and realizing they supported my ancestors and how they can support me too, with life, with fruit, with shade, with animals. Knowing
that every footstep I took, is a footstep that Abraham, Isaac, or Jacob
might have taken, makes hiking in Israel a more intense experience than
anywhere else in the world."

Similarly, Diane excitedly exclaimed: "I'll never look at a tree in the
same way that I used to. He [Daniel] just totally connected me to Israel.
Like me – Diane – to Israel. Because this is where everything happened
and this is where my ancestors came from and this is the tree that they
depended on. And now I'm looking at it and I'm walking through those
fields and looking at those trees. Wow, it's so cool."

At the same time as they take part in an Israel felt to possess essential
meaning because of its perceived connection to participants' ancestors,
chevre are also presented with an Israel that is inherently profound,
owing to the link that Livnot makes between the physical land and
Judaism. At Livnot, Israel is constructed as a highly mythical land, possessing an inherent meaningfulness, depth, and potency that needs only
to be watched for to reveal itself. The physical land of Israel is offered
as the quintessential location of Jewish symbolism. After they had been
eating wild grapes and pomegranates on a hike through Nahal El Al in
the Golan Heights, Daniel offered participants his view of the land:

In the Land of Israel, everything you see stands for something.
Every one of the seven kinds of fruit that we eat, that we are

eating, that we ate, they all stand for something. This olive tree is incredibly symbolic. Olives are symbolic. Leaves are symbolic. For instance, the olive leaf. In the bird from Noah's ark. Everything you see is a symbol of something much deeper. That's it. That is, in my own humble opinion, the most profound thing about this land. It is like another land. It has trees like other lands, it has plants and animals like other lands, but there is a deeper layer than anywhere else. First of all, the fact that our ancestors lived here thousands of years ago. But besides that metaphysical connection. Everything here is symbolic.

It is particularly through the weekly hikes that participants are extended a mythical view of the land as they learn about the relationships between nature and Judaism, between Israel's agricultural cycle and the holiday cycle, or between carob trees and creation. Participants come to develop a strong sense that compared to other countries, there is something inherently different about the physical land of Israel. Fern most deftly expressed the idea, echoed by many participants:

It's really weird thinking about going back to the States and going out to some random mountain. The Land [Israel] is different. It's just different. There are beautiful places in the world. There are beautiful places in the States. I feel like saying that there's something that does truly feel holy about it [Israel], but it seems too cliché. The Land here is so deep, it's just so deep. The trees are deep ... It's so connected. I just don't see the United States like that. I don't see Canada like that. I don't see anywhere else in the world like that. Nowhere. It's so deep, it's so symbolic. And the reason why it's so powerful, that whole feeling is that it's who I am. It's not just that I'm an American therefore I connect with Montana. It's different and I understand that now. Whereas before I thought I could connect as much with Montana, or should connect, as much with Montana as an American, as with the Land of Israel.

CONTEMPORARY ISRAEL: HIDDEN AND ROMANTICIZED

The portrait of Israel that is painted by Livnot is a selective one, owing to both active constructions and features that are absent. This Israel is primarily rural and physically beautiful, possessing an inherent, essential meaning by virtue of its connection to Judaism and to historical Jews. As already noted, aside from the visit to the Har Herzl military cemetery on a trip to Jerusalem, contemporary Israel as a modern state is encountered only abstractly, in the classroom or through brief discussions of the daily news. Participants do not experience modern Israel to anywhere near the degree to which they experience the historical and mythical aspects of the land. Livnot offers no actual classes on Israeli history or society, although there are semi-regular classes on Zionist history and current events.

While contemporary Israel and Zionism are relatively neglected compared to biblical and ancient Israel, specific aspects are given some attention. The history of the state is presented romantically, in either tragic or heroic terms that depict Israel as a country struggling to survive against impossible odds. The occasional classes on security issues given by Brian Ellis paint a compelling picture of Israel under siege, and outline the potential threat it faces from neighbouring countries. Any attention given to the philosophy and phenomenon of Zionism focuses on its unique, revolutionary nature. At the same time, these classes suggest that modern Zionism fulfills basic religious obligations and goals by enabling the return to the land so often spoken of and yearned for in Jewish tradition.[17] On one occasion, a Livnot teacher explained to participants that contemporary Zionism stems from the fact that "the burning desire to be in the Land of Israel is part of the genetic makeup of our [Jewish] souls."[18] Classroom treatment of Israel and Zionism presents a romantic, idealized construction focusing on themes that possess great emotional appeal.

Equally, there are occasional hikes that address contemporary Israel, but they do so in a narrow and dramatic fashion, emphasizing tragic or heroic aspects of its history. For example, when a regular hike was cancelled owing to bad weather, a bus trip to various sites in the Golan Heights was arranged in its place. One stop was at an army base to distribute snacks and greetings to the soldiers, in honour of *Rosh Hashana*. This experience was exciting for participants, who were titillated by intimations of danger, the base's "secret" location, its proximity to Syria, the fact that cameras were prohibited, and the difficulty encountered when seeking permission to enter the base. The encounter with good-looking young men stationed in the wilderness to protect the country against a hostile presence "just over there" encouraged a romantic heroization of the army and the conscription system. Livnot participants were excited to be bringing food to soldiers, perceiving themselves to be doing a good deed and thrilled to be somehow helping the country through caring for its soldiers. The soldiers themselves were somewhat bewildered by the episode, and seemed to think it was a little weird.

On the same day, the group sat in trenches near the Syrian border, once used for military surveillance. Participants were informed that this area is called Emek HaBacha, or the valley of tears because of the heavy Syrian losses incurred there during the Yom Kippur War of 1973. Daniel suggested that no other army in the world would name a battle site to commemorate enemy losses, and that normally a victorious army seeks to emphasize its own gains. However, according to Livnot staff, the Israeli army is more sensitive and caring than other armies, and able to recognize that "even when you've won, you're supposed to be depressed because you've caused a loss of life." Daniel then outlined the overwhelming danger to Israel posed during the Yom Kippur War, and told stories of the incredible individual heroism, courage, and self-sacrifice with which the Syrian military threat was met. At the nearby outdoor memorial called Oz 77, there is a tank from 1973 and a ring of trees to commemorate fallen Israeli soldiers. Daniel read aloud the moving memorial poem posted there, then spent a moment in heavy silence.[19] Placing a stone marker on the memorial,[20] he turned and dramatically walked away. Participants slowly, seriously followed his example, and everyone boarded the bus in silence.

In this hiking event, which offers participants a rare look at contemporary aspects of Israel and Zionism at Livnot, the romanticism of its construction of Israel is immediately apparent. Even the rather limited portrait of Zionism and contemporary Israel that Livnot offers is profoundly idealized, based around the emotional, wrenching themes of heroism and tragedy, threat and survivalism. This lack of extensive, basic engagement with Israeli or Zionist history made it possible at the end of the program for one participant to ask in all seriousness, and with group murmurings of equal confusion, who David Ben-Gurion was.[21]

Livnot avoids dealing with the modern state of Israel (*medinat yisrael*), with its modern problems and dilemmas, in favour of the mythical, trans-historical, biblically-based *eretz yisrael* (Land of Israel). As a result, the few participants who even notice the absence of contemporary Israel can be frustrated. Marni was perplexed by the lack of understanding she felt for contemporary Zionism and the state, which she contrasted to her strong sense of connection to the biblical, ancient Israel:

I feel an intense connection with Tzfat and this place and Livnot and the land that I walked over. But Israel as an entity and what it

stands for, I still have a lot of issues clouding my mind about it.
The whole aspect of Zionism. So feeling connected in that sense,
I don't get it. I get the biblical connection, I really do. I get that
and I feel it and I'm so amazed with it. It's a really beautiful thing
to me ... Certainly the hikes and the hike to Gamla really affected
me. Touching the flint. Walking across the land in three days. Being
in the desert affected me profoundly. That was a whole unique,
amazing, wordless experience unto itself. Being in the desert I really
did connect with the biblical sense out there and felt its power. It
was more through the *tiyuls* than anything that I got that. As far
as Zionism and the State of Israel, that was more in class, but
I didn't get the connectedness. I didn't get it. I still don't get it.

A DEPOLITICIZED ISRAEL

In its treatment of political issues, Livnot U'Lehibanot emphasizes ideals
of tolerance, mutual respect, and compromise, based on the particularly
non-Israeli idea that political views are private personal opinions and
that the attempt to persuade is somehow coercive. In what is perhaps
the more "real" Israel, everyone has an opinion, expresses it often, and
tries to persuade anyone who will listen. Most Israelis have lifestyles,
schools, friendships, and even neighbourhoods that are directly related
to their position on the political-religious spectrum. Livnot's carefully
controlled attempt to create an environment of respect, mutual tolerance, and privacy concerning political opinions serves to shield participants from some of the unappealing and divisive or fanatical aspects
of Israel and Israelis. Livnot staff themselves readily acknowledge that
Livnot is a distinctly North American idea, and one that makes little
sense to most Israelis, since it neither serves ultra-Orthodox efforts to
make people more religious, nor addresses secular Israeli concerns
about religious coercion. The Israel presented at Livnot is one that is
highly depoliticized, and thus an Israel that appears less foreign and
radical to participants.

The Israel presented in the Western media, the Israel of occupation,
of bulldozing Palestinian homes, of curfews and human rights abuses,
is completely absent at Livnot. Widespread poverty and suffering in the
Occupied Territories do not play a part in Livnot's portrait of Israel,
nor does the "second-class" status of Arabs who are Israeli citizens.
Certainly participants never meet a Palestinian or Israeli-Arab, nor are
their claims presented or addressed except when it seems useful to
underscore Livnot's narrative of persistent threat to the Jewish state.

In each three-month Livnot program, participants spend one *shabbat* on a Jewish settlement in the West Bank. Although this event is optional, participants are given no information about why some people might choose not to participate. According to staff member Eliyahu Levy, the aim of the settlement *shabbat* is to counter what he sees as a "vilification, or even demonization in the American Jewish public's eyes" of settlements in the Occupied Territories. As a result, Livnot fosters the impression that Jewish settlements, whose presence in the West Bank is a hotly contested national and international issue, are really just misunderstood suburbs. The settlement *shabbat* serves to "declaw" the settlement issue, and to turn it into a non-issue for *chevre*. To avoid tensions for participants, Livnot deliberately places them for *shabbat* with families that are not political extremists. However, this decision also contributes to presenting the settlement movement as a group of people who simply want to escape big-city Israel, with little in the way of ideological motivation or moral and political consequences. For Livnot participants, settlers are often viewed as just regular families living in small communities. Staff member Daniel explains:

People love families in – although I don't want to use that word but you used it first – in settlements ... It's mind-opening ...
I think they see a part of Israel that they could never really see if it wasn't through Livnot. I also think that it breaks a lot of myths. One could make a good argument that you can't ignore the fact that there are politics here in Israel and it's very one-sided to do that kind of a thing, because of course I'm going to come back happy about that [settlements]. Then why don't you give the other side, for instance? So the question is, how would you give the other side. Would you send them to Ramallah [in the West Bank]? Would you send them to Tel Aviv? Would you let them hear a different political view? The truth is, the people here are sharp cookies. They go to a family and that's saying, "This [territory] is ours, it was promised to Abraham, and I'm just going to be here and if the Arabs have a problem with that, that's just tough." They don't like that, and it turns *chevre* off. We always monitor people. If we knew that people were really into the politics part, that was like a big thing ... I mean, obviously they're going to be a right-wing family, politically. And that's going to come out somehow. But if we hear people preaching? Just like if we hear people preaching about Judaism, we pull the rug from underneath the family.

And while participants may well be the "sharp cookies" Daniel speaks of, they are also open-minded enough to revise their opinions based on what they see. Some participants are simply bored by the settlements, finding the experience banal, and conclude that the experience was the same as celebrating *shabbat* anywhere in Israel. Others view the settlements simply as a safe, community-oriented escape from big-city life. The notion, however, that the settlements are nothing out of the ordinary, that the West Bank is just like any other part of Israel, and that the settlements are not political, is a highly political conclusion, and one that carries significant implications. Fern's description of her visit to the settlements demonstrates the depoliticization of this hotly contested element of Israeli political life:

> I thought it was great ... it totally surprised me ... I just never really understood what settlements were all about ... it totally changed my view of them. I always saw the people who lived on settlements as being kind of nutty. I mean, what are you doing living there? But they're not radical people, they're just people who want to live outside of the big cities, have more space, don't necessarily feel that they should not move into Israeli land just because of everything that's going on. They're moving on with their lives. We can create wonderful communities with big houses and live very nicely in land that's open and there's lots of it. My stereotype was that most people lived in settlements because they wanted to prove a political point.

Clearly, the Livnot lens through which participants are invited to see Israel is one that is basically religious and, at least nominally right-wing in orientation. This direction does not, I believe, stem from any real attempt to encourage Livnot participants to support right-wing policies, but rather from the desire to inspire in participants a basic sense of Jewish nationalism and love of the land. At the time of my fieldwork, there was, to my knowledge, only one quietly left-leaning staff member at Livnot, who felt some conflict about Livnot's political message. He explained his position to me:

> On the one hand, I don't want to teach them that their relationship with Israel should be with a right-wing political slant. On the other hand, I think there is a certain need. For instance if they want to become left-wing one day, that's fine. But first they have

to be right-wing. I don't think it's healthy – for instance, Israelis. Israeli left-wingers, if there's somebody who is "I am all for giving the Palestinians back the land, because I couldn't care less about the Land of Israel and the Jews," that's a problem. But if it's "I'm tired of seeing my friends killed in war. I love this country more than anything in the world. I'd give my life for it. But maybe there's a solution." That's different. That's fine. But you need first the basis of what it means to have a love of Israel. I think it's a natural thing that the love of Israel is first going to be more kind of right-wing and more that slant.

A HOMOGENEOUS JEWISH SOCIETY

As mentioned above, Livnot focuses almost exclusively on Jewish Israel, which is presented as unified and homogeneous. In Livnot's narrative, Arabs exist solely in the context of the West Bank and Gaza Strip, or in unfriendly neighbouring countries. The Druze, discussed only because the three-day hike passes directly through the Druze village of Peki'in, are presented as a kind of "good Arab" because of their loyalty to Israel. There is no discussion at Livnot of Israel's struggle with racism toward Jews of Ethiopian descent, or the systematic exclusion of eastern *Mizrachi* Jews from the higher echelons of achievement and recognition. These *Mizrachim*, who form the majority of Jews in Israel, are discussed at Livnot only in the context of their friendliness and synagogue seating in the round, which is presented as being more sociable than European pews. The Israel constructed at Livnot is one that is significantly unmarked by secular-religious divisions and violence. For participants at Livnot, contemporary Israel is largely obscured, or idealized as Jewish, unified, and idyllic.

Through Livnot's construction of Israel, participants come to understand Israel as a country that offers a Jewish society and the freedom to express one's Jewishness in public. Participants often contrast this freedom to North America, where they recall feeling somehow misunderstood or unable to enjoy a public Judaism in such a secular or nominally Christian society. This perception of Israel as offering a uniquely free place to express one's Jewishness can both result from and lead to a deeply romantic view of Jewishness in Israel. Many participants, for example, expressed their joy at being in a place where everything shuts down on *shabbat*, from stores and restaurants to public buses. While Livnot is not responsible for constructing this feature of Israeli society, by avoiding the issue of secular Jews and their concerns about religious coercion in Israel, Livnot can help foster the misleading notion that *shabbat* closures are uncontested. A number of participants were enthusiastic about the idea of being Jewish in what they perceive to be a society in which Judaism is a shared, common feature of life. Steven's suggestion that "everybody's on the same page" when it comes to Judaism in Israel is undeniably romantic: "It's just the strangest feeling. I take it for granted now. That everyone's Jewish. No one really questions anyone about what they're doing. I mean, as you get more into religion, there are divisions that cause tension. But besides that, everybody's on the same page and everybody understands what's going on. Everything shuts down on Saturday. It just shuts down. Everybody deals with it, they understand it."

Similarly, Robert was quite moved when he came across a large group of Chassidim dancing in the streets of Tzfat one *Rosh Chodesh*, celebrating the start of a new month in the Jewish calendar:

> As we got closer, we thought it was a dance party or whatever. We saw all these Chassidim dancing around, just in a big circle. Absolute madness. Just a huge party ... I'm just sitting there looking at it in awe. Then these two Chassidim run out of the circle and grab three of the other guys in Livnot and myself and just dragged us in. Within seconds we're in the middle of prob- ably a hundred Chassidim. Just jumping around and running in circles. The mutability of the dance too was pretty amazing. In such a strict group of people, you could do anything. You could be jumping up and down or be in the centre looking like you're clog dancing. It was all fun. They put their Chassidim hats on us ... It was amazing to be a part of that! There again, just like *shabbat*. You couldn't do that in America. This is very much a part of Israel. You can't do this as a minority. Part of it is being sucked into the majority where you realize the awesome power of the people.

While Robert is correct in his observation that this public Chassidic display is less likely in America, such a scene is also a relatively unlikely event in most parts of Israel. The event is also not as ideologically neutral as it might have appeared to him. However, since Livnot does not discuss secular-religious tensions or problems caused by the reli- gious nature of the state, it becomes more possible for participants to become caught up in the collective Jewish effervescence of the moment. As a result, participants tend not to realize that the complex question of whether one can live a better or more fulfilling Jewish life in Israel than in North America cannot be addressed without considering some of the more complex social, cultural, and political realities of life in contemporary Israel.

DISJUNCTURES

Regardless of the picture of Israel painted by Livnot, there are various aspects of the "other" Israel outside Livnot that participants do encounter on their three free weekends during the program. The disjuncture between the Israel that participants experience at Livnot and the one they discover during their travels often leads to surprise, dislike, and confusion. Many participants, even by the end of the program, know nothing about secular Jews in Israel, and their often acrimonious relationships with religious Jews. Thus Fern was surprised and extremely upset on a free weekend to hear anti-religious and anti-Israel feelings expressed at a dinner party of an Israeli friend:

It's not that I feel lied to, but it's been a shock. Based on my feelings about Judaism. On my free weekend I went to my cousin's house and she had a dinner party. There were three other couples there. So here I am, I'm having this wonderful, amazing experience at Livnot and here I am with Israelis and other Jewish people who've made *aliyah*. If I were to have done everything we do at Livnot [on *shabbat*] they would think I'm weird, they would totally judge it, they would be negative about it. They were negative the whole time about Israel and 8 million things about Judaism and religious Jews and how horrible they are. And assuming that anyone who wears a yarmulke is part of that horrible group, not just black hatters. I was like "Wow!"

However, such experiences rarely challenge the developing worldview of Livnot participants, presumably because free weekends do not occur often (every three weeks, on average) and participants return to Livnot after each one. What is presented at Livnot is felt by participants to be the "real" Israel, the "true" Judaism, the authentic portrait untarnished by factionalism and fads. As Fern puts it: "If anything, Livnot has been a saviour because had I not done Livnot and had I just come to Israel,

I could be sitting at the table saying 'Wow.' I might have formed much different impressions about Israel and Judaism without Livnot. Livnot has helped me stay grounded in a belief of what Judaism is truly about, not what politics and counterculture have made it out to be."

In a similar experience of dissonance, Hannah's visit to a secular *kibbutz* was an unpleasant experience for her, awakening her to the fact that not all Israeli Jews are as positively inclined toward Judaism as she had expected. Hannah's surprise was coupled with extreme disapproval, which included the suggestion that secular Jews should not live in Israel:

> I have very negative issues about the secular society and how they're just – to me, I just perceive it as anti-religion. *Don't be here if that's how you are.* That's my personal feeling on it. I didn't know it was like that! I knew that everyone wasn't religious, but I didn't know that there were people who would actually refuse to do Jewish things. That people would go out of their way to be as un-Jewish as possible in a Jewish country ... The main place I saw it was when I saw my brother at his *kibbutz.* Someone said that the bar was open on Friday night and I said "Really? On *shabbat?*" And she was like "Oh, we don't do that here"... It was really disturbing.

By the end of Livnot, Warren had also come to share a similar vision of Israel as a conservative, religious state: "I am becoming really pro-Israel and I really see the necessity of it. I feel very protective of Israel. Extremely conservative. My views are conservative. I lean towards a religious state. I know there are problems with that. But if we let things erode like they have in the United States, then what is the purpose of Israel? What's going to bind it together if it's just a Jewish state by name, just that we're Jewish. What does that mean that we're Jewish? It means nothing if we're not behaving and living in a Jewish way."

AN ISRAEL THAT NEEDS THEM

At the same time as it is portrayed as rural, homogeneous, and apolitical, Israel is also constructed for participants as a country that needs them, through the process of daily manual labour. Rather than simply signing a cheque to the United Jewish Appeal, as they might have seen North American Jews do for Israel, participants at Livnot are given the opportunity to make what they view as a practical, physical contribution to the country. The director of Livnot U'Lehibanot, Benjamin Green, admits that while in the early days of the program participants worked in order to build the campus, manual labour is currently performed primarily for the physical release, sense of accomplishment, and connection to Israel that it provides. Through this experience of demanding, regular manual labour, participants are offered a chance to relate to Israel through building the land, and thereby to participate, at least to some degree, in the core Zionist narratives of pioneering and settlement.[22] For Wendy, the experience of rebuilding was significant: "We saw the destruction of the earthquake here in Tzfat and what Livnot did to help it be rebuilt. That connection is pretty important. Rebuilding the destruction of Israel ... I think it's extremely important to have work, not just for the physicalness of it, but to be a part of a rebuilding. This whole country has been rebuilt. It's still happening from different destructions or different attacks ... It helped me to acquire a connection because I was rebuilding it."

The feeling of helping, of making a difference to Israel and to the Jewish community there, was deeply satisfying to many participants. For Diane, as for many others, the feeling of satisfaction that came from helping the community was a surprise:

> In the beginning I hated it [working]. I hated waking up at 6:30, to be out the door at 7:30 to be working until 11:30. To me that was ughh! And it was really hard to get into it. But now, in the galleries specifically, at first it was oh my God I have to chisel this straight line and I don't know why. But then when we had that opening ceremony, it was totally amazing. Because that's work that we're doing! We're helping these galleries be restored ... even if it's a small contribution. Today I was helping to paint the mural and people were walking by and saying, "Oh that's so great!" ...
> There was this guy who works upstairs and he was giving us cookies for snacks. It was so cool. I can see how it's really helping the community.

When Livnot alumni return to Tzfat, a common highlight of their visit often involves walking through the Old City and pointing out the buildings or parks that they helped build. The experience of making a concrete contribution, of helping to shape the country and making a difference is powerful, causing participants to gain a stake in what happens to Israel: after all, it is now partly theirs since they have contributed to its development. Israel becomes a country marked by their effort, a country they helped with their own labour, rather than simply from afar, with money. Like many participants, Fern had not expected to find the work component of Livnot as satisfying as she did: "It's actually pleasantly surprising how much I do enjoy it. I really do feel like I will leave feeling like, *wow*. Whenever I come back to Tzfat, I'll feel like I actually contributed to building it ... I love the idea of being able to contribute to the community and give of myself in that way." And again: "I was walking around the other day and looking and I saw all these Livnot plaques all over the place. Livnot is literally part of the history of Tzfat ... The sense that I helped build and maintain one of the cities of Israel really is mind boggling. It's an immediate connection."

In fact, while some residents of Tzfat express appreciation for the work that Livnot participants do for the city, more than one resident has suggested to me that, in fact, Livnot projects are of little real value to the community, that they are often left unfinished and tend to create significant amounts of garbage and debris around the old city.

AN ACCESSIBLE ISRAEL

At the same time as it is a Jewish, unified, mythic, and rural land, the Israel offered to Livnot participants is also highly accessible and a plausible option as a place to live. This Israel has few linguistic barriers as the language of the program is English, with a few token Hebrew words used for things like "the group," "cleaning duty," or "hikes." To ensure that participants do not feel uncomfortable, staff refrain from speaking Hebrew to each other in front of them. While occasionally informal, optional Hebrew classes are offered during free time, they operate at an extremely basic level and are usually abandoned by participants early on in favour of sleep and running errands. Close to the end of the fall program of 1997, a number of participants were deeply shocked to learn that they might have trouble finding a temporary job in Israel after Livnot without some ability to speak Hebrew.

As participants have very little contact with people born in Israel, and almost none with non-*Ashkenazi* Israelis, they also experience an Israel possessing few cultural hurdles. Since the vast majority of program staff have backgrounds similar to those of participants, having been raised in North American and non-religious homes, participants come to feel that Israel is less foreign and more comfortable than they might otherwise experience. Livnot presents an Israel with little in the way of cultural difference, run by North American Israelis who share a common cultural vocabulary with North American participants. At the same time, however, the Israelis of North American backgrounds that they do meet are committed to the country in a unique way, having actively chosen to emigrate to Israel rather than live in North America. Steven expressed the power of seeing the choices made by Livnot staff: "When I first came here [I thought] the people who run the program are all American-born or Canadian-born?! I was like, that's kind of stupid, because it's an Israel program they should be Israelis. But at the same time, you see people who came over, started their whole life, and it's comforting in a way. 'Ah, look at us, we're having a great time. We've got kids, and the kids love it over here.' You see that and it's as if to say, 'We've done it, so can you,' in a way."

This construction of Israel as accessible and comfortable, combined with living in an environment that is populated with North Americans who have chosen to forgo an "easier" life in the United States or Canada for the relative hardships of living in Israel, transforms Israel into a significantly more plausible option for participants to consider as a place to live for the future.

FINDING ROUTES TO ISRAEL, FINDING ROOTS IN ISRAEL

Traditionally, nations and cultures have been conceived of as discrete, singular entities that are linked in some natural, essential bond to a particular territory. Whether as a result of popular language use, nationalist ideologies, anthropological studies, or community activism, particular peoples are thought to be organically "rooted" in particular territories.[23] It is through the standard image of the world map, Gupta and Ferguson explain, that "schoolchildren are taught such deceptively simple-sounding beliefs as that France is where the French live, America is where the Americans live, and so on ... we assume a natural association of a culture ('American culture'), a people ('Americans') and a place ('the United States of America'). Both the ethnological and the national naturalisms present associations of people and place as solid, commonsensical, and agreed on, when they are in fact contested, uncertain and in flux."[24]

Increasingly, anthropology has come to recognize that the presumed associations between people, culture, and place assume static, bounded, homogeneous groups that rarely reflect the multiple, mobile, mixed realities of contemporary life. Ethnographers have begun to address "in-between" spaces and concepts such as borderlands, diasporas, and transnationalism.[25]

In a similar vein, this chapter has proceeded on the assumption that what Gupta and Ferguson call the "processes and practices of place-making" need to be interrogated and laid bare in order to problematize the "natural" associations of people and place.[26] Like all presentations of Israel, the Israel of Livnot is a selective construction which emphasizes certain features of the country while downplaying others. This chapter has sought to investigate the vision of Israel that Livnot U'Lehibanot offers to participants. Particularly through their weekly hikes, and, to a lesser degree, in the classroom, participants at Livnot experience an Israel that is deeply meaningful, marked with the presence of ancestors, inherently Jewish in nature and society, apolitical, and rural, a "home-land" that belongs to them as Jews. The Livnot construction of Israel is a portrait that tends to ignore both contemporary and troubling aspects of the state, focusing rather on romantic, heroic, or tragic events that possess a strong emotional appeal. Livnot's construction is grounded in the concept of *eretz yisrael*, the land of Israel, instead of developing a relationship with or understanding of *medinat yisrael*, the state of Israel. Livnot encourages the development of a personal, religious, symbolic relationship between participants and "their ancestral land," rather than a nationalist connection to the political entity of the contemporary Israeli state.

Without a doubt, this construction of Israel is highly selective, idealistic, and deeply romantic. In many ways, it is precisely the selectivity of the portrait that makes it "work," enabling it to appeal to a young audience, imbued with a post-1960s, somewhat New-Age reverence for nature, roots, and spirituality. In contemporary North America, the sense of being indigenous, or otherwise rooted in one's "native" soil, is "power-fully heroized,"[27] a phenomenon that Lowenthal labels the "mystique of native antiquity."[28] Equally, the "new strands of 'green politics' that literally sacralize the fusion of people, culture and soil on 'Mother Earth,'" serve to romanticize and valorize the grounding of people and cultures in what is conceived of as their natural place.[29] Livnot participants are often environmentally aware, sensitive to the land claims of indigenous groups in North America, and deeply sensitive to nature. An Israel that appeals to participants' own desires to be indigenous, and that does so in a way that is natural, rural, and spiritually significant, is powerfully attractive to them.

For many North American Jews, the complicated relationships between such historical and political factors as immigration, anglo-conformity, the allegiance demands of the modern nation-state, Western education, and assimilation have caused their sense of personal or religious connection to Israel as a "homeland" to become erased and forgotten. At the same time, the perception that North America provides an equality of opportunity and religious freedom unheard of in other diasporic communities ensures that there are few "push" factors inspiring Jews in North America to dream of a utopic, safer, more complete Jewish life in the land of Israel.[30] Finally, modern Jewish religious thought outside of Israel has generally sought to demystify, re-symbolize, and politicize the idea of *eretz yisrael*. This trend, argues Arnold Eisen, has been very successful in the diaspora, resulting in a political view of Israel as "a reality cherished and supported but kept separate from one's religious identity as a Jew."[31]

Financial and general political support for the state of Israel has been a regular part of public Jewish life in North America.[32] Through the popular media, Jewish community institutions, and public political life, liberal North American Jews are accustomed to relating to Israel as a modern nation-state. However, while most American Jews would claim a profound commitment to Israel, that connection is, generally, entirely political and public, and lacking in either a spiritual dimension or impact in the private realm.[33] Even though "echoes of Israel" might still be heard in common Jewish rituals, like the breaking of a glass at the wedding ceremony to recall the destruction of the Temple, that meaning, Steven Cohen asserts, "is probably lost on most members of the wedding party."[34] I suggest that even if the members of the wedding party shared an intellectual understanding of the traditional rationale behind the practice of shattering the glass, most contemporary North American Jews would not possess the emotional connection, the deep attachment to the land of Israel that would imbue such a gesture with meaning. It is precisely the feeling of a spiritual, emotional bond to the Land of Israel that most moderately affiliated North American Jews lack, and which Livnot encourages participants to develop. Livnot allows North American Jews to feel that Israel possesses some inherent religious meaning, value, and significance beyond simply its political importance as a modern nation-state.[35]

Through the process of Livnot, Judaism becomes (re-)territorialized for participants, and, correspondingly, participants as residents of

North America, become (re-)diasporized.[36] While it is entirely possible
that the biological ancestors of Livnot participants were among those
who left Palestine some 2,000 years ago, we must recognize equally
that diaspora is more than just a neutral term of location. Rather,
"diaspora" is a loaded label that suggests periphery, and which necessarily implies an organic, original, more authentic sense of rootedness
in a "centre" elsewhere. Without such an emotional attachment to
another place, centre, homeland, or nation, diaspora is simply an empty
technical term denoting nothing more than a physical location other
than somewhere else. Diaspora necessarily suggests a dual loyalty
toward places, and assumes some connection to the location currently
inhabited, alongside a continued involvement with and relationship to
the "homeland." It is only through the territorialization of Judaism, its
grounding in the land of Israel, that Livnot participants, as North American Jews, become "diasporized." Through this "(re-)centring" of Israel
from vague space to holy place, participants are transformed not only
from tourists to potential pilgrims, but, paradoxically, into diaspora Jews.

Doubtless, Jewish understandings of the land of Israel – its role,
importance, requirements, and implications have changed significantly
according to period, place, and historical circumstances. Nonethless, for
almost 2,000 years between exile from the land under the Romans and
the creation of the state of Israel, the idea of the land of Israel has
consistently functioned as an integral part of Judaism. Much yearned
for in religious imagination, Israel was an abstract, spiritualized, mythol-
ogized construct that possessed little grounding in earthly reality or in
the actual situation of Palestine of the time. In traditional Jewish thought,
eretz yisrael functions at least as much as a spiritual destination as it is
a concrete piece of geography.[37] It is easy, and some would even say
desirable, to imagine a Judaism without the modern nation-state of
Israel. But it is impossible to imagine Judaism without the love of and
longing for the mythic ancestral Land of Israel. The symbolic, romantic,
religious Israel displayed by Livnot allows these disaffiliated, alienated,
or Jewishly illiterate Jews to tap into a powerful historical sense of longing for a utopic Israel that can never be fully realized. Regardless of the
ambivalence that exists in biblical and Talmudic literature toward political possession of the land, a longing for return to the idealized land of
Israel, regardless of how spiritualized and future-oriented, has formed a
central part of the Jewish experience until the modern era. This connection to Israel is paralleled by a conscious sense maintained among Jews
living outside of "the Land" that they constitute diaspora communities.[38]

Livnot makes the "traditional," religiously significant concept of Israel and the longing for it, a palpable, plausible possibility for participants. The program offers neither a detailed nor a complex understanding of the land's religious significance. Difficult questions such as Israel's relationship in Jewish thought to notions of exile and redemption, the cause of the land's holiness, or the implications that it suggests are not engaged at Livnot. What Livnot does, however, is to offer participants "the Land" as a potent category, as an effective entity possessing significance. In so doing, Livnot's construction of Israel allows *chevre* to participate in a mainstay of Jewish tradition: the yearning for an idealized Land of Israel, a romantic attachment to "the land of our ancestors," and an Israel which has profound religious significance.

4

Routes to Other Jews

Most participants come to Livnot with little attachment to the concept of Jewish peoplehood, whether as a historical or contemporary entity. Livnot seeks to alter this situation by encouraging a relationship between participants and other Jews, be they Orthodox Jews, Jews of history, or their peers, and based on familiarity, similarity, and relevance to participants' own Jewish selves. As participants come to perceive these other Jews as increasingly like themselves, a mirror process begins in which the participant comes to recognize his own inner-otherness, his particularity as a Jew, and his own difference.

Many *chevre* arrive at Livnot possessing little more interest in traditional Judaism than a curiosity about a radically different, remote, exotic culture. Certainly, most participants tend to feel that Jewish culture is more relevant to them than are other cultures, however vaguely this is articulated. But while Livnot participants might intellectually understand Jewish history to be "theirs," it remains alien and inaccessible to them. Orthodox staff members and other particularly observant Jews are fascinating but distinctly foreign to *chevre*. Over time, and using the mechanisms that will be discussed below, Livnot tries to overcome the alterity of different (and sometimes similar) Jews for participants, and encourage a sense of familiarity, community, and kinship.

For participants, this process of getting to know other Jews is myth-breaking and one that challenges preconceived stereotypes. At the same time, the process offers a profound sense of community and belonging that transcends time, space, and lifestyle. Basic Livnot features of "historical" hiking, empathy between religious staff and non-Orthodox participants, and the experience of living in close quarters with Jews of similar ages and interests transform the way that many participants view other Jews, and thus, inevitably, themselves as Jews. Arriving as individuals, participants come to see themselves as rooted in a larger polity that includes the ancient, the different, and the similar.

LOOKING FOR ANCESTORS: ROUTES TO HISTORICAL JEWS

In addition to introducing participants to the natural world of *eretz yisrael*, as discussed above, many Livnot hikes include journeys to sites or areas perceived to have historical significance, including Gamla, ancient villages, the desert, and several ancient synagogues. Great effort is made on these hikes to explain the historical importance of a site through creative, colourful descriptions that seek to make the ancient past come alive for participants. Often these explanations imbue Jewish history with personal relevance to the present and to participants' lives. This is done by drawing out moral lessons from Jewish quests for independence, adding insights into the contemporary Jewish community, or demonstrating the importance of commitments to Israel and the need to ensure Jewish survival. In this manner, the primary purpose of *tiyulim* at Livnot is to concretize historical episodes for the participants by journeying to the site and teaching the living relevance of Jewish history.

During a night hike through caves from the Bar Kochba period (early second century) in the Beit Rimmon valley, participants sat together in a wide, pitch-dark room at the opening of the cave system and, before exploring the caves themselves, listened to Daniel's description of historical events. By the light of a single flashlight, Daniel explained the use of caves during the Bar Kochba revolt. His narrative weaves together colourful historical description with moral lessons and the theme of Jewish pride:

Turns out that, after, the Romans with the Caesar Hadrian chased the Jews during the Bar Kochba revolt, because the Jews dared to stand up against the Romans with Rabbi Akiva and Bar Kochba at the helm. And the Romans brought in no less than twelve legions from Europe. Now a legion consists of, depending on what researcher you are, between 15,000 and 35,000 soldiers. We're sixty years after the Temple was destroyed and the Jewish people were decimated. What do we have left? Twelve legions had to come into this country by boat in order to stop the rebellion. The twenty-second legion, which came by foot from Egypt, we never hear about again, because apparently they were totally wiped off the face of the earth by the Jews. We're the comeback people. We are that bush, we're the caper bush. We just keep on coming back with that *chutzpa*. You can't get rid of us. Every other country fell, just like us. Every other country accepted being Romans, except the Jews. It was amazing … every civilized nation in the world puts a head on the side of a coin. Except the Jews. We put olive leaves and clusters of grapes and things like that.

Daniel's story continues, explaining how the Jews gained a military advantage by concealing themselves in caves, until finally the Romans forced them out of their hiding places with smoke. Using this theme of being "smoked out," Daniel then explicitly links the Bar Kochba revolt of the second century to the Warsaw Ghetto uprising of 1943, a recent, heroic, yet ultimately tragic event, one with which participants are familiar and emotionally connected. This linkage aims to render the Bar Kochba event and the people involved less remote and foreign, and their struggle more comprehensible to a twentieth-century audience:

And then the Romans did one more thing that beat us. What did they do? What's the one way you can get people out of this cave? Smoke 'em out. I'll read you one verse from the Talmud, just one verse: "They smoked the house upon us, they smoked the cave upon us." They smoked us out. That's how they beat us. Billows and a fire and the very beginning. And we choked to death … They died by smoke inhalation. What's the first thing you think of when you hear that story? Tunnels and smoke. What association does anybody have? Warsaw … Jews lived in tunnels, and Jews survived the Nazis. How can a Jew survive the Nazis, c'mon, it's a joke. And the only way they beat them was the smoke, the poison gas. And that's history repeating itself. This is our Holocaust museum, guys. Because this and the Holocaust are twins, and neither time did they succeed. But it seems as if they did. You know, you can look at this and say we lost, look at everything that was lost, we lost. But you can also look at the big picture.

Despite the immediate, tragic outcome of both the Bar Kochba revolt and the Holocaust, Daniel explained to Livnot participants that the Jews ultimately came to win, simply by their survival.[1] The Jewish people were actually victorious, in this narrative, because both the

Romans and the Nazis were relegated to history books and museums, while the Jews are alive and free. Livnot's explicit connection of the Bar Kochba revolt, the Holocaust, and the State of Israel, based on themes of resistance and of long-term survival against the odds is also part of a heroic Zionist re-imagining of history.

Zionist rhetoric and ritual minimizes the defeat and tragic results of the Bar Kochba revolt, and uses it instead as a model of struggle for national liberation.[2] One of the ways in which the defeat of the Bar Kochba revolt is minimized is by showing the ultimate short-term victory of the Romans. The example that Daniel uses in his explanation to participants is common in Israel:

> We could say, you know, we lost. There's only one way that we can say that we didn't lose. And this a historian once wrote, on the Ninth of Av[3] each year, on the day that the Temple was destroyed and the Bar Kochba revolt fell, every Ninth of Av he goes to the Israel Museum in Jerusalem, and there's a place there called the Bar Kochba room. There's a bust there of Caesar Hadrian. Hadrian's the guy who engineered the mass murder of the Jews in the Land of Israel. And every time that his name is mentioned in the Talmud, he has a little nickname that the rabbis gave him. You know what his nickname is? "May his bones be crushed." "Hadrian the emperor, may his bones be crushed." We don't say that about a lot of people. Only one guy, may his bones be crushed. That's Hadrian. And this guy goes and stands every Ninth of Av in the Bar Kochba room of the Israel Museum and looks at this bust of Hadrian ... and he stands there and he looks at it there and he says, "You are in a glass case in a museum, and I am walking freely in the land of Israel." You know, that's what the Nazis tried to do, to have a museum. And you know, in the end, that's who's in the museum. Not to rub it in, not to take revenge. It just happens. We're still around. And that's a miracle. This is a place where you can come and appreciate the miracle. We get to walk upright in the land of Israel today.

Finally, in a concrete attempt to make the historical experience of the Bar Kochba revolt more realistic for participants – and thus the hardship of all Jews under threat – Daniel describes the complete, impossible silence required while hiding from the Romans. Offering participants the opportunity to share in that historical experience, Daniel invited *chevre* to experience a brief taste of hiding from persecution, in the same cool, dark caves where it happened almost 2,000 years earlier:

> You know what happened when the Romans came; they tried to find people. They would try to listen just like the Nazis did, to Jews that were hiding out in the attics. They would try to listen for breathing. The Romans would walk around with sandals that were studded with nails. So when you heard somebody walking on top of the cave, you knew they were within seconds of finding you all and killing you all. You couldn't breathe. You couldn't leave the cave. Because if you left the cave, a Roman might be watching and would see where the entrance to the cave was ... That's terror. That's when they had to be totally silent. Just to see what it was like, let's take just sixty seconds, not two years, not a month, not like three hours until the all-clear is given. Sixty seconds, of trying not to swallow, not to breathe, not to giggle, not to move any limb. And you'll see how hard it is. Try! Sixty seconds not to move.

The Jewish history taught at Livnot is aimed squarely at fostering a relationship between participants and their cultural heritage. Rather than providing an intellectual study of history, Livnot seeks to link these young Jews to the Jewish collective by encouraging their participation in Jewish collective memory.[4] Contrasting the pursuit of "heritage" with that of "history," David Lowenthal suggests that most of the criticisms made against "heritage" are because it is perceived to threaten "real" history with bias, political motives, or outright fraud. Recognizing that history is hardly a pristine, transparent lens on past reality, he writes: "Heritage is scolded for swerving from the true past – selecting, altering, inventing. But history also does this. Like heritage, history cannot help but be different from, as well as both less and more than, the actual past ... The most crucial distinction is that truth in heritage commits us to some present creed; truth in history is a flawed effort to understand the past on its own terms."[5]

In contrast to history, the purpose of heritage is to encourage the development of particular worldviews or values. At the same time, Lowenthal notes that heritage tends to be far more engaging for people, owing to its vitality and immediate relevance, than are the more distant, alien, dull facts of history. For people more inclined toward heritage than history, "such an unrevised [historical] past is too remote to comprehend, too strange to be exemplary, too regrettable to admire, or too dreadful to recall. It may also be too dead to care much about."[6]

Livnot clearly offers participants an encounter with Jewish heritage, rather than a factual study of Jewish history. It is consciously aimed at affecting participants' understandings of themselves as Jews, and what that means in the present. Jewish heritage at Livnot is not taught as a collection of cold, remote classroom facts, but rather as "an experience" in which participants can share. Jewish heritage at Livnot is also not portrayed as one culture's history among many, of equal importance and relevance to any other history. Rather, Livnot understands itself to be teaching participants *their* heritage, a past privileged by virtue of the perceived kinship between its protagonists and present-day Jews.[7]

Participants are highly conscious of the impact of this kind of experiential teaching on their understanding of the Jewish past. For Steven, the ability to relate to Jewish history is bound up with his feeling of relationship and community with other Jews: "The weird thing is learning US history in school – it just didn't seem very tangible. I just couldn't connect ... [At Livnot] you feel like those [Jews] are people who have been fighting for something that you belong to. I guess it's the belonging to something. America's so big, you're American ... So many things have happened to the Jewish people over years and years and years. They just keep coming back fighting. It's not like they want to take over the world. They just want a place for themselves."

Brenda was positively surprised to learn that, in contrast to her stereotypes of passivity and victimization, Jews actively fought against the Romans. Knowledge of Jewish heroism and activism made her feel a great pride in "her" history: "What is more exciting than the idea or the knowledge that the Jewish people actually fought and conquered the Romans or whoever were the invaders of the time? They weren't just sitting around reading books or something. They were real warriors, fighters, which I love. That is just amazing to me."

Livnot's construction of historical Jews as fighters and ardent Jewish survivalists in a threatening world affects participants's own views of their role in and responsibilities to Jewish survival. As Steven explained, he has learned "why it's important to know who you are and what you've gone through. Your past. I just feel, not paranoia, that people are always after us. But there's not a very big community who is on your side. And if anything, it's just the Jews. So why should I turn my back on the Jewish people, the Jewish religion ... it's like the Jewish people are one big family. Just the way they relate to one another."

These stories of historical Jewish suffering and martyrdom inspire some participants to feel responsible to continue a heritage and a people for which others have sacrificed their lives. Historical examples of people fighting and dying for the right to practice Judaism imbue Judaism with a new kind of value for participants. Referring to Gamla, where, in 67 CE, the inhabitants leapt to their deaths from steep cliffs in order to delay the Roman approach to Jerusalem, Nancy commented:

> I was thinking, there were many people ... who totally gave their lives for Jews to have a free place to live. Especially at Gamla. I thought that was our best hike. They gave their lives, they died, they jumped over, just so it would keep the Romans from getting to Jerusalem for like, another day. What we do is nothing. Who are we fighting? ... Being Jewish and having that passed down is what I've learned here. It's a responsibility. I don't think we have any right not to pass that on and learn. It kind of bothers me now, my friends who are Jewish but ignore or don't observe or you wouldn't know they were. I think it's selfish. Because our ancestors, to give us a free place to live and freedom, died for us. So how dare we not respect that?

At Livnot, historical Jews are portrayed almost exclusively as fighters, resisters, and martyrs for the cause of Jewish survival and independence. Great effort is made to ensure that participants connect with those Jews of history, and come to feel that their struggles are neither remote nor irrelevant. For many participants, this presentation of the past creates a sense of Jewish community over time, and inculcates a greater respect for Judaism as a tradition worth fighting and dying for. By identifying themselves with a group that has been singled out for persecution through history, participants develop a sense of their own particularity, their own difference as Jews.

JUST LIKE NORMAL PEOPLE: ROUTES TO ORTHODOX JEWS

Beyond presenting Jews of the historical past, Livnot also encourages participants to develop relationships with and alter their perceptions of other, contemporary Jews. Prior to attending Livnot, the vast majority of participants recall viewing Orthodox Jews as distant, exotic others about whom they possessed many negative stereotypes. At Livnot, however, all of the staff with whom participants have regular daily contact are observant.

The attempt by Orthodox Jews in Israel to relate to young North Americans whose Judaism is largely peripheral to their lives is one that must cross a potentially substantial gap of culture and lifestyle. To promote the development of empathy between liberal North American young people and the Orthodox staff, Livnot requires at least one partner of the coordinating couple to be from North America. In addition, most of the regular teaching staff are from North America.[8] From Livnot's perspective, the advantage of a shared North American background is that it enables staff and participants to more easily establish connections with each other through references to North American popular culture and a common idiom. Both in the classroom and in other learning settings, staff regularly make references to North American music, movies, politics, and sport. According to Daniel, staff with a North American background share "a common vocabulary" with *chevre* that enables staff to understand participants' culture on its own terms. This permits staff to address subjects that the average Israeli with a religious background might not feel comfortable discussing:

> So for instance, drugs, right? If an average Israeli – at least at Livnot, not in Tel Aviv – would be reading an application that says, "Well, I used to smoke pot when I was in school, but now it doesn't appeal to me anymore," an average religious Israeli would say, "God, this person's a criminal. We can't have such a person on the program. Drugs, are you kidding?" What percentage of North Americans who go to universities today don't smoke pot? C'mon. It's infinitesimal. How can you explain that to an Israeli? To an Israeli that's like, the worst thing ... In the traditional fold it's totally out of bounds. Totally out of bounds. And that's part of life in North America today. People want to know, they've asked what's wrong with drugs, what's wrong with marijuana. If I can drink a little too much *Kiddush* wine on *shabbat* and get a little buzz, what's wrong with drugs? Now how can an Israeli answer that? Now that's just an example, but it could be thousands of things. A question on homosexuality. There's no possible way that an Israeli who comes from a religious background, can answer that. They'd be [sputtering] "Uh, we don't deal with that." It's such a taboo.

In addition to the North American experience that staff members share with participants, many of the Livnot staff did not grow up in religiously observant households. Most staff members, like participants, come from Reform, Conservative, or unaffiliated Jewish families. A common upbringing allows the experience and attitudes of staff members to resonate with participants and permits a level of intimacy that can come only with staff and teachers having "been there" themselves. Daniel explained that, in addition to coming from North America, a non-Orthodox background is important for staff members:

> Because it also has to do with a common vocabulary. In other words, the more worlds that you've been in, that you've dabbled in, the better ... if we could get someone who did LSD and was already married three times, the more the merrier. The more distant, the better, so that you can communicate. There's a limit, of course, and a stability someone should have. But it [similar life experience] does open doors to a lot of people. Someone who rebelled against Judaism, a lot of people here rebelled against Judaism. That's great, because they [staff] know exactly where they [participants] are talking from. They know exactly where they're coming from. And they can discuss on a more real level, not just in theory. It's the "I was there. I know what you're talking about. I can tell you how it was from my outlook." That's good discussion.

This empathy enables the staff to serve as role models and exemplars of Judaism in action. It is the interactions that *chevre* have with Orthodox staff members that allows participants to learn about observant Judaism by seeing it in practice and watching people live according to its precepts. The lifestyles and daily behaviour of staff form a kind of litmus test that enables participants to examine and evaluate what they learn in classes about Judaism. Clearly, staff are aware of their effect on participants and their role in displaying Judaism. Staff members actively try to keep conflicts among themselves private and stay on their best behaviour in public. As Ariela, one partner in the coordinating couple, explains: "Being an example is really important. It's something that we take very seriously. Which is why we try to keep all the garbage inside. And outside, it's not like we're faking something, but it's showing them the best we have to offer."

The development of a connection between staff and participants at Livnot is aided by the staff's cheerful acceptance of personal questions from participants. Staff members readily discuss their backgrounds and paths to observance. This kind of openness inspires trust and helps build empathy between non-observant and observant Jews. Ariela describes the value of honesty and intimacy with participants: "I think that it's important for them [participants] to see, wow, I'm normal.

With certain limitations, but not a lot, my past is really open to them and I'm comfortable talking to them about where I've come from and what I've gone through, if I think that they can value from my life experience ... I think it is important that they see that somebody who chose a religious life can also relate to them and where they're coming from. I think that it helps me be less untouchable."

Participants are frequently surprised to learn that religious Jews are not necessarily judgmental and that they do not perceive themselves to be superior to others. Similarly, participants discover that observant Jews also make mistakes and experience internal conflicts. Such honesty on the part of an Orthodox Jewish teacher transmits the message to participants that, appearances aside, everyone struggles and doubts, and that such experiences are a normal part of being human and Jewish.

Fern explained how Livnot caused her to reassess her preconceptions of religious people as somehow abnormal and inaccessible: "I've never gotten to know religious Jews like I have here at Livnot. From the families to Ron and Ariela, and Daniel or Eliyahu. It's not like I look at them and think they're so weird or different. They're great! They're funny. They can totally roll up there sleeves. It's not like they're so pure, like you can't touch me, or you can't be yourself around them. They're just like normal people. That's been a big revelation."

The attempt to develop trust and empathy between staff and participants is also aided by the keen sense of humour that many Livnot teachers bring to the classroom. The use of humour to convey serious information (including carrying a chair on one's back to demonstrate what constitutes work on *shabbat*, using funny voices and accents, or poking gentle fun at religious Jews) enlivens the learning process. Employing such humourous techniques also gives the impression that Orthodox Jews can be funny, and challenges participants' expectations that traditional Judaism is necessarily a sombre, serious, sober affair. Referring to one particular teacher, Nancy exclaimed: "He is such a great teacher. You don't even want to get up and go to the bathroom because you'll miss one minute of what he's saying. Not only does he teach, but he does it in a way that our generation and our kind of people and our age can relate to. He gives personal experiences with it ... you can relate easier. He doesn't always quote the Bible every second. He's more of reality. Just the way he teaches. He's entertaining, he keeps you enthralled, he makes you think. He doesn't just lecture to you."

For participants, the process of developing relationships with Orthodox Jews can sometimes involve shocking revelations. Many participants express their surprise to learn that Orthodox Jews can be in touch with the modern world, open-minded, and even "cool." Sharon, a woman very sensitive to issues of racism and cultural stereotypes, explained her surprise "that I would accept somebody who's Orthodox! That I would learn that not every Orthodox person isn't the same as the next Orthodox person! That you can wear *tzizit* and *payos*[9] and still have fun. It sounds so stupid. But working with Uri [the work foreman], he kids around, these people have pasts, they're not afraid of things, they're open and they joke around and they talk to you and you can tell them things and you don't have to be worried about their perceptions … Holy shit, he [Uri] is religious [laughing]! You know it but you don't know it. This is a normal person. This is a normal person."

Certainly, one of the most deeply embedded stereotypes with which participants arrive at Livnot concerns Orthodox Jewish women, whom they expect to be passive, docile, and subservient. The experience of spending time with articulate, intelligent, questioning, assertive religious women is striking for *chevre*. The female Livnot staff members participate eagerly with male staff members at hard work and long hikes. Far from the repressed or uneducated individuals that participants expect, the Orthodox women on staff at Livnot both know, and are comfortable expressing, serious Jewish information, as well as their own minds.

As liberal, well-educated, young North Americans, participants generally categorize themselves as open-minded and tolerant of diversity. Many participants do not even realize the extent of their stereotypes about Orthodox Jews until those stereotypes are challenged at Livnot. Sharon continued: "It's really funny, because in my life I'll be the first one to say 'Stop generalizing! You can't generalize, everyone's an individual.' But when it comes to Orthodox Jews I was so not like that. I was so the opposite. Thinking that they're all closed-minded, they're all like *Chabadniks*,[10] or just crazy fools or so extreme."

Learning that religious people can be "normal" and fun, as well as questioning, open-minded, and critical, comes as a significant shock to many participants. Fern explained that before Livnot she had

the stereotype that I think for some reason that it's easy to have about religious Jews, that they're a certain kind of person. That's totally changed. Totally changed … They're so cool. I relate to them like they would be some of my friends. I see them talk about Judaism and question and challenge and not take everything. I see them being open-minded to other ways of thinking that others might subscribe to that might be different from theirs and being totally okay with that. I guess there's this image that I've had, and maybe it's a myth, that all religious Jews will be judgmental on non-religious Jews. And while I think that that is sometimes the case, it's not always the case.

Personal, empathetic relationships with staff members foster the impression among participants that Orthodox people are not necessarily insular, and that observant Jews can have experiences of and be able to relate to what participants deem to be "the real world." Such realizations make it more difficult for participants to dismiss Orthodox Judaism itself as irrelevant or antiquated.

This experience of finding religious Jews in any way similar to oneself contrasts with participants' experience of Jewish life in North America. In the liberal Jewish community, the individuals generally perceived to be religious tend to be rabbis or Hebrew school teachers. Participants have rarely encountered "ordinary" people living committed Jewish lives. Robert expressed his surprise to learn that religious Jews can be average, regular members of society: "Even the idea of an Orthodox person! My rabbi wasn't even Orthodox. The average Joe, the foreman of the construction group that we work with, is more religious than my rabbi was in the States. And he doesn't act like that. He isn't haughty about it. He's not a rabbi. His daily life is more religious."

Beyond simply displaying themselves as Orthodox people to participants who have had little or no previous contact with them, the staff members at Livnot also demonstrate the option of Judaism as a daily, lived tradition. On *tiyulim*, participants can see male staff members unobtrusively drift away from the group to put on *tfillin* [phylacteries] and perform their morning prayers under a tree at a rest stop. Equally, participants might be present when one of the coordinators patiently teaches his children the blessing that is to be recited before eating an apple. This experience of observant Judaism as a regular daily lifestyle helps render the traditions understandable and plausible as potential life options. Rachel found that the experience of watching staff members' Judaism on display helped her make sense of religious observance: "I'm seeing people who are living the lifestyle that I heard about before, but I didn't understand how they could do it. I didn't understand why you'd want to move here and cover your hair all the time and do all these things. Even though I heard a lot of the traditions before, I just didn't understand why someone would want to do it. And now I'm coming to understand more the feeling of coming here and doing those things."

Participants' experiences of contact with Orthodox staff at Livnot also affect how many individuals view observant Jews outside of the program. The religious population of Tzfat is mostly ultra-Orthodox, and, with their distinctive dress and insular lifestyles are even more obviously "other" to Livnot participants than are the Livnot staff. Yet the dismantling of stereotypes that results from interactions with Livnot staff members reaches beyond the confines of Livnot. Tamara described the process she went through of "getting to know stereotypes as individual people. The men you see in the street, walking along in their black coats and their black hats and speaking with them. And speaking with the women who cover their hair and cover their arms. Seeing them as people and not just as icons for something that you're either supposed to fear or you're supposed to accept. Or something otherworldly."

The Livnot construction of observant Jews is one of familiarity and similarity rather than exoticism and distance. For many participants, Livnot represents the first time they have even spoken with a religious Jew, let alone developed a relationship with one. The feeling of connection that most participants develop with Orthodox Jews fosters a sense of community and kinship across differing lifestyle choices. This perception of commonality often causes participants to believe that there is some essential, if not biological link between Jews that makes them different from others and members of a unique community, sharing something special purely by virtue of their common Jewishness.

IMAGINING STABLE FAMILIES: ROUTES TO A JEWISH FUTURE

In addition to there being Orthodox Jews on display for participants at Livnot, the Jewish family is also present. The family and home are presented as the true locus of Judaism, in contrast to the synagogue-centred Judaism with which *chevre* are at least nominally familiar. There are three kinds of family dealt with at Livnot – the family that participants come from, the families they see on display, and the idealized families they will make for themselves in the future.

Without being explicitly critical, Livnot creates a distancing from one's birth family that is not just physical. In a class that was devoted to the Genesis story (12:1) which relates Abraham's travel to Canaan, it was suggested that sometimes one must go far from home and birth-family to be open to new, transformative experiences. Many *chevre* come from divorced or seriously conflicted families whose examples of domestic life they are not eager to emulate. Finally, participants' families are the unspoken arena of "inadequate" Judaism, and can, as will be discussed in chapter 6, create significant conflict for participants following the program.

There are also Orthodox Jewish families on display at Livnot, whom participants contrast with their birth-families. *Chevre* interact regularly with the families of staff members and families in the Tzfat community with whom they visit on *shabbat*. Certainly the value of staff members as individual role models is heightened when their lifestyle involves their families. Participants have the opportunity to selectively interact with religious families who are, of course, conscious of being watched and judged. *Chevre* get to watch parents bless their young children on *shabbat*, teach them simple prayers, and coax ethical behaviour from them.

Like many participants, Hannah was inspired by the apparent coherence, stability, and healthiness of the families she encountered. She explained how significant it was for her to be "seeing a bunch of families with large numbers of children and that seem pretty stable. They're all growing up with this [Jewish] ethic. Seeing the families that we've seen who are examples of people who do all these things. They just seem way more together than any family at home. I figure there's definitely something to it [Judaism]."

The sheer importance that staff members seem to accord their families at Livnot and the seriousness with which adults took parenting were commented upon by numerous participants. As Irene noted, this focus contrasts with her experience of life in North America: "I admire their lifestyles. The family, the importance of the family. The importance of community. It's not so much individualistic. It's not so much me, me. And taking pride in things other than monetary things."

Participants interact freely with the children of staff members, and, depending on the age of the children, can offer some limited, selective caretaking. As one staff member mentioned to me, participants have rarely had extensive contact with children, as participants normally come from small families. Spending time with Livnot children is significant for *chevre*, often awakening maternal or paternal longings. Livnot takes marriage and children seriously, and encourages participants to think seriously, often for the first time, about the kinds of families they want for themselves.

While this focus on family is important for both male and female participants at Livnot, the significance of this emphasis appears to be far greater for women. Female *chevre* are particularly struck by the frank talk about practical, marriage-oriented dating, and seeking a partner based on common values and goals, rather than just emotional and sexual connections. Female participants are extremely conscious of the potential pain in dating for fun and possible conflict in choosing partners based solely on feeling. Many women at Livnot want to marry "suitable" partners, but have not felt comfortable expressing that desire or pursuing that goal without feeling parochial or un-liberated. Livnot gives them the opportunity to speak their minds and validate their feelings about topics that participants feel are faintly illegitimate for feminist women – the desire for marriage and stable families.[11]

JEWS JUST LIKE ME: ROUTES TO JEWISH PEERS

Beyond encouraging the development of relationships with historical and Orthodox Jews, Livnot also enables participants to live in extremely close contact with Jews their own age who possess similar backgrounds and values. Many *chevre* come to Livnot feeling alienated from Judaism, and have not always pursued friendships with other Jews. Some participants simply did not grow up in Jewish neighbourhoods where they might have had the opportunity to meet other Jews at Temple or Sunday School. In some cases, this lack of exposure to other Jews was heightened due to economic or social marginalization from the Jewish community due to class differences.[12] Other participants had the option of involvement in the Jewish community, but did not want to be exclusive or restrictive in their friendships and pursued ideals of multiculturalism and diversity in their social lives.

Some *chevre* recount that prior to Livnot their encounters with Jews their own age were generally unpleasant. These participants often expressed dislike for other Jews, who they described as snobby, elitist, or materialistic. In sharp contrast to stereotypes of Jewish affluence, Livnot creates an environment that is antithetical to materialist, pampered luxury.

Doubtless, there exists at Livnot an element of young adult rebellion against the "bourgeois" Judaism of their parents and the established liberal Jewish community they have encountered. While most participants come from middle to upper–middle class backgrounds, Livnot *chevre* themselves do not, or perhaps do not yet, enjoy or seek a similar lifestyle.

Unmarried and childless, many participants are still in university or are only beginning their first serious employment. The values they cherish are authenticity, spirituality, and diversity rather than the emphasis on social status, financial security, and conspicuous consumption that they perceive to characterize "other Jews." Simply the experience of meeting religious staff members who work with their hands, get dirty, dress simply, and live modestly is surprising for participants who might never have met a committed, actively Jewish farmer, carpenter, or musician.

The program offers participants a chance to look beyond their stereotypes of other Jews their own age as upper-middle class and sharing in those class values. Livnot provides alienated and isolated participants the opportunity to engage meaningfully with other young North American Jews. For those participants who have had negative perceptions of their Jewish peers, the experience of meeting "regular" Jews can come as a pleasant shock. Laura observes that she found it

a little surprising because ... my experiences with most Jewish people was that they were really kind of stuck up and snotty. And it's not like that here. There's cliques and that kind of thing forming, sort of, kind of, but it's not anything like growing up at all. I kind of was afraid of that before I came here. I thought everybody was going to be these really snobby, jappy[13] people that are just so untouchable and who are professionals. And it's not like that at all.

I've learned that not all Jewish people are Jewish people that people stereotype and that I stereotype. There was somebody I met here yesterday [not at Livnot] who was your typical person that I always think of Jewish people as. Sarcastic, obnoxious, thinks they're better than everybody. Not everybody's like that. People here are like me. They don't have to be so sarcastic and all that stuff. They can just be regular. That's something I've learned.

Wendy recalls experiences with North American Jews that were very similar to those that Laura mentions, but Wendy found that she disliked the Jews she met so much that she was reluctant to be identified publicly as a Jew. In contrast to her expectations, Wendy explains that when she met other Livnot participants on arrival in Israel, both she and the others were thrilled to find that they shared similar attitudes and values, perceiving themselves to be cool, down to earth, and not materialistic:

The first myth [that was challenged] is the American Jew. I was
active with the Young Jewish Professionals and I didn't like it
because they had this stereotypical American Jewish snobbery.
I had a huge problem with that and I never wanted to be identified as a Jew. It's a terrible thing to say, it really is ... I really don't
feel like I fit in. But it started at the airport, the myths started
breaking ... Almost all of us said the same thing. It's so nice to be
around Jews like us. We didn't think that we existed, this ground-
edness, not so snobbish. We didn't have the materialistic qualities.
It was really embracing ... We all said to each other on the flight,
"Gosh, I didn't know you people really existed." That there were
really cool Jews.

Some participants feel alienated from the Jewish community as a
result of their cynicism toward religion, negativity toward Judaism, or
their "alternative" opinions. At Livnot those individuals are offered an
environment of Jews where such attitudes are the norm. Josh, for example, was especially happy to find Jews that, he felt, were like himself,
questioning, doubting, and investigating Judaism rather than simply
accepting traditions and beliefs: "I didn't know there were Jews like
this, period. All the Jews who I've met here are really confused. Not
really confused, but wanting to learn more, instead of getting it shoved
into their faces to the extent that they don't want to learn it for themselves, they just want to believe what they're told. They [the people
here] are kind of skeptical. I still feel a lot more skeptical than everybody else here, but not as badly as I did when it was me and everybody
else ... everybody is at that age when they don't know what they want.
It's very important. It makes me not feel as alone in the world as I have
in the past."

Livnot provides an opportunity for young Jews to interact in an
intense, meaning-oriented environment. Late-night discussions address
serious topics of faith, ethics, ritual, personal growth, doubts, and God.
Certainly, conversations also include "mundane" subjects like drinking,
sports, and the opposite sex, but interaction among participants often
reaches far beyond the superficial level, permitting and encouraging a
rare depth of communication between people. Nancy compares Livnot
discussions favourably to the kinds of conversation she recalls having
with her friends at home: "Some of us were having a conversation last
night, and somehow we got on the subject of Leviticus and something
we read yesterday. We all looked at each other and started laughing.

And we're like, okay, it's Monday night, normally we'd be discussing Melrose Place [a popular TV show] and now we're discussing Leviticus."

Similarly, Hannah expressed surprise at the depth of conversations in which she was taking part. She found her interaction with fellow *chevre* to possess what she identified as a greater degree of authenticity and substance than the conversations she was used to having in North America:

> I don't know if it's the people who are on the trip and it's deep people who have all these deep conversations, or if it's what we're learning ... there's a lot of Jewish and biblical and stuff that we've learned being talked about. And it's really weird, actually. It's mentioned in probably every conversation. Even if we're talking about relationships, we'll bring in something that we learned in class. That's cool, actually. I realized I'm having all these deep conversations with people. Even if it's not about what we're learning, but it's not just about bullshit stuff. People are talking about real stuff, like their feelings.

At the same time that Livnot provides an environment in which young North American Jews are encouraged to relate to each other in meaningful ways, it is also a milieu focused on community building, mutual support, shared responsibility, and quality interpersonal relations. Participants at Livnot are expected to put classroom lessons about ethics to practical use in daily program life. For example, in conversations it is common to hear someone stop mid-story, realize they are about to spread gossip, and refuse to continue. *Chevre* are expected to, and often do, help each other physically and psychologically on difficult parts of hikes, support each others' personal growth, and volunteer to help carry groceries together. Together they share group work, communal dining, and tight quarters. Although such a rigorous community orientation can sometimes make it difficult to find a quiet moment alone, there is a strong group spirit at Livnot and a feeling of social cohesion. Participants are more than just participants, or individuals simultaneously taking part in the same program. Rather, they are, ideally, *chevre*: a group, a gang, a society, friends. For many, Livnot constitutes their first meaningful, Jewishly-focused community.

Clearly, the Livnot program itself is a highly liminal period for participants, who undergo transformation, learning, and personal growth while "betwixt and between" the familiar structures of home.

The communal living, eating and labour, simple clothing, shared chores, deep personal interaction, intense friendships, and mutual aid shared by participants all contribute to the "communitas" ethic of program life. This "communitas" characteristic of Livnot provides an opportunity for participants to engage in an extended experience of close-knit, meaningful, shared Jewish community.[14]

FINDING ROUTES TO JEWS, FINDING ROOTS IN JEWS

Jews have traditionally viewed themselves as comprising a people, a nation, a community, referring to themselves as *am yisrael*. They have historically shared a sense of common ancestry, collective history, mutual responsibility, and kinship with each other, over time and across space. While this feeling of ethnic group attachment has certainly increased in importance as a response to modernity, secularism, and declining religious authority, the Jewish sense of community and kinship is one that has evolved out of concepts deeply rooted in Jewish history and religious tradition.

Clearly, the Jewish community that participants encounter at Livnot is a construction, designed to appeal to them. The other Jews that participants meet through the Livnot program are hand-picked to share things in common with participants, and to be neither too different nor threatening, neither preachy nor radical. The Livnot portrait of the Jewish people includes almost no Israel-born Jews, ultra-Orthodox Jews, or secular Jews. *Sepharadi* and non-Orthodox (Reform or Conservative) Jews are also virtually absent, although participants sometimes encounter poor *Sepharadi* as recipients of Livnot's community service efforts. Jewish history is mined for its emotional power, relevance to the present, and contemporary lessons, making historical Jews appear immediate and meaningful to participants. It is clearly apparent that Livnot presents a partial, biased, and incomplete look at the Jewish people, designed to instill a positive sense of Jewish community. At the same time, it must be recognized that all portraits, all accounts, all Jewish communities are similarly limited and only somewhat true.

According to Jonathan Woocher, survivalism, with its emphasis on Jewish peoplehood, forms the core of Jewish civil religion in North America.[15] It is precisely this kind of group-focused Judaism that many Livnot participants experienced growing up. In such milieux, children are often encouraged by their parents to believe that Jews are somehow different, that Jews should stick together, that there is a difference between "us" and "them." Uncomfortable with such blatant ethnic particularism, many participants chose to have little to do with the Jewish community before attending Livnot. Some participants made special efforts to avoid building relationships with Jews. Other participants found that most of their friends were Jewish, but were so by accident rather than by design. Finally, some participants, as a result of the choices made by their parents, simply did not have any sustained exposure to other Jews.

Many participants found it confusing to grow up in families that espoused both liberal values and a commitment to Jewish survivalism. An acute tension exists between particularism and universalism, especially in Western Christian societies. Liebman and Cohen argue that

> Unlike Israeli Jews, American Jews face pressures that militate against Jewish familistic feelings and behavior. American Jews need to square their Jewish familistic sentiments with American conceptions of equality and Western conceptions of liberalism and humanism. In these conceptions there is something archaic, unenlightened, and intolerant about asserting the primacy of one's kin or clan. In the liberal humanistic vision, the individual is the center of concern, not the family or the tribe or even the nation. And the primary attachments of people ought to be to their friends or coworkers or to those with whom they share acquired traits, not to those among whom they happen to have been born.[16]

Kinship, difference, and Jewish cultural specificity are suspect notions in a Western world that is heir to a Christian discourse of universalism, sameness, and individualism. For many Livnot participants, raised as they have been in what is at least a nominally Christian North American society, Jewish community was not always a real, plausible option for them prior to Livnot. Owing to either a lack of exposure or a desire to avoid engaging in something as "archaic and unenlightened" as Jewish peoplehood, the experience of meaningful relationships with other Jews is new for some participants. Those participants who came to Livnot feeling more connected to ideas of Jewish unity and community, and had more Jewish contact as a result of accidents of neighbourhood and class, often lacked compelling, Jewish reasons for their relationships with other Jews.

Livnot is an antidote, both to the Western Christian tendency to avoid Jewish peoplehood and to the superficial communalism of Jewish community organizations. Through various mechanisms, Livnot allows participants to engage in a sense of *am yisrael*, of the Jewish community, in a more complete and deeper sense than they might have experienced it before, if they experienced it at all. Moreover, Livnot offers participants access to and the opportunity to participate in the collective memory and history of that people, however selective, through the program's presentation of Jewish heritage.

5

Routes to Judaism

The impact of the Livnot experience on informants' feelings about Judaism as a religious system is highly significant. Generally speaking, participants commonly characterized their post-Livnot relationship with Judaism as "meaningful," compared to what they understood to be the more "meaningless" or "empty" Judaism they had encountered growing up. Also, many participants explained that through Livnot they had developed a significantly more "personal" and "spiritual" relationship to Judaism than they had previously experienced. Doubtless, the current manner in which an individual understands her life story affects the way in which she perceives her past. Past events are always edited, relabelled or recategorized to fit into the current narrative that the individual uses to make sense of her life. Thus, toward the end of Livnot, when participants reflect upon changes in their relationship with Judaism since beginning the program, their current feelings about Judaism obviously affect their understandings of their previous Jewish experiences:

My relationship with Judaism, I think it's personal now. It's not someone else's. It's a religion that, okay, I was born with it, but what is it? I had no attachment to it. So I held the Torah when I was thirteen [at my *bat mitzvah*]. Now, it's more of a personal thing. NANCY

It's a total paradigm shift really. That is what's happened at Livnot ... The Judaism that I grew up with was fundamental to my life but there certainly wasn't anything personal to it. There was nothing personal about it. To the point that I felt like the people who were in all those Jewish organizations like UJA [United Jewish

Appeal] and stuff and all those people who went to my *shul* [synagogue] regularly, somehow they were more Jewish. I never felt not Jewish but somehow there was something more for them than me. I totally don't think that anymore. I would feel so comfortable right now, even if I don't practice the way the most religious person practices, going anywhere and feeling more equal with them. And that the way I go through Judaism is just as valid. That there's room in Judaism for lots and lots of different kinds of people. I didn't really realize that before. And that's one of the reasons that through my adult years, through college and afterwards, it [Judaism] wasn't part of my regular life at all ... I did not know anything. There was no meaning behind it. There is so much more meaning attached to Judaism now ... there is just so much more meaning attached to my Judaism than ever in my whole life. And it really feels like a basis for the rest of my life in a lot of ways. FERN

It's this spiritual essence. I was seeking it out and I found it. It was actually there [in Judaism]. There is that in Judaism, and I didn't know that before. For me that's really huge, that was my quest, that was what I was looking for. I found that in so many things about my experience at Livnot. In everything, there's meaning and there's substance and there's depth. That's a huge connection for me. I didn't know it was there. I honestly didn't ... It's surprising. It's been surprising since the very beginning. MARNI

I really had no idea what Judaism was. None before I came. I had negative feelings about it. Not from knowledge about what it was. I'd always been made fun of for being Jewish when I was younger. I just didn't think there was anything useful in it. I never knew any substance to Judaism. I just knew about things I was forced to do, like going to *shul* on the High Holidays. But not connecting to it. Not knowing there was anything to connect to. Never really seeing any meaning in it, so why the hell do it? ... So *everything* I've learned has been a myth-breaker. The connection between Judaism and nature. The spirituality in nature. The symbolism. Learning about the High Holidays. Now I believe that Judaism can be a part of my life, that there is something to grab hold of. It's opened up an entire world for me. WARREN

[Growing up] It [Judaism] just was. There wasn't an idea of
fulfilling or meaningful or spiritual. It just was. It just was. Before
I came to the program and I would talk about being Jewish before
the program and people would ask me how am I Jewish,
I couldn't really grasp it. I couldn't put my hand on it. So what
I ended up saying is that my family is very culturally Jewish ...
Livnot brings Judaism into everyday life. You recognize it as a
2,000-plus–year-old religion but you recognize it as something
that's applicable and everyday. Livnot shows you how you can
bring that into the real world ... Livnot is one big visualization of
Judaism. It brings this thing that you could feel totally discon-
nected from, it connects you in a real-life way. It's just putting you
in there. SHARON

IT'S PERSONAL NOW

Clearly, participants' attitudes toward Judaism are strongly affected by
the experience of Livnot U'Lehibanot. Livnot exposes participants to
an articulation of traditional Judaism, and enables them to develop a
relationship with the tradition in which their cultural roots are perceived by staff and participants to lie. The program offers access to the
culture of traditional Judaism via a multitude of routes. This chapter
will illustrate Livnot's portrait of Orthodox Judaism as debatable, personal, accessible, flexible, multiple, ethical, egalitarian, universalist, and
environmentally-friendly. This construction of Judaism is potentially
appealing and relevant to its audience of young North American Jews,
speaking as it does to participants' values, concerns, and priorities.

In their comparison of Israeli and American Judaism, Charles Liebman
and Steven Cohen explore and compare the Israeli and American Jewish
communities' concepts of Israel, Jewish peoplehood, anti-Semitism, and
religious life.[1] A central feature of their findings is that American Jewry's
understanding of Judaism is significantly characterized by four elements:
personalism (the tendency to judge and transform the tradition according to its usefulness or meaning to the individual), voluntarism (that is,
a feeling of choice over obligation), universalism (the idea that Judaism
has a message for all people, and that Judaism should be open to the
messages of other traditions), and moralism (that is, having an ethical,
rather than ritual emphasis). These concepts of personalism, voluntarism, universalism, and moralism are closely related to the political and

social liberalism that is, at least for non-Orthodox Jews, a core feature of American understandings of what it means to be a Jew. Clearly, some of this liberalism stems from, or is in agreement with, social thinking in the Jewish religious tradition. However, Liebman and Cohen assert that the emphasis placed on personalism, voluntarism, universalism, and moralism in contemporary American Judaism is disproportionate to their historical presence in Jewish thought, and ignores other, more particular, ritual, or obligation-focused tendencies in traditional Judaism: "We do not suggest that personalism, voluntarism, universalism and moralism are entirely new, much less that they are alien to Judaism. They certainly can be found within the tradition itself. But they now have become major dimensions or instruments through which American Jews interpret and transform the Jewish tradition."[2]

Most Livnot participants grew up with at least some participation in precisely this liberal, urban North American Jewish culture that Liebman and Cohen describe. *Chevre* have been much more involved in the dominant North American social world than they have been in Jewish culture. As a result, their encounters with Judaism must pass the test of the contemporary, mainstream North American values to which participants subscribe. In their efforts to overcome participants' negative attitudes toward Judaism, lack of affiliation, and weak Jewish knowledge, Livnot offers a portrait of the tradition that appeals to the values of liberal Jewish culture. At the same time, Livnot's Judaism also presents a gentle critique of North American materialism and superficiality that offers Judaism as an effective alternative to late–twentieth-century excess. Livnot has selected a Jewish tradition that can speak to participants in their own language, addressing their commitments to personalism, voluntarism, universalism, and moralism, while simultaneously questioning contemporary popular values. This chapter will provide a detailed description and analysis of Livnot's construction of Judaism, and the features that help make the program's portrait "work" for participants.

A DEBATABLE JUDAISM

One of the fundamental ways in which Livnot transmits a message about Judaism is through the way it is taught in the classroom. For the overwhelming majority of participants, Livnot is the first Jewish education they have experienced in many years. The program staff are highly conscious of this fact, and of their role in providing an alternative model of Jewish study for participants. One of the classes in the first week of the program deals directly with Jewish education, allowing the staff to articulate Livnot's approach to learning. Livnot presents the ideal Jewish classroom as active, participatory, and emotional. Students are encouraged, even directed, to ask tough questions of the teacher and to argue with the ideas being taught: "During these classes, you won't sit down and just 'Yeah, uh huh, yeah, wow, uh huh.' That's not cool. It should be more like this, 'Now wait, now hold on! I have a problem with that and I'm going to tell you! Like, what is this chosen people thing? That's not ethical. We're better than other people?' Things should bother you! ... So say it. Don't be afraid, ever, to ask any question. And don't be afraid to be heretical ... You can say anything you want ... you can believe whatever you want. And unless you're trying to make somebody feel bad, there's nothing you can say that's out of line. There's no such thing as a heretical question."

While regular daily classes at Livnot usually begin with a lecture, they are commonly focused around a vital core of active student input and vibrant group discussion of the material. Teachers at Livnot actively seek out and encourage an honest, challenging exchange of ideas and opinions about the subject under debate.

For most participants, this kind of Jewish education is an exciting change from their earlier experiences, and is radically different from their recollections of Hebrew school. Livnot's teaching philosophy offers participants a Judaism that is located squarely in the realm of the debatable, and a religious tradition that is open to investigation, contestation, and dispute. Participants come to view Judaism as a tradition that encourages many opinions and that can accept disagreement and challenge. This kind of active investigation of issues and the staff's openness to treating difficult questions make a strong impact on participants, who are used to what they describe as a more passive model of Jewish education. In contrast to her childhood experience of Hebrew school, Fern remarked that Livnot "gives us the opportunity to feel that it's totally okay to think what we want, to take what we want, to leave the rest of what we don't want. Whereas in Hebrew school the dynamic is to accept what the teacher is telling you. It's not so much, I think, encouraged to question from the standpoint of 'Do I believe in this or not [at Hebrew school]?' It's more like 'This is what I'm feeding you, so this is what you accept.'"

Similarly, Sharon explained that she was "thinking at a deeper level about these things and they're really making sense to me. Maybe it has to do with the way things are presented here, too. Take this and look at it and question it and don't accept it blindly, but really explore it. That's not anything I ever once did in my Jewish background. It was blind acceptance. [At Hebrew school it's a case of] this is what they're teaching you and this is your mom sending you here. It was not why; it was just, that's it."

A Judaism that is open to serious debate and that welcomes disagreement and challenge is popular with participants who are used to questioning and critically evaluating ideas, rather than simply accepting them on the basis of authority. Livnot's Judaism appeals to participants because it is a tradition with which they can argue, and one that can accommodate their criticisms.

JEWISH TEXTS AS RELEVANT

In addition to lectures and discussion, most classes at Livnot also include a textual component, taken from traditional Jewish sources, including the Hebrew Bible, Talmud, and Midrash. These sources are carefully examined by individuals in pairs, known as *chevrutot*, patterned after a traditional format for Jewish textual study. Participants read a section of translated text related to a topic discussed in class, and are asked for their reactions to the text or given a particular question to pursue. Thus, a class in preparation for *Yom Kippur* might involve an investigation of Maimonides' Laws of Repentance. A class on Jewish ethics, for example, might have *chevrutot* discuss Leviticus chapter 19. After working in pairs on the textual material for a fixed period of time, the class regroups to share insights, problems, and complaints evoked by the passage under examination.

In the initial class on Jewish education, Daniel described *chevruta* study as an engaging learning situation which encourages the quest for personal meaning in texts:

So here's this text. You get a text, and you haven't the slightest idea what it means. But what does it really mean? You decide. You sit with the other person, and you talk about it. You argue. Even if you don't really disagree, you find a way to disagree ... two people, getting together, and discussing – usually in a proactive way – a text, an idea. That's the way it works. There's no shush, as in the library. We actually, purposely, disturb each other ... we think it's a better way than just sitting and listening to some lecture. It's being active. And it's getting a text and not being told

what it means. "Let me tell *you* what the text really means."
Because in the end, *you* decide what it means. And the way you
decide is by arguing or discussing with your *chevruta* partner.

Chevruta study at Livnot presents a vision of Jewish learning to
participants that is profoundly personal, active, and participatory. This
pressure-free, small-group study format helps make Jewish texts accessible to student inquiry, and removes the texts from the restricted realm
of the scholarly or the sacred in which participants might have placed
them. This method of learning, based on small groups exploring textual
meanings together, promotes a vision of traditional Jewish texts as argu-
able, open to discussion, and available for personal interpretation. It
was precisely this element of personal interaction with the text that, for
Diane, made the *chevruta* sessions so useful: "You can take any piece
of literature and have a whole different view than your partner. That
helped me to look into myself to see how I relate to different issues and
different pieces of literature from the Torah and Maimonides and that
kind of stuff. It made me think about how *I* feel about something out
there. It helped me to internalize what it means for *me*."

In addition to the regular classes held every afternoon at Livnot,
participants may also choose to study rather than work for one morning
each week, and to participate in small group discussions on two special
topics. Usually the first of these small group classes addresses a biblical
theme, figure, or story. Using directed discussion of the traditional texts
and commentaries, these small groups allow students to work more
intensively with textual sources and to develop a basic level of comfort
with Jewish scriptures. A study day might be offered, as mentioned
above, based on the text of Genesis 12:1, in which Abraham left behind
his homeland, birthplace, and family on a quest. This passage might be
related to undertaking a process of finding oneself or to the ways in
which Abraham's travels might be similar to the paths that *chevre* have
taken to Israel and Livnot.[3] In this manner, Jewish texts are rendered
meaningful, familiar, and accessible to participants.

Beyond classes and small-group study, Livnot also encourages active,
individual engagement with traditional Jewish texts. Each participant
is expected to present a *dvar Torah*, or short *shabbat* talk on the weekly
Torah portion, at least once during the program. This requirement provides an opportunity for *chevre* to work alone on the text to seek personal significance and group relevance in the Bible. Often, participants
start out wary of this project, and feel inadequate about performing a

task that is deemed something that "only rabbis could do." As the program progresses, however, *chevre* become increasingly comfortable and competent at working with traditional texts, and find themselves intrigued by the possibility of locating personal meaning and contemporary relevance in scripture.

The *chevruta* method and Livnot's emphasis on relating scripture to personal life help make sources once perceived to be inaccessible, dry, or "too religious," more open to inquiry, potentially interesting, and applicable to "real life." It was this process of coming to see the Bible as meaningful to her own life that had the greatest impact on how Rose viewed the text: "We were talking this morning in class about how the characters in the Bible – what do they mean and how do they speak to you. It was just incredible thinking about it. In one area it's just a historical story, and then another area is this person – I guess you can look at them and see insights into your own thoughts and feelings ... The feeling and the thoughts and learning about Torah and the connection is new for me. It's usually just done in a strictly historical 'this is what it is' and 'this is the story' and 'that's what it means' kind of sense. In this way it's more connected [to me]."

Similarly, Wendy felt that she was developing a perspective on Jewish scriptures that differed radically from her previous beliefs about the Bible. Prior to Livnot, Wendy had perceived the Bible solely as a repressive and oppressive force, based on how she understood it to function in a Christian context:

At first I couldn't handle reading the *Tanach* [Bible] at all. So when they asked me to do a *dvar Torah* weeks ago I said no, I can't handle it, I can't get anything out of the text ... for me it was like "The Bible." It's like this bad thing. I don't know it to be good ... [At Livnot] I've been realizing it's a set of morals and lessons and fables. But it took a long time to be comfortable with it. Living in a Christian society it's like "The Bible" [spoken with a Southern drawl]. And everything about "The Bible" is just ugh, these people are just Bible-lovers. But people really don't know what's in there. And that's an amazing thing, what really is in there. And how many interpretations there are. How beautiful it really is. It is amazing.

Robert, too, had felt fundamentally alienated from the Torah based on his experiences of Christian American society and its interaction with the Bible: "For me, the Bible always seemed a very Christian thing. In my community there was always the Christian right-wing. All the kids in high school would always be writing Job 5:12 on their letters to each other or on their notes.[4] Or on their t-shirts. They would walk around and there was almost this arrogance of showing off what they knew about the Bible. It made me really polarized from the Bible. Now at Livnot I've realized that there's a great deal of wisdom in the Bible, if it's not a showy thing, if it's not like 'Look, I'm reading the Bible.'"

Classes involving argument about Judaism present a vision of the tradition as one that is open and encouraging of debate and challenge. Similarly, an approach to normative Jewish texts that investigates them intensively, discusses them openly, and seeks personal relevance from the material portrays these texts as accessible and potentially meaningful for participants. These basic teaching methods at Livnot have a profound effect on the way that Judaism and traditional Jewish texts are perceived, challenging the negative view of Judaism and Jewish education that participants developed earlier, particularly at Hebrew school.

Clearly, Livnot offers a particular view of Judaism that is implicit and embedded in the medium of its teaching methods. As will be illustrated below, Livnot also constructs a portrait of Judaism at a more explicit level, presenting the religious tradition as flexible, tolerant, and multiple, as well as egalitarian, universalist, focused on ethics (rather than ritual or God), and grounded in rational authority.

THE JEWISH SUPERMARKET

One of the primary ways in which Livnot displays Orthodox Judaism to participants is through a metaphor which compares the program to a supermarket. Staff explain that their role involves "stocking shelves" with a range of traditional Jewish "products." The task of participants, as staff express it, is to spend three months symbolically wheeling a shopping cart up and down the aisles, taking those products off the shelf, investigating them, and possibly returning some or even all of them. Staff members insist that what participants end up with in their carts at the end of the program is up to the individual. Thus, traditional Judaism at Livnot is offered not as a monolithic system which must be accepted in its entirety, but rather as a collection of separate practices that can stand alone. Livnot's approach to religious observance is one of radical voluntarism and freedom of choice, and rejects an "all or nothing" understanding of Jewish tradition.

The supermarket metaphor is introduced to participants at the orientation when they first arrive at Livnot, as Ariela explains: "Livnot is a supermarket. What does that mean? You are all now being given out your shopping carts. Here they are, take them, they're yours. Your job is to take your little shopping cart and walk up and down the aisles. Our job is to stock the shelves. Your basket might stay empty the whole time. It might get so full that you have to take another one. You might go down the first row and pile it up, then you take a turn and you put a bunch of stuff back. What you do at the checkout, when you finally get to the checkout, is totally your business. You might take a raincheck. That part is totally and completely up to you."

Livnot's supermarket analogy, with its rhetoric of picking and choosing, is highly appealing to a young North American Jewish audience. The feeling of control over the contours of one's Judaism, together with the notion that different combinations and forms of Jewish observance are acceptable, fosters an impression of Orthodoxy as pluralistic and flexible. Sharon explained that the metaphor "really hit home ... I don't want somebody to tell me that in order to be Jewish, or for anything, I don't want someone to say you have to do all these things or else you're not [Jewish]. Because the way that I've defined myself as being a Jew is not by you have to do all these things, it's by I choose to do what I choose to do. I choose to take what I want, the traditions that I want, and I leave the rest ... You do what makes you feel comfortable. I'm all about that."

At the beginning of the Livnot program, many participants voice concerns about brainwashing or the possibility of religious coercion. Yet it is precisely this supermarket metaphor which enables participants to feel welcome as individuals, free of pressure to conform to external models of religiosity or Jewishness. Fern described the calming effect that the metaphor produced for her:

> I had a little bit of a fear as I was thinking about what Israel program I wanted to come to, that I would get involved in a program that would try to somehow convert me into something I either didn't want or wasn't ready for. That there was some underlying agenda. When I heard that Livnot is a program that is like, "we want to stock the shelves. We want you to take your shopping cart and go around and put into your shopping cart what you want," that to me felt very safe. It made me feel like I was allowed to be an individual. It wasn't that Livnot wanted to

make me into some cookie-cutter graduate that left [the program] and started wearing skirts and *sheitels*.[5] That was really important to me.

The Jewish supermarket metaphor works well for participants. It speaks to their desire to create a Judaism in their own images, and to adapt the tradition to their personal needs and interests. Even in the late 1960s, Luckmann identified a "pervasive consumer orientation" toward the sacred, in which the individual approaches a range of possible ultimate meanings as a buyer.[6] Livnot's supermarket analogy presents a traditional Judaism that can appeal to the deep individualism that is a core element of North American culture.

SEVENTY FACES OF JUDAISM

Another commonly stressed idea at Livnot, one closely related to the supermarket metaphor, is that there exist seventy equally valid faces to Judaism. This concept is based on a *Midrash*, or a traditional exegesis of the Hebrew Bible, which sought to interpret the "one bowl weighing seventy shekels" (Numbers 7:13) brought by tribal leaders to the desert Tabernacle. The *Midrash* explains that this bowl represents the single law of Torah which can be expounded in seventy different ways.[7] This metaphor of seventy faces is regularly used at Livnot to suggest to participants that there are a multiplicity of acceptable paths to Judaism and ways to be Jewish. Specifically, the emphasis placed on this idea serves to counter a common perception among participants that Orthodox Judaism insists on a single, normative, restrictive form of Jewish observance. Sympathizing with this perception among participants, one teacher commented: "The biggest problem with Judaism, at least for me, I can only speak for myself, I can't speak for anybody else, is that it's a cage ... This is our biggest problem. It's a cage! ... We have a bad image. Because Judaism has been portrayed for thousands of years as being restrictive. You can't just blame society. We haven't gotten out the message that there are seventy faces, that you can go whichever way you want ... That's our biggest problem. We think Judaism is a cage."

Because the *Midrash* forms part of the normative Jewish tradition, it is reasonable to assume that this metaphor of multiple facets and levels of interpretation was not meant to endorse a non-observant life as equally valid to living an observant life. However, at Livnot the concept of seventy faces suggests to participants that there are both no wrong

answers in traditional Judaism, and no authoritative "right" way to be
Jewish. All options, combinations, and permutations are deemed acceptable, according to this notion, because they simply represent other,
equally valid faces of Judaism. Clearly, for participants informed by a
late twentieth-century North American ethos of individualism and pluralism, a multiple, partial Judaism is both more palatable and certainly
much easier to experiment with than one that is conceived to be abso-
lute or the sole true path. Fern explains what this meant to her: "It's
something I've never heard before, that there's seventy faces to the
Torah. To me, that basically means there's no one way to be Jewish. If
someone comes along and says, 'This is the way, this is what you must
follow,' that's dogma. That's not what Judaism is all about. It makes
me feel like Judaism is much more open-minded than I thought it was."

The idea of seventy faces was also new to Laura, who, like Fern,
describes how the freedom that it offered made her feel more positively
disposed toward Judaism: "I've never actually heard of that [seventy
faces] before. And that meaning that there's different ways of approaching the Torah, more or less. That could be seventy different ways of
approaching Judaism. You can be a Hasidic Jewish person, a Reform
Jewish person, an Orthodox. I think you find what's most comfortable
for you. You don't have to take everything that they say ... There's
really no right or wrong."

Just as the metaphor of Livnot as a Jewish supermarket encourages an
individualistic approach to Judaism, the notion that Judaism possesses
multiple, equally valid expressions validates any individual, personal,
or hybrid constructions of Judaism that participants might develop. If all
Judaisms are simply different facets of the same gem, then all articulations
of Judaism are, in the eyes of participants, acceptable Judaism.[8]

AN ETHICAL JUDAISM

At the same time as it portrays a construction of Orthodox Judaism
that is flexible and multiple, Livnot also offers a Judaism that is primarily informed by ethics rather than by rituals or beliefs. The primacy
that the program assigns to ethics is indicated by the fact that the first
week-long theme for classes and activities at Livnot is devoted to Jewish
models for interpersonal relationships. During this week, ethical behaviour
is presented as constituting the essence of traditional Judaism.

Livnot constructs an ideal vision of Orthodox Judaism that is not
commandment based but rather is oriented toward treating people well,

pursuing non-exploitative relationships, and creating a just society. Thus, for example, *shabbat* is extolled as "earth day," while *halachic* restrictions on sexual relations both outside and within marriage are portrayed as practices which ensure that women are not sexually objectified. Equally, on *shabbat*, participants are expected to observe traditional, normative restrictions on their activities solely out of respect for the religious neighbourhood of Tzfat's Old City. Outside of the Old City or at the more isolated citadel area, participants are free to "desecrate" the sabbath by smoking, writing letters, or listening to music. Similarly, in deference to the religious sensibilities of others, *chevre* are requested to follow a very basic degree of *halachic* modesty requirements by avoiding tank tops and "short shorts" when off campus and around the Old City. Again, however, participants are welcome to dress in any clothes they choose while on campus, and may even wear bathing suits on hikes. While observance of Jewish dietary regulations is expected in the campus kitchen so that teachers and community members can eat with participants, there is no expectation that participants will or should eat only kosher food outside of Livnot. Likewise, participants are neither expected nor encouraged to attend synagogue on *shabbat*, and there are neither daily prayers at Livnot, nor even grace after meals.[9] Thus, most of the ritual requirements placed on participants are presented as deriving from tolerance for the beliefs of others rather than any religious authority. For participants who have been raised in religiously and politically liberal Jewish homes, such themes as respect for the beliefs of others, concern for the community, and care for the earth resonate far more strongly than would an appeal to tradition or the commandments of God.

Livnot offers a portrait of Judaism that is also more ethical, home-based, and personal than the ritual-focused and synagogue-centred traditions of North American Judaism that most participants have already come to reject. Daniel focused on this difference in one talk to participants: "The truth is, in Israel the synagogue is always secondary. Most of Judaism isn't going on there. You go there for a few minutes every day. Most of Judaism is going on at home, and in the workplace. Unfortunately, in many cities in North America, that's not true because in a lot of cities there's not a lot of Jewish things going on except for *shul*. So unless you're going to play raquetball with somebody Jewish at the JCC [Jewish Community Centre], there's not a lot to do out there that's really interesting ... You can be a fine Jew without being in *shul*."

An opposition between ritual and ethics is frequently drawn in contemporary Western society.[10] Certainly participants commonly use these ideas as dichotomous religious categories. Discovering the ethical component of Judaism comes as a significant and welcome surprise for most participants who tend to classify observant Judaism as "ritualistic." *Chevre* are often excited to realize that Judaism has opinions on correct behaviour toward others and that these values coincide with their own, previously developed ideas. For Marni, "It was really this shocking notion that all these values that I hold and all of these things that I think are right, they're Jewish! Like, whoa! They're Jewish. Like the gossip thing, *lashon hara* – that was a huge revelation that that's some-thing that's talked about in Judaism. That was a big revelation that has unfolded on lots of different levels on different topics, to find out that things are 'by golly, that's Jewish!' It had been right under my nose the whole time … it was right there under my nose and I didn't even know it. Now I have words, whereas I didn't have words for it before."

At the same time as it presents a "traditional" Judaism that is not primarily focused on commandment keeping and ritual, Livnot also portrays a Judaism that is not particularly God-centred. This absence of an explicit theistic framework permits participants who are unsure about the existence of God to continue to learn about and participate in Orthodox Judaism without feeling uneasy or excluded. Daniel points out that "the mission statement of Judaism is not 'Hear O Israel.'[11] The mission statement of Judaism is found at the end of [Leviticus chapter 19, verse] 18, 'Love your fellow as yourself.' That's the mission state-ment. That's what Rabbi Akiva said. So where's God? It [the issue of God] is not really number one here. It's not really a priority. It's there … but that's not the main thing. That's not the main event."

In this construction of Judaism, there is room for everyone and for all ideas, with no possibility of heresy or of giving offense. However, as participants investigate and discuss traditional Jewish texts, the issue of God does arise simply by virtue of the material, and in ways that cannot easily be ignored. Speaking to *chevre*, Daniel approached the subject early in the program:

> Once we start going into the Bible, somewhere around the second word there's this three-letter word called God. And some people don't believe in God. So some people may say, "Well, then this just isn't relevant for me" … someone could say that "If I don't believe in God, and God is the basic premise of the Jewish reli-gion or way of life, then really, you know, there's nothing to talk about." If you think, and it's another myth, that the most important sentence in Judaism is "Hear O Israel, the Lord our

God, the Lord is One," is the most important thing about Judaism, and you don't believe in God, bye! Bye. Why waste your time for three months? … I would suggest that those who are atheists or who don't believe in God, or who are agnostics, you don't have to feel out of place. That's fine. No pressure.

While respect for the community is presented as the rationale underlying the ritual observances that participants must follow, the observances presented to participants as comprising a traditional Jewish lifestyle are shown to derive their authority from utility. The motivation for ritual observance, Livnot suggests, is not obedience to God, tradition, or scripture, but rather that observing traditional Jewish precepts makes rational sense, offers practical benefits, and leads to a better, healthier, happier life. Accordingly, it is suggested that *shabbat* provides an opportunity for the individual and the natural world to rest and rejuvenate, dietary practices encourage a greater respect for animals and for oneself, and the laws of family purity offer both a more mutually satisfying sexual relationship and time for a woman to focus on herself. In the Livnot portrait of traditional Judaism, one observes the traditional strictures of Judaism not necessarily because it is commanded by God, but because it makes practical sense to do so as a result of the physical and psychological benefits that derive from observance. According to Livnot, the individual may determine the degree and nature of his or her ritual observance through voluntary, rational choice. As a result, participants come to regard Judaism as sensible, practical, and useful rather than as the authoritative or restrictive system they had envisaged before Livnot.

AN INCLUSIVE JUDAISM

As a tradition that is primarily ethical or moral in focus, the Judaism constructed by Livnot is portrayed as radically accessible to all, regardless of class, status, or sex. For participants who are products of the egalitarian ethos of late twentieth-century North America, this kind of accessibility is vital to their ideals of justice and equality. This portrait of a Judaism that offers equal opportunities to all is explicitly spelled out by Ariela's introduction of the concept of *ben adam le chavero*, or interpersonal relations:

One other idea I'd like to put forth for the "entire congregation" thing is accessibility. We're in the middle of *Vayikra*, of Leviticus, talking all about the priestly this and the Levites that. Not everything is accessible to everybody. Not everyone is going to do all the ritual stuff that's going on. And this [Leviticus 19] needs to be separated out. Because they're for everybody, even the highest and most noble person. Call these some of the highest and most noble principles of Judaism, even the lowest and least noble can achieve them. These are being spoken to everyone. You have as much access to achieving this as you and you and you and the priests and Moses and Aaron and everybody. Equal access to high moral standards. That's really significant. Mister Jew over here sitting on the sidelines who doesn't think so much of himself, should not think that he has any less access or any less ability to achieve this "be holy as I am holy," and of this stuff, than anybody else. That's really important. That's really important for us to establish right now, because welcome to the club, guys. As much access as you want to anything Jewish, here you go. Judaism is anything but elitist.

Often, Judaism is presented as the antithesis to status based on wealth, intelligence, or ability presented as secular, North American values. In a class discussion of a teaching in the *mishna* on wisdom,[12] Addressing the question "Who is wise?," Daniel suggests that in Judaism, intelligence or knowledge is not of central importance:

A professor being wise is not specifically a Jewish ideal. I'm not saying that professors can't be wise, but there's a reason why it doesn't fit so well. That is, that if a professor is our, like it was for me, the archetypal wise person, what that often will mean is, what is wisdom? Knowledge. In other words, the amassing of things in your brain. Or IQ. "I'm a professor of physics and I'm *very* right. I know all kinds of formulas. I can send people to Mars. I'm amazing." According to the Jewish angle you could be very wise, but that's not what's going to make you wise. In other words, it's not the amount of material, of binary numbers of zeros and ones in your brain. That's not what makes you wise. That maybe will make you intelligent. Maybe that will give you a high IQ. But that [knowledge] is not going to make you wise. According to Ben Zoma, it's not knowledge that makes you wise. It's attitude. In other words, I could be somebody who never went to school, not only somebody who never went to school, but who doesn't have a very high IQ, I can even be somebody who doesn't have the capability of being intelligent, of being a professor of physics. But I can be very wise.

From envisioning a Judaism in which everyone has equal potential, regardless of intelligence, Daniel continues to offer a Judaism in which everyone has equal access to wisdom, regardless of physical or mental capabilities: "No matter even if we can't even move or talk or even use our brains." This focus on wisdom rather than intelligence, like the idea that Jewish ethics are for everyone, suggests to participants that "traditional" Judaism possesses a radical egalitarianism.[13]

At the same time as it is fundamentally egalitarian, the Judaism presented by Livnot is also strongly universal. Judaism is portrayed as the sole Western religion that embraces non-members and allows them a role, without any expectation of conversion. In a class dealing with the traditional concept of Jewish chosenness, Eliyahu Levy addresses the question of non-members:

I'm only speaking now for Western traditions, because Eastern traditions are a very different critter. But it's not true within Jewish tradition, that if you're not Jewish, you don't get a part of whatever this ultimate reward is. Judaism and its offspring religions, Christianity and Islam, all share a concept which comes from Jewish tradition, and that is a notion of ultimate reward. A balancing of justices in some kind of afterlife. But the important point to note is, if you are not a Christian, you have no part of it. If you are not a Muslim, you have no part of it. If you are not a Jew, no problem! You can still have a part of that ultimate, after-this-life reward. Not only that, it's actually easier.

For participants who have grown up in the pluralistic, urban environments of North America, this kind of apparent tolerance for other religions is appealing, as Nancy explains: "I don't know about the Messiah thing ... but if it does happen, we're the only religion where it will happen for everyone. It won't just happen for us, which I like. Because it's not really exclusive. Yeah, we're the chosen people, but we're not selfish chosen people."

Beyond being simply universalistic, Judaism is also constructed as a religion that is involved in the world, rather than one that rejects it for religious solitude. At Livnot, Judaism is compared favourably to Eastern religious traditions, which are presented as encouraging meditative isolation away from distractions of work, family, and society. In contrast, Judaism is presented as a tradition that remains engaged in, challenged by, and challenging of the more "mundane" world. Participants who are used to a high level of participation in the social world, and who are not seeking any radical rejection of society, find it comforting and appealing to know that they can still pursue conventional goals of career, family, and possessions within Judaism. The Orthodox Judaism of Livnot allows participants to be critical of specific, troubling aspects of contemporary North American society, without requiring renunciation of that society for meditative solitude or monastic asceticism.

PROTECTING WOMEN'S INTERESTS

Particularly in its treatment of sexuality and gender roles, Livnot offers a Judaism that serves as an alternative to what *chevre* perceive to be the excesses of modern society. Livnot presents participants with a Jewish world in which sex is not a matter of casual physical relations, however pleasant. More than simply special, the sexual act is portrayed as sacred in Judaism. Sex, Daniel explained, leaves more than just

> an impression on your body. It makes an impression on your soul … I know it sounds very Victorian. I know it sounds very old-fashioned. But according to the Jewish tradition, and in some cases you might say Jewish law, if it's only going to be physical, it's usually not good … This is going to upset a lot of people, because we have been brought up with the idea that two consenting adults can do whatever they want, and what does it matter. If I want to have sex with x, y or z and x, y or z also wants to, then so what? I'm not hurting anybody. Judaism says no, it's not enough. It [sex] is too special.

Raised after the sexual revolution in North America, the Livnot audience is one that would not respond to any notion of sex as somehow "dirty" or purely for procreative purposes. Livnot *chevre* are aware of and speak frankly about sexual issues. Most participants have been sexually active outside of marriage for several years. The notion that just because sex is pleasurable, permissible, and available this does not mean that it must be meaningless or trivial resonates deeply for them.

According to Livnot, this pro-sex stance of traditional Judaism is also one that is sensitive to women's needs and is carefully designed to protect women's interests. Teaching a class entitled "Intimacy," Daniel explained that the frequency of sexual intercourse in a marriage is determined by the wife's level of desire, rather than that of her husband. This ideal is presented as a case of the Jewish sages recognizing the physical differences between men and women, and stepping in to protect women from the possibility of sexual coercion:

There is one gender that decides if there's going to be sex tonight. And that's the female ... The sages gave the keys to the bedroom to the woman, in Judaism ... The wife has rights. The man has obligations. It's not symmetrical, but it will lead to unity. We're used to thinking that if everything is balanced exactly on the women's side and the men's side, it will lead to unity. Judaism is saying something that is not politically correct ... If a woman has a headache and doesn't want to have sex, and the man *really* wants to have sex ... What do you do in those cases of un-unity? How do you balance out the un-unity? You balance it out as follows: If a woman has a headache and doesn't want to have sex, and the man does, begs, forces, whatever, it can be very, very painful in many ways for the woman. So says Judaism ... If the man has a headache and the woman wants to have sex, so the poor man who has the terrible headache will sacrifice his little headachy-poo and will have sex [in sarcastic, condescending voice]. And you know something? He's going to have a great time! Because you know something? That's just the way people are. I know that's not a good thing to say anymore. I'm para-phrasing in a big way, in a big way. But it's not going to be so painful for the man. But it could be very painful for the woman ... We want to unbalance the natural unbalance, so in the end it will come out equal. How do we do it? You've got to stack the deck. How do you stack the deck? Give the keys to the woman. Not acceptable today ... The idea of the sages was to cause the least pain possible. That's what this is all about ... And there's so much pain going on in the world today because of sex. There's so much pain being caused to people because they're treated like objects, because there's no equilibrium, because there's no equity in the end. The sages are trying to prevent hurt ... The sages are saying if a woman does not want to have sex and is asked by the other person to have sex, but she does not want it, it can cause her much pain. It seems that the sages are saying that a man will have less pain. In fact, you know, sometimes he might even like it.

Perhaps even more striking is Livnot's presentation of the traditional Jewish practices that regulate marital intimacy based on a woman's menstrual cycle.[14] Livnot presents what can appear to be some of the most anti-woman laws in Judaism, the observance of "family purity" (*taharat hamishpacha*), as the epitome of respect for and protection of women. Like the quotation from Daniel above, Naomi suggests that Judaism understands human sexual desire, and argues that the laws of periodic separation between husband and wife preserve a marriage from sexual boredom:[15]

> The observing of the laws of *taharat hamishpacha* is the renewal of this wedding ceremony every month. It's the intimate ceremony between husband and wife. Because your first union is such a powerful one. It's one you never want to let go of, of a newly wed couple coming together. You just want to cling on to that moment and never let go of it. Well this is giving you that opportunity to monthly renew it ... We should only want, both of us, totally, mutually desire each other when we come together. It's such an ideal to come together, that when we come together, we're coming together both of us with the same desires. I've been married almost twenty years, and I've never had to say, "Not now dear, I have a headache." Because when you can be together, you appreciate every minute of being together. And if you look at *Newsweek* research surveys, it's getting sadder and sadder. Every now and then they have these surveys, the average American couple, how many times a month do they have sex? It's down to one, once a month. Because it's like "I'm tired," "I don't have time," "She went to sleep," "Tomorrow night." But when you have a time that this is your time together, you work your schedule around that too. You want to go to bed together. Because this is our time together ... And when you come to the point of menopause, that's a point, if you look statistically at marriages in America, so many women go through the kids are going off to college, the woman is full of anticipation, and all of a sudden the husband says, "I'm bored of this marriage, dear," and he goes off with his secretary. Here, in a couple that has observed this their whole lives, I'm just saying this from women that I've spoken to at this point in their lives, and the answer is "Hey, free sex now!" It's like, the kids have flown the coop, we don't have to be quiet, there's suddenly a rejuvenation between them. When you've had

a life of respect and borders and everything, and raising your family, and all of a sudden, instead of a woman going into a depression that she doesn't have her period anymore, all of a sudden there's a different point of relationship between them.

Doubtless, the ideal of a marriage that includes intense and lasting physical desire is one that appeals to participants. Based on comments I overheard, female *chevre* found it difficult to forget the compelling image of a pious middle-aged woman who had never had to plead a headache. Beyond keeping alive the spark of marital desire, the observance of family purity laws is also portrayed as a practice that preserves female autonomy, encouraging and validating a woman's non-sexual, independent time:

There's a point of, I need to be with myself. Thank God, I've never ever felt to say, "Not now dear." That's wonderful. Because I've had my time when it's just me. Sometimes I need to unwind. To sit up when everyone's asleep and just read. Or learn. Some women feel that they need to get together more with other women, and sit late at night learning with a friend … I'm torn between my giving of myself. But there's this certain time of saying I am to myself. I can take advantage of that and relax and not feel guilty, to say, "My body is to me right now" … There are times when a woman needs to be with herself and her body. This is saying not just that it's allowed, it's revered. Your time for yourself is important, and it is respected. Use it. Use it whatever way it's important for you to use it. This is your time for your own spiritual delving into yourself.

Finally, Livnot suggests that the laws of family purity and the prohibitions against physical contact between husband and wife for almost two weeks each month serves to build deeper relationships and enhance non-sexual communication between partners: "This is the time that we take advantage of developing our relationship in other spheres. When you can't even with your own husband reach out physically, you know, when he comes in and he's had a hard day and you want to just put your arms around him and say, 'How was your day honey?' and you can't reach out physically, you have to reach into the other resources of yourself. This building of the concept of respect, and space and borders, it gives a lot to a healthy relationship."

A Judaism that recognizes the reality of female sexual desire and
sacralizes sexuality, while at the same time protecting women from
(male) sexual coercion and boredom and preserving time for women to
be non-sexual, is extremely appealing, particularly to female participants.[16] As Fern explained, she feels that Judaism accounts for human
nature in a way that makes sense to her: "And if you truly follow *halacha*,
there's reasons for it. They're not even illogical reasons for it ... From
the standpoint of *shomer negiah* [cross-gender physical contact] or
lashon hara [gossip] or even the way women deal with their period and
the *mikvah* [ritual bath], they're very natural strands in human relations
that Judaism's found a way to capture and accommodate. Judaism is
not going against nature."

For Tamara, Jewish approaches to sexuality are difficult, but seem
potentially rewarding from a romantic point of view. She described her
impression that

> Jewish women are considered holy, but there are certain things
> that they're forbidden. Resolving that conflict within myself,
> coming from the open society in which I was raised, is a pretty
> tough call. I don't mind so much covering myself up [modesty].
> I don't feel that that's an attack on me as a woman. Both women
> and men have to practice that and there's something beautiful
> about that; it's very simple in its beauty. And it makes the slightest
> peek or the slightest look a million times more loaded, a million
> times more powerful ... You catch someone's eye, you catch the
> eye of a boy dressed in black and it's wow, this huge thing. I can
> really envision being in *Fiddler on the Roof* or *Yentl* and catching
> someone's eye and having it be huge. It means a hundred times
> more than what it means now, where you're looking people up
> and down every day. It [Judaism] takes a lot of the dirty connota-
> tions out of sexuality and of the body and really turns it into
> something simple and beautiful.

Many female Livnot participants perceive themselves to have been
hurt by men in the sexual arena. At various times they have felt objectified, used, and sometimes abused by men operating within a worldview
of free sexual expression without responsibility. When confronted with
the religious Jewish practice of avoiding all physical contact with the
opposite sex prior to marriage, participants are often shocked. Women
performing their National Service at Livnot will simply not touch male

participants.[17] Many women, however, are positively intrigued by the idea of restricting their pre-marital physical contact with men as a means of getting respect and countering the potential for being used solely for men's sexual gratification. Even those female *chevre* who feel able to maintain self-respect while participating in pre-marital sexual relationships believe that the Jewish practice of restriction makes fundamental good sense for them as women. Many participants agreed that sexual desire between men and women is inevitable, and that restrictions on physical contact make male-female friendships truly possible when the option of expressing that desire is radically precluded.

Rather than seeing them as anti-woman, many religious women in patriarchal traditions feel that the strict gender roles and pro-familialism better promote women's interests than does feminism. Sociologist Judith Stacey observes in such religious tendencies toward the "incorporation, revision and depoliticization" of feminist goals an emerging "postfeminism" rather than sexism or anti-feminism.[18] Livnot's construction of gender roles in Judaism and female participants' responses to it are strikingly similar to the discourse of newly-religious women concerning sexuality and the family.[19] Ideals of heightened sexual desire, bodily autonomy, respect, and more communicative relationships were all cited by Debra Kaufman's informants, as was Jewish legitimation of sexual pleasure, as advantages of the gender roles offered by traditional Judaism.

It would be incorrect to give the impression, however, that all issues of traditional Jewish gender roles are received so generously by Livnot *chevre*. Women are particularly shocked by the synagogue inequalities they see. However limited, participants' synagogue experience prior to Livnot has occurred almost entirely in contexts of liberal traditions with mixed gender seating. While the rare situations of prayer at Livnot take place without a physical barrier between men and women,[20] all Tzfat synagogues in the Old City include a separation (*mechitza*) between the sexes. Additionally, because most Tzfat synagogues are quite old, the women's sections are often cramped, ill-kept, and impossible to see or hear well from. While many female *chevre* at Livnot are deeply upset with this obvious inequality, it remains a minor issue since participants are rarely required to attend synagogue services.[21]

The traditional Jewish ritual differences between men and women include not only separate seating in synagogue, but also different religious obligations. At Livnot, this difference is explained with appeal to the idea that women are naturally more spiritual than men are, and so have fewer ritual obligations. Another variation on this theme explains that women are more connected to issues of time, by virtue of their menstrual cycle, and are thus exempt from numerous time-connected commandments. Female participants are surprised and pleased by such explanations. For Fern, they represent a new outlook:

> We were talking the other night about the passage in Genesis where it talks about after Eve bites from the apple, her punishment, which is basically to be subservient to men. I'm putting my words to that. But Eliyahu gave an unbelievable explanation as to the role of women. It's the very first time I ever thought about the fact that women, from a Jewish standpoint, could be considered on a higher plane in some ways than men. And that the reason that men have to do certain things is because for whatever reason they're just naturally further from God than women are. It has helped me to understand certain things. I'm not at all okay about covering every inch of my body, not being able to wear bathing suits, covering my hair … But that being said, my myths about the way Judaism treats women are being challenged.

The idea of a religious Judaism that treats women as separate but equal (or somehow superior) appeals to female participants who are eager to locate a non-sexist tradition. Through its teaching of Jewish perspectives on sexuality and gender roles, and its explanations for obvious ritual inequality, Livnot offers its audience a woman-friendly Judaism that both remedies the excesses of modern society and does so without subordinating women.

AN ENVIRONMENTALLY FRIENDLY JUDAISM

The Judaism presented at Livnot is one that is profoundly involved in the physical world, as well as the social world. Particularly through the weekly hikes, staff encourage participants to perceive meaningful associations between the natural world and Judaism. From highlighting the relationship between the seasons and the Jewish holiday cycle, to explaining the religious significance of carob and olive trees, hyssop and caper bushes, or extolling the "naturalness" of Jewish burial practices, Livnot fosters an impression of Judaism as a tradition that is deeply in tune with natural cycles and that is, ideally, fundamentally committed to protecting the environment. Fern commented on the impact of this association: "The hikes were a very, very important part of exploring Judaism in the field. It's like, being in the field of Judaism. You need to take certain things that you learn in class, like the seven species[22] or whatever, and then to go into the hikes and see olive trees and grape vines and fig trees. All of them right there. It's very powerful. And then to learn about how they relate back to the holidays, like *Sukkot*. Judaism is so grounded into nature and water. All of that was brought out through the hikes."

For many environmentally aware participants, the discovery that Judaism is embedded in the natural world comes as a surprising and welcome revelation. Prior to taking part in Livnot, some participants had felt so strongly about the importance of their own spiritual connection with nature, and so pessimistic about finding such an orientation in Judaism that they had actively sought out other religious traditions and philosophies. Wendy explains how this affected her:

I didn't know Judaism had a place in nature and *vice versa*.
So I just kind of went on in my life and developed my own little nature rituals and found it within other organizations. It was a wonderful discovery because I feel like you have to have a connection to the land and to what's going on in nature to be able to have a connection with spirituality and a connection with religion. If you don't have that, it's very difficult in my eyes to exist on a spiritual level ... It was a wonderful thing to learn that everything [in Judaism] is really dominated by a lot of nature. So blessing the grapes, blessing the bread, it's like thanks [God], this is nice.

Of course, at Livnot, the ideal point of intersection between Judaism and nature is found in the land of Israel itself. As the formative environment for Judaism, according to the program, the land of Israel possesses inherent meaning and deep religious symbolism, as was discussed above in chapter 3.

DISSONANCE

Livnot is deeply committed to its carefully drawn portrait of traditional Judaism as relevant, accessible, and palatable to participants. As a result, great effort is expended to protect these constructions from any serious dissonance that might threaten their plausibility. Sometimes program staff find themselves engaging in a kind of "damage control" or "impression management" to protect the image of Judaism that Livnot

seeks to communicate. On one such occasion, after a group of participants had worked for several hours preparing a large vat of soup, staff
members realized that because of a simple mistake[23] a point of the
dietary regulations had been violated, rendering the huge amount of
soup unkosher. This situation created a serious dilemma for staff members, who had to decide how to explain to participants that so much
perfectly good food, as well as their precious time, had to go to waste
because of what would appear to participants to be a minor, ritualistic,
dietary technicality. It was decided, not surprisingly, that the soup had
to be thrown out, as it was not *kosher*. Significantly, however, staff
members also agreed to hide this decision from participants, so that
they would not develop a negative view of traditional Judaism as ritualistic, overly strict, or wasteful. As a result, the staff hurriedly tried to
recreate the soup in secret, in a chaotic scene of staff members scurrying
around while trying to appear nonchalant to participants, cutting vegetables in a locked office, and attempting to make a soup that looked
exactly the same as the one that had just been thrown out. A staff
member explained the situation to me: "People's feelings are really
important and it's really important to handle it sensitively, but you can't
eat the soup. Our job is to find a way to not eat the soup in a way
that's not going to ruin the way these people see Judaism for the rest
of their lives. And that was the biggest difficulty in that situation.
Because we could not come to these people who had spent their entire
morning making this soup and say, 'Sorry, you used the wrong knife,
we have to throw out the soup.' You can't say that to these people.
They're not in a place where they can hear it."

The possibility of dissonance between the portrait of Judaism suggested
by Livnot and participants' experiences is not always deterred in such
dramatic ways. In particular situations, participants can feel conflict
between specific practices or emphases or experiences and the Judaism
they encounter at Livnot. At certain points, some staff members too
perceive the attempt to construct Jewish tradition in a way that appeals
to participants as clashing with the goals of the program or with *halacha*.

The difficult issue of intermarriage is one that almost inevitably arises
in each Livnot program. In a Jewish community highly concerned with
ensuring its own physical and cultural survival, intermarriage represents
a threat to these values, and is viewed as the potential or probable loss
of a Jewish family. Yet intermarriage is common in the North American
Jewish community, and occurs with greater frequency among Jews with

lower levels of Jewish affiliation. On almost every program, there is at least one participant who has a serious non-Jewish boyfriend or girl-friend back home. At Livnot, discussion of such difficult topics as inter-religious dating, intermarriage, and assimilation are left until the final week of the program. Classes during this week include the announce-ment of many dire statistics on Jewish population loss through assim-ilation, intermarriage, conversion, delayed childbirth, and decreasing family size. Participants are told in emotionally-laden terms that the disappearance of millions of Jews owing to these demographic factors is known as "the silent Holocaust."[24] Small discussion groups are con-vened on the topic of "Assimilation and Intermarriage," allowing par-ticipants to share feelings about their personal lives in an intimate, supportive setting.

Particularly for participants in romantic relationships with non-Jews, the subject of intermarriage, with its link to assimilation and culture loss, is acutely threatening. After three months of an intensely positive Jewish experience like Livnot, participants often come to the conclusion that there is something in Judaism worth perpetuating and that this goal can most easily be achieved with a Jewish life-partner. For some participants, this implies no immediate, painful consequences. But for those who are committed to non-Jewish partners, and now simulta-neously infatuated with Judaism and aware of a developing sense of responsibility to the Jewish community, the topic of intermarriage and assimilation is especially painful. The attempt to reduce possible inter-marriage is taken so seriously at Livnot that a participant's relationship with a non-Jew is considered important information that would be freely shared between staff members. Participants are sometimes shocked and upset to learn that their private lives have become topics of discussion at staff meetings. It is in addressing the subject of intermarriage that Livnot's policy of non-coercion is perceived by participants to be the most seriously challenged, since clearly the staff does want participants to do something: marry other Jews. Those participants actively wres-tling with the issue of intermarriage often feel subjected to uncomfort-able levels of pressure to leave their non-Jewish partners. The issue of intermarriage is also perceived to be at odds with Livnot's construction of Judaism as tolerant and open-minded. As Sharon explains, "I still have a problem with the whole intermarriage and inter-dating thing. About how Judaism seems to be so accepting but all of a sudden it's not." Participants involved with non-Jews express the feeling that discussions are being aimed pointedly at them, as potential intermarrieds, and that they are constantly being monitored for their reactions by staff.

While most staff members express the view that reducing intermarriage is at least, as Ariela describes it, a "positive by-product" of Livnot, one staff member disagrees, at least on a personal level. This individual clearly acknowledges the dissonance between Livnot's treatment of the intermarriage issues and the program's policy of non-*kiruv*, which refrains from pressuring people to live in a particular Jewish way:

> Officially, Livnot doesn't believe in *kiruv* ... And yet there are certain things which even Livnot official policy says we are trying to make them do. One or two things like not intermarry. You could say that *is* making them live an observant life, in other words you don't want them to intermarry ... My sense is that there are staff members who think for instance if someone intermarried, that would be a failure. I personally don't think so ... Because I'm the extreme of non-*kiruv*. Those are the one or two things we do of *kiruv* here, and officially I do them because that's my job and I'm fine with that. But me on a personal level? I don't want to make anybody do anything. It's your choice, it's your life. And I'm totally fine with that. And it doesn't hurt me if you decide to marry someone who is not Jewish. That's your decision, it's your life. You're responsible, not me.[25]

Another area of potential dissonance between the Judaism taught at Livnot and certain practices or emphases that the program upholds involves the issue of "who is a Jew." On occasion, a participant comes to Livnot who, although raised as a Jew, does not conform to the *halachic* definition of Jewish, because his or her mother was not Jewish or underwent a non-Orthodox conversion to Judaism. Livnot's policy is that people in this situation are permitted to join the program, but the issue of their *halachic* status as non-Jews is discussed with them at some point during their stay at Livnot. The discovery that one is, according to traditional definition and in the eyes of many Jews, not Jewish, can be extremely unsettling, particularly for participants who are becoming increasingly interested in Judaism in a positive way.

One blazingly hot day in the summer of 1996, Rachel sought me out for an urgent talk, insisting that we meet "in town," away from the Livnot campus. I wondered what could possibly be wrong – Rachel seemed to be having a good time on the program, participating fully and thinking seriously about all that she was learning. Rachel's encounter with Judaism at Livnot was obviously transforming her previously negative attitudes toward Orthodoxy, until that very day, when the staff broached the subject of her Jewish status with her. She met me in tears, shocked, and not a little angry to learn of what she perceived to be an elitist, in-group mentality in Orthodox Judaism that denied her entrance to a community to which she felt she already belonged.

While Judaism can be understood in an extremely tolerant, flexible, open and multiple fashion, there are limits to such interpretations, even at Livnot.

WITHOUT THE WARTS AND PIMPLES

Although Livnot clearly offers a selective and carefully chosen portrait of Judaism to participants, that construction is not presented as being partial. Participants are frequently told that they are learning about "Judaism the way it's been practiced for 3,000 years." *Chevre* simply do not have enough information to challenge the construction they receive and are rarely suspicious of what they are learning. One clearly articulated exception was expressed by Rebecca upon learning about Jewish attitudes toward sexuality. Using a dating metaphor to describe her introduction to Judaism, she explained:

> I think I would like to get to know Judaism better, although maybe not spend too much time with Judaism because it might become overwhelming. Know what I mean? … I like that Judaism says that it's a woman's due to get her ration of sex from the man. It's something the woman wants. That it's not just lie back and think of Mother England. That says that it should be like a sacrament … It should be something incredible … Cynically I wonder what they picked and chose to tell us about that. Because somehow I'm guessing that along the way there were a bunch of rabbis who didn't think you should be enjoying that at all. Somehow I don't think we're taught about the schools of thought that believe women are a temptation and lead men away from prayer and into sin. I'd bet some money there's a lot of that out there … This isn't a get to know the warts and pimples. This is hello. Look at this nice person. Like all people she has a few flaws, but let's not dwell.

Certainly, staff members convey the impression that they are teaching an authentic, traditional Judaism that has remained virtually unchanged since its inception and is universally practiced by all Jews. Livnot also steadfastly refuses to address the various different articulations of Judaism that have arisen since the Enlightenment. According to Eliyahu Levy, the education director: "Livnot takes people up to the end of the eighteenth century. We studiously avoid taking positions on Jewish identity affiliation and the answer to the Jewish problem after the Enlightenment. Because, we think, who are we to do that? In many cases, it's the individual's choice. What we simply try to do is expose them to all the stuff that went into bringing a Jew up to the eighteenth century, and then, boom, they can deal with it themselves ... we don't get into Orthodox, Conservative, Reform type things."

The Judaism taught at Livnot is never actually called "Orthodox" Judaism, although most participants label it as such.[26] Rather, staff members consider themselves to be illuminating "traditional" Judaism. There is no acknowledgment that the kind of Judaism they offer is just as informed by the post-Enlightenment age as any of the other contemporary manifestations of Judaism.

While the portrait of Judaism presented to participants at Livnot is partial and more appealing than the practices of the larger Jewish world, the construction of Judaism that staff members offer to participants should not be understood as completely contrived or manipulative. Rather, it is an ideal that is sincerely derived from the staff members' own beliefs and worldviews. Staff members feel that they are honestly portraying the best of Judaism, and thereby putting participants in touch with a more real and authentic tradition than they might otherwise experience. This perspective is clearly apparent in a comment made by Zahava, a young woman who grew up in an observant family and who was performing her National Service at Livnot: "It [the Livnot construction] is definitely a part of Judaism. It's just a part that, unfortunately, for many religious people, has died. Many religious people treat *halacha* as Judaism, and that is it. They would not like Livnot because it's not *halachic* [following Jewish law]. The staff is *halachic*, but the *chevre* aren't. But there's a side of Judaism that Livnot has, that many places don't have. It's not a fake Judaism, I think it's the real Judaism ... Livnot is definitely a real Judaism; it's just not a Judaism that exists so much in the world nowadays. I don't know if it ever did."

Ariela explains that, in her view, Livnot's emphasis on ethics and interpersonal relations is in line with God's will, even if, as an observant

Jew, she also believes ritual observance is a fundamental requirement of Jewish practice: "I don't think that God wants us ... to ghettoize and turn off the rest of the world, and be so focused on how big a piece of *matzah* I should eat at the Passover *seder*,[27] that I'm ignoring the fact that the person next to me doesn't know what I'm talking about."

The Livnot staff believe that this emphasis on ethics, personal meaning, flexibility, and tolerance aims to counter the distorted vision of Judaism as ritual-focused and synagogue-based that they perceive to have developed in the West. Staff members often agree with participants that the kind of Judaism that both they and participants experienced growing up is worthy of rejection. Mainstream North American liberal Judaism is abandoned as formal, meaningless, cold, hypocritical, and materialistic. Equally, Livnot registers a quiet protest against more religiously right-wing Orthodoxy, viewed as ritualistic and unwelcoming. In its stead, the Livnot staff offer what they believe to be a truer, more authentic portrait of Judaism, as Ariela explains: "I think it's *really* important that people know that, that people know that Judaism *is* a well-rounded religion. Because so much of what you see out in the world is, what is Jewish? Jewish is going to a very stale synagogue and reading a prayer book of things I don't understand three times a year and lighting *shabbat* candles. That is not Judaism. Nor is Judaism saying that anybody who isn't religious is bad."

This subtle protest against stricter articulations of Orthodox Judaism does not always have such quiet outcomes. Livnot's celebration of the *Simchat Torah* holiday in 1995 ended in violence when some ultra-Orthodox residents of Tzfat converged on a synagogue and harassed celebrants for allowing women to dance holding a Torah scroll.[28] Accusing those present of violating Jewish law, the individuals physically attacked Livnot participants and community members. Zahava, who was performing her national service at Livnot when the event occurred, vividly described the scene for me in detail:

This year for *Simchat Torah*, Livnot was at Beirav [a local synagogue]. And there the women danced with the *sefer Torah*. Which in many shuls isn't accepted ... The men danced outside in the street, and the women danced inside with the Torah. Suddenly a bunch of *haredim* [ultra-Orthodox] came from the side and were yelling and shouting ... They were shouting and saying, *"Hillul sefer Torah"* [desecration of the Torah scroll]. They threw a rock and it broke a glass and it came inside. Then the men came in from the street. They were being very violent and yelling, "Women dancing with *sefer Torah. Hillul sefer Torah.*" They grabbed a *sefer Torah* and they were hitting women with it. It was crazy. I couldn't believe it. I was the only one shouting at them because *chevre* couldn't say anything. I was saying to them, "*Sefer Torah gam shel nashim*" [The Torah scroll also belongs to women]. And they said, "*Sefer Torah lo shel nashim*" [The Torah scroll doesn't belong to women]. Then the battle moved out into the street and there was actual violence. They were hitting the men. One girl also got a little hurt. One *chevre* had his glasses swept off his face and broken. All I wanted and all the *chevre* wanted to do was stay and fight it out with them. Then the women *chevre* started singing "*oseh shalom bimromav*" [He who makes peace on His heights]. Which is very nice but because of *kol isha* [the prohibition on hearing a woman's singing voice], it made them even angrier ... The police came and cleared them away ... It was pretty much resolved, but the *chevre* were very, very upset ... Daniel explained about how in Judaism, or at least the way Livnot sees Judaism, the basis is *ben adam le chavero* [between man and his friend]. That's why we have that as the first seminar. And later on you get to *ben adam la Makom* [between man and God]. The basis of all Judaism is first interpersonal relations. And they [the *haredim*] got that wrong. They got their priorities skewed. That was the problem.

Since then, Livnot has made it a priority to celebrate *Simchat Torah* in Jerusalem, where more liberal Orthodox synagogues and their practices are tolerated.

While Livnot fosters the impression among participants that its teachings are examples of "traditional" Judaism, the staff freely admit, when questioned, that they display a Judaism with a particular emphasis. Such partiality is, the staff feel, a necessary and reasonable method in their efforts to break participants' stereotypes about Judaism and repair the damage of early, negative Jewish experiences. Using the example of teaching about *shabbat* at Livnot, Ron describes how the program tries to achieve this goal:

When you look at the Torah, what does it say about *shabbat*? Keep *shabbat* because God rested on that day. It says it in a few different ways. Then other times it says if you don't keep *shabbat*, the penalty is death. Now, for instance, you could look through the whole Talmud tractate of *Shabbat*. It doesn't talk very much about the beauty of *shabbat*, and what does that mean, exactly. It's technical laws about what things you do you're liable to be killed and when you're not. That's the way Judaism was for hundreds of years. Now there's another side of Judaism which was less developed ... which many people knew because they just knew it, they didn't have to learn it. But now you're dealing with people from the outside who don't know it. So it has to be presented in a very safe way. Not that we're saying that these issues don't exist. But when we're going to explain *shabbat*, we're not going to jump in by saying "*Shabbat* you have to keep, and these are the technical rules of what you have to do." But rather, what is the idea of *shabbat*, what does it mean to us in the modern world, how can we relate to it.

Staff members are clearly aware that they are presenting a selective portrait of Judaism to participants. Zahava, the national service woman quoted earlier, explains that initially she was surprised by Livnot's particular construction of Judaism. She recounts that during her first program as a staff member she was concerned about the unrelentingly positive view of Judaism on display, and how she discussed her misgivings with another staff member: "I said to him 'Shouldn't we also be teaching them the bad side of Judaism, the things that are wrong with it?' Because I definitely have things that I struggle with in Judaism. He said that people coming here have enough of the negative side of Judaism. They've gotten that part quite well, and the other side is what they need."

As the education director, Eliyahu explains that Livnot's particular construction of Judaism is goal-oriented, and designed to appeal to participants to help them become open to learning about Judaism. Staff members feel that without a vision of Judaism that appeals to the interests and needs of *chevre*, as young, liberal North Americans, participants would not be inclined to investigate Judaism at all. Eliyahu notes that "this isn't a special brand of Judaism. It is, to my mind, certain emphases of Judaism and Jewish tradition, Jewish life, at their best. But it's definitely true that in order that people even hear, see, experience, listen to some things, that we tone some things down. Jewish teachings are full of talk about obligations and things like that. We talk a little bit [about it], I do my little thing on *mitzvot*, we mention obligations, but we might stress the idea of the voluntaristic side involved ... We certainly stress certain things."

As part of Livnot's construction of Judaism, the program also uses a careful method of presenting the tradition, one designed to gently challenge participants without turning them off. For young, non-observant, North American Jews, many aspects of Jewish tradition are foreign and difficult to assimilate. Prayer, belief in God, the restricted role of women in ritual, and the concept of the Jews as the "chosen people" can be distinctly alien for participants who grew up in more liberal, secular environments.

One of the ways in which Livnot tries to make these topics more accessible is by moving from "easier" subjects to "harder" ones, from those ideas that are familiar, and thus more readily accepted by participants, to those concepts and practices that are more difficult for them to assimilate. Classes at Livnot follow weekly seminar topics, beginning the program with approachable subjects like ethics, and moving slowly toward more contentious issues like the centrality of Israel to Judaism, sexuality, Jewish spirituality, and intermarriage.

According to the Livnot staff, this progression is a process of gaining participants' trust by encouraging an initial, positive inclination toward Judaism through material with which they already agree. By starting out with "easier" topics, staff members hope that participants will be willing later in the program to engage concepts that might be more challenging or problematic. According to Ariela

> It is not a coincidence that *Ben Adam le Chavero* is the first seminar and *Ben Adam la Makom* [spirituality] is the second to last. It's not a coincidence at all ... I really try to play down the God part. Because first it's let's give them stuff that they see as objectively valid and let's let them say, "Wow! That's Jewish. That's really cool. I can get into that." Not that it's manipulative. The intention is not for it to be manipulative. The intention is, you learn one plus one equals two, before you get to calculus. And you relate to Jewish things that you can hear. First let's show the part how Judaism parallels my life. That "Oh, I could have a place in Judaism. This is something that's relevant to me." Then move onto things that blow their brains out and are so totally different than their lives. Because if you do that first, forget it. They're outta here. This is not about saying "Do this." This is about saying, "Look at it and see where your part is in it. Look at it and see if it has any relevance to you. Here's the part that for sure has relevance to you. Now look at the part that might be a little more

difficult to swallow." Once they see that there is something in here that's relevant to me, then they can be more able to not totally put their walls up to things that are foreign.

Staff members do realize that these routes to roots include potential dangers and might have unintended consequences for the way in which participants understand Judaism. Ideas such as picking and choosing from elements of Jewish tradition, multiple interpretations of texts, and practices, and an overwhelming emphasis on ethics, for example, when taken to their logical conclusions, can end up directly at odds with basic tenets of "traditional" Judaism, even as Livnot staff understand it. Ron outlines this dilemma:

> We try to walk a very fine line between presenting Judaism the way it traditionally has been for thousands of years and allowing people to go off different ways with it. It's a very difficult line that we walk, and we're not always comfortable with it. We could get a letter from a past *chevre* and the letter says, "The best lesson I learned in Livnot is that Judaism is really important to me, and that Judaism is whatever I make it and whatever I understand it to be." Which on the one hand is wonderful: here's this person who has developed a wonderful, caring relationship with Judaism, but, on the other hand, they're walking away saying Judaism is whatever I make it. And that's not true. So it's this very, very difficult balance. Where even something like, there's a very big analogy at Livnot about the supermarket, where you go up and you take whatever you want. But what does that mean? Does that mean I don't have to keep the whole Torah? Does that mean we don't think that Judaism is everything but just little pieces? No. But on the other hand, we're saying take things for where you're at in life. If you're into *shabbat* and you're happy with that, that's fine, that's cool. But we can't say that's what Judaism exactly wants you to do. It's a very difficult balance and we try to stay in the middle … I think we purposefully leave it very vague, to stay safe.

FINDING ROUTES TO JUDAISM, FINDING ROOTS IN JUDAISM

Using this construction of "traditional" Judaism that is at once tolerant, flexible, multiple, rational, environmentally-friendly, accessible, and pluralistic, Livnot U'Lehibanot makes Judaism an appealing, plausible option for its young North American participants who are lacking in Jewish background or who possess negative attitudes toward Judaism.

Livnot moves adhesion to Judaism from the de facto, automatic realm of familial descent to the realm of a freely made choice. In anthropology, descent relations point to relations conceived to be inherent in biology and blood, while consent relations suggest those freely chosen, like marriage in North American society: "Descent language emphasizes our positions as heirs, our hereditary qualities, liabilities and entitlements; consent language stresses our abilities as mature free agents and 'architects of our fates' to choose our spouses, our destinies and our political systems."[29]

As a result of increased knowledge about Judaism, greater familiarity and ease with traditional Jewish customs, and a feeling of the personal relevance and potential meaning to be gleaned from religious observances, participants are better able to make choices about the shape and nature of the Judaism they want for their own lives, rather than simply doing Jewish things from a sense of survivalism or familial obligation. Toward the end of the program, participants often eagerly explain that they now possess the "why's" of Judaism, as the following series of interview responses attests:

Now I know *why* I'm saying certain things. I don't have to just read the Hebrew. I can read the English and see if it has meaning for me. If it has meaning for me, I can read that out loud. And if neither of it does, I can read my own prayers and my own thing, or just feel the group. And that helps. REBECCA

Before, I didn't do anything Jewish. I didn't do any Jewish things. I mean, I broke the [*Yom Kippur*] fast with bagels, and I went to services once or twice a year. But I didn't know why. Being Jewish is more about knowing why, and this [Livnot] has pretty much done that. NANCY

I think the best thing about Livnot is ... it created more questions for me. It brought up questions that I wanted to ask, to get the why. And they answered them. But then I had ten more for each one I asked ... it inspired a desire in me to learn more. NANCY

Now it [Judaism] has so much more meaning. As a young child I was taught to do blessings, but now I understand why. It has so much more meaning to it. If I would have had that knowledge back then, I would have been a much happier kid. DIANE

It's different [from growing up]. I'm here because I want to be here, number one. It [Livnot] is explaining [Judaism] to me, rather than just saying well you are what you are, and just follow these rules. We're learning why's of everything and how it ties in to our lives. LAURA

Yeah [I feel more comfortable with Jewish things]. Because I know why. Rather than somebody telling me to do something. I know why. And if I have a question, they answer me. That makes me feel more connected to it [Judaism]. Rather than just being told, like if somebody just tells you to go to *shul* just because, then you're not going to get anything out of it. LAURA

Here, we're learning the reasons. And maybe those people at home knew why they weren't tearing toilet paper or turning on lights [on *shabbat*]. But there's more to it than that. Here, I think we're learning the more to it. Because we have the ability, we can ask the questions. I can ask one of the teachers, "Why am I doing this?" And they're going to answer me. They're not just going to say, "Because it says in the Torah blah de blah. Go away." They're giving you the explanation why, and that means everything. LAURA

I never got meaning behind actions and meaning behind why we celebrate holidays and the meaning why we lit candles on *shabbat*, because we did until I was about six or seven when we stopped. There was no open environment to do that in and no real interest even to do that. My mom certainly wasn't interested and my dad is a professional Jew but has no spiritual or religious aspect to his Judaism. MARNI

I want my sister to do it [Livnot] because when you call yourself something and you don't know why you call yourself that and there's a place that can help you to find this in a really amazing, beautiful way. MARNI

I'm at Livnot because ... I chose to explore Judaism. That's why I'm here. I got to the point of [wondering] "What does religion mean to me?" I grew up this way, fine. I don't know why I'm doing what I'm doing. It doesn't mean anything to me. So now I want to go explore that. FERN

Possessing greater knowledge and having had a positive experience of "traditional" Judaism, participants are both better equipped and more inclined to make choices about their own Judaism than they were when they came to the program. Through Livnot, the rituals they observe and the Judaism they participate in become more a matter of active, adult choice than simply a result of the accident of being born a Jew. In different ways, to greater and lesser extents, and in more and less traditional ways, Livnot participants are empowered to engage consensually in their descent, and to make choices concerning their ancestral culture.[30]

Many participants experience a fundamental transformation in their religious lives, from perceiving Judaism as meaningless to believing it meaningful, from a religious affiliation that results from chance to one based on active choice, from group membership by descent to participation by consent, from a Judaism focused on survivalism to a Judaism possessing traditional religious content. Social-scientific observers of North American Jewry have noted a pronounced emphasis on survivalism, coupled with an increasing sense of peoplehood and community, and a diminished connection to Judaism as a spiritual, religious tradition since the 1950s.[31] Livnot provides participants with the opportunity to experience Judaism as a vibrant, living, meaningful religious system, rather than the occasional, ambivalent, spiritually empty, status-oriented, or survivalist Judaism that they felt themselves to have grown up with. As such, the program's construction of the Jewish religious tradition, no matter how selective, "works" for participants. Livnot's portrait of Judaism allows participants to become active "choosers" of Judaism in ways that are meaningful and relevant to them, rather than simply be Jews by accident.

6

Life after Livnot

The impact of Livnot does not end with the program's emotional "final circle," held on the last night. Rather, it extends deeply into participants' lives following the program. Almost all of the Livnot alumni I spoke to describe their experiences at Livnot in positive terms, speaking of the program as a profoundly significant, transformative episode in their lives. There are several possible reasons for such generally positive responses. First, is the simple possibility that, by its very nature as a challenging, novel, stimulating situation, many participants enjoy the experience and find it meaningful. Second, efforts to facilitate the interviewing of past participants resulted in a sample that was skewed to favour past participants who had maintained a current telephone number with the Livnot office, or who were in touch with other past participants. The technique of snowball sampling that was used for this research tends to result in a study sample of respondents who are part of a social network of other respondents, and can exclude people who have chosen to isolate themselves from other members of the group. The people who stay in contact with the program or with other alumni are those who had at least a basically positive experience at Livnot, although I did actively seek out participants who had a negative experience on the program. Finally, there are several strategies that Livnot uses to help ensure that participants have a positive experience. One of these strategies is the careful selection of both who is accepted into the program, and who remains at Livnot. In a practice that can be perceived by many *chevre* as arbitrary or even draconian, participants who, in the opinion of staff, are consistently negative, unable to accept the

demands of the daily schedule, spreading dissent, having problems getting
along with others, or engaging in drug use, excessive drinking, or other
problematic behaviours can be, and often are, asked to leave the program. I have even heard it said among staff members that there is something wrong if no one is asked to leave during the trial period of each
program session.

The first three days of the program are treated as a mutual trial
period, a time in which staff and participants have the opportunity to
consider and evaluate each other. During this time, intensive staff meetings are held every night, in which each participant is discussed in detail,
on the basis of his or her behaviour and encounters with staff members.
Staff members are expected to spend some time talking with each participant in order to get a sense of their background and attitudes, and
to determine how the individual will fit in and contribute to the program. Participants are encouraged to be honest about any concerns they
might have during this three-day period. At the end of this time, each
participant meets individually with the coordinating couple for a discussion of why they have come to the program, and what they hope to
get out of it. Sometimes these discussions lead to what is usually a
mutual decision that Livnot is not the right program for a particular
individual. Since the group has not yet formed tight social bonds at this
early stage of the program, the loss of participants in the first few days
is, generally speaking, not a traumatic process for the *chevre*. It also
sometimes happens that in cases where an individual participant seems
ambivalent in his or her participation in the program, staff members
will *threaten* the individual with expulsion. The goal in such cases is
to precipitate some serious thought and inspire an impassioned defense
by the participant for remaining at Livnot.

Such careful control over admission to the program is understood by
staff members as an attempt to ensure that the people who come to
Livnot are seriously willing to engage with the Jewish material, will
survive the various challenges, and will participate enthusiastically.
Rather than manipulation or an artificial control of the environment,
this selection process is, according to staff members, simply part of their
responsibility in attempting to provide a serious, positive community
for those people who seek it. Livnot staff, quite reasonably, do not want
participants who do not actively want to be there or who will disrupt
the experiences of others. It must be stated clearly here that such control
over participation in the program does not imply that Livnot wants
chevre to be passive, non-confrontational, excited about Judaism, or

perpetually enthusiastic. However, the program does require that they be willing to participate and engage, seriously, with everything from hiking to learning, from working to singing. Livnot is by no means a holiday or escape from structured existence, and those that seek such an experience are advised to go elsewhere. As noted above, participants rarely come to Livnot because they are especially committed to Israel or necessarily eager about Jewish learning. Most often they seek an easy, temporary escape from North America as a diversion, an adventure, or an attempt to "buy time" before deciding what to do next. As a result, it is not uncommon for potential participants, especially during the summer months, to be seeking more of a relaxing, unstructured, holiday type of environment than what is actually offered by Livnot.

While participants are in some sense almost hand-picked to have a positive experience, and while the vast majority certainly do so, there are daily, regular difficulties encountered by most participants at some time during the program. No matter how positive the memories of any individual past participant may be, life at Livnot itself is often remarkably difficult. A severe shortage of free time, personal space, luxury amenities, solitude, sleep, and control over one's environment can result in interpersonal tension and friction. Disagreements or personality clashes between particular participants are not infrequent. The experience of a "bad day" at Livnot is easily compounded by what can sometimes feel like the irritating enthusiasm or positive attitudes of other participants. The actual daily process of the program is, regardless of participants' happy memories, not always smooth. Rather, life at Livnot is regularly challenging to participants, on physical, emotional, intellectual, and spiritual levels.

Beyond the regular daily annoyances and difficulties of program life, there are more serious problems that participants experience at Livnot, and that become clearer when viewed from the physical and emotional distance that individuals achieve following the program. While almost all past participants who were interviewed articulated evaluations of the program that range from the generally positive to the overwhelmingly enthusiastic, many past participants also voiced criticisms of specific aspects of Livnot. These criticisms range from mundane complaints about insufficient free time, poor living conditions, and lack of sleep, to more substantive concerns. Some participants express more serious critiques of the program's administration, the pressure they felt regarding *aliyah* or Jewish observance, the treatment of gender and sexuality issues, and Livnot's political slant. While the range of these criticisms is wide, none of these more serious concerns were ever espoused by more than three individual past participants. This suggests that while there are obviously complaints about the program that become more substantial when considered following the program, no specific issue is particularly glaring or perceived commonly to be a problem. In fact, for some of these criticisms it is possible to find several past participants who state the exact opposite to be the case. An element of Livnot that one participant might criticize, another might see in a radically different light, and praise.

Staff members also express disagreements among themselves, and their own criticisms of Livnot. These include complaints about the laxity of *halachic* standards in the program, concerns about the idealism of the Judaism presented, and tensions over administrative and financial issues. There are, of course, the inevitable daily tensions that flare up in such a close working and living environment, although these are carefully kept far from the eyes of participants. And while these disagreements do exist, the staff themselves characterized their relationships as low in conflict and described themselves as sharing general agreement about the goals of the program.

While participants are encouraged to have a positive experience, and while the great majority of my informants spoke enthusiastically and lovingly of Livnot, this is not always the case. Some participants, as a result of personality clashes, depression, an inability to cope with the schedule, feelings of coercion, or homesickness do not have a good experience at Livnot. Most participants in such situations do not complete the program, either as a result of their own choice or suggestions from staff. This dynamic ensures that participants who complete the program and have an intensely negative experience at Livnot are in fact quite rare.

While some participants express serious criticisms of the program, and all participants experience difficulties and tensions during the program, I was able to locate only two people who had both completed the program and found it to be an overwhelmingly negative experience. Laura, the twenty-seven-year-old receptionist from the southern United States who was profiled in chapter 1, had been directing her own life and schedule for many years. As a result, her greatest criticism was that she found Livnot's program schedule to be both too structured and too rigidly enforced:

I really felt like I was treated like a child. Maybe at times that was something that we needed. But you know what? I'm not a child.

I'm not a teenager. I really, really felt like that, a lot ... I think when we didn't want to go to class, it was a big deal. I felt like I was back in school. And we were in school, I guess. But it made me feel really rebellious, and like a teenager again. Like "Well fine! Then I'm *definitely* not going to go to class" ... I felt like I was going to get in trouble if I didn't do this or if I didn't do that. I think they need to lay off on that a little bit. I don't think it needs to be so strict, you know? It was everybody's choice to come there.

While she was at Livnot, Laura was depressed, homesick, and felt unable to keep up with other participants physically. She recognizes that these feelings significantly coloured her Livnot experience. In our conversation, she expressed discomfort at the idea that someone might take her experiences as truly representative of Livnot, and felt that her disappointment was due to personal issues that had little to with the program itself:

It [Livnot] answered a lot of questions for me. I learned. I think it helped a lot of people more than it helped me. I would hate to use myself as the example. Because I had a hard time. I was going through a hard time and I had a hard time when I was there. Maybe if I had a different outlook when I started, things might have been totally different ... I had a hard time adjusting to being away. I didn't think I would ... I guess I was going through a lot of changes, and maybe I went there a little more depressed than I thought I was ... I had a hard time on the hikes, which was a really big part of it for me, and the working. Just the physical part of it was really difficult for me.

Melissa's recollections about her experiences at Livnot are even more intensely negative than were Laura's, owing to a series of personality conflicts and situational disagreements with certain key staff members. Melissa felt herself inexplicably singled out as a target of criticism, judgmentalism, sexism, exclusion, and general mean-spiritedness. Livnot was a lonely, miserable period for Melissa, and she describes how strange it felt for her to watch other people participate so enthusiastically when she was having such an unpleasant time. Her negative experiences at Livnot, and the dissonance that Melissa perceived to exist between how she was treated and what Livnot taught about ethical behaviour, actually turned her off Judaism for several years: "There were so many times when they said that the most basic thing is that you need to be a good person. Above all the traditions, you have to be kind to other people. And I felt like the first one wasn't obeyed by the people who were teaching us ... [some staff members] I just really had a problem with ... I couldn't really take the message seriously from people who I didn't respect."

A different kind of negative response to Livnot is found in the dissonance that can arise in cases where, following the completion of the program, a past *chevre* acts as *madrich* for another Livnot program. The role of *madrich* is a volunteer position of liaison between staff and participants. Responsibilities of *madrichim* include working in the kitchen or at the work site, making *toranut* and *nikayon* schedules, lending a hand with everything from shopping to organizing food for hikes, providing informal counselling, generating enthusiasm, and keeping an eye out for problems among the *chevre*. *Madrichim* take part in all regular staff meetings, and staff feel that their input is critical for understanding the group dynamic and individual participants.

The opportunity to take part in Livnot "behind the scenes" can be a mixed blessing for past *chevre*. While it does give particularly interested participants the chance to spend more time in Israel, further their Jewish learning, and develop closer relationships with the staff, the position of *madrich* almost inevitably brings a realization of the degree to which the Livnot environment is manipulated and controlled by staff members – a feature that is hidden from *chevre* during the program. This loss of innocence can pose a challenge to past participants' beliefs about Livnot. Lisa describes her surprise and concern when, as *madricha*, she learned of the extent of staff discussion, information sharing, and background strategizing about participants, and realized that much of the program that appears spontaneous to *chevre* is really carefully contrived:

It bothered me that the staff would get together and report back to each other about how everyone was doing. It was like, "So, Lisa. Did you have any deep and meaningful conversations with Jennifer? Because you know, she has a non-Jewish boyfriend at home and we were just wondering what's going on with that. Have you talked with her about it?" Just this whole big-brother feeling. The thing is, now I see that it's for the welfare of the participants and everyone is very caring. But it bothered me a lot. The excitement when "Guess what? So and so just broke up with his non-Jewish girlfriend! Isn't that great?" And all the staff huddling together, [saying] "Well so and so did this and so and so did that." Also, on the hikes, on the three-day hike, everyone gets people to talk to. Like, "Go have deep conversations with so and so, so and so, so and so." I just found it really calculated and awful ... I remember on my program that Hagai [a staff member], we had had a lot of tension throughout the program. Then on the three-day hike he approached me and we talked for a long time. I just found out later he specifically chose me to talk to. I was so upset. I was so upset. There are a lot of things like that about Livnot. You think it's so spontaneous and really, it's been planned.

When asked about her time as *madricha*, Sharon expressed surprise at some of the Livnot politics she encountered during a period of tension between the Tzfat program and the Jerusalem campus: "You just wouldn't think that a program like that, that's supposed to be like, 'We're so family and so lovey-dovey and cushy-wushy,' you just wouldn't think that the Jerusalem campus and Tzfat campus would be fighting at all. That was so strange. That was weird ... It took away some of the niceness of all the people involved. It took away some of the genuine 'I live my life every day, every single minute by Jewish laws' of everybody involved ... You find out that they're human."

Another participant, Ruth, was shocked and angered to learn more about one of her "ritual" roles as *madricha*. As mentioned in chapter 5, some participants at Livnot had non-Jewish mothers, while others had mothers who had converted in a non-Orthodox manner, rendering their conversion illegitimate according to Orthodox Jews, and their children non-Jews. Ruth was expected to ensure the permissibility of food prepared in the kitchen by making sure to stir all food cooked by any *chevre* who were not halachically Jewish. As a ritual requirement that participants would almost certainly find offensive, both in its attitudes toward non-Jews and the implicit assumption that non-Orthodox Jewish conversions are inadequate, it is not discussed with *chevre*. To learn of this practice as a *madricha*, both as a characteristic of observant Jewish practice and one that is part of the worldview of Livnot staff, was an unpleasant realization for Ruth and other *madrichim*.

GENERAL PATTERNS, POST-LIVNOT

Following Livnot, past participants choose Jewish lives for themselves that are characterized by individualism, radical diversity, and creativity. While some preliminary, general patterns emerge from respondents' narratives, such generalizations unfortunately sacrifice the thickness and nuance of specific, individual articulations of Judaism, which will be presented below. One of the most common patterns of Jewish involvement among Livnot alumni involves an initially intense religious enthusiasm and commitment that becomes modified after a period of time. This modification of observance appears to result from several factors, including negative responses from family and friends, and tensions or discomfort with the Jewish community. Also, alumni find Jewish religious participation significantly more difficult in North America than they found it in the more supportive environments of Livnot and Israel. The numerous past participants who characterize their experiences as one of initial observance followed by less observance over time tend to describe their process as one of realistic modification of tradition, and the adaptation of Judaism to the realities of their own interests, priorities, and location, rather than in any sense a failure. It must be noted, however, that regardless of their declining Jewish observance or commitment relative to the immediate post-Livnot period, almost all past participants in this category still characterize themselves as significantly more involved in Judaism and the Jewish community than they were before they went to Livnot.

A second general pattern found among Livnot alumni is one of steadily increasing religious observance. Through continued Jewish study after the program, usually in Israel, a significant number of former *chevre* become more observant of religious tradition and *halacha*. Similarly, many past Livnoters choose to pursue a relatively stable route of increasing participation in the Jewish community over time. Of course, this route of increasing observance or community involvement "ends" when the individual reaches the level or degree of Jewish commitment she desires, owing to lifestyle choices. Past *chevre* who have become significantly more observant were found most commonly among individuals interviewed in Israel, or in North American informants seriously planning to emigrate to Israel. This is because Israel offers an abundance of serious Jewish learning opportunities and it is substantially easier to live an observant Jewish life there. Such a supportive environment both attracts Jews who are already Orthodox and can encourage observance among those who are not.

Finally, a small group of participants complete the Livnot program with levels of Jewish interest and involvement not markedly different from those they possessed prior to Livnot. Although these alumni often describe having more open-minded attitudes toward Judaism and a greater understanding of observant Jews following the program, the experience did not effect a highly noticeable or quantifiable change in their own practices and Jewish commitments. This pattern was commonly expressed by these past participants as the feeling that Jewish observance was not a major part of what they wanted for their lives at the current time. Significantly, however, none of the alumni interviewed in this group viewed the Livnot program as a waste of time in terms of Jewish learning and experience, a matter that will be discussed at greater length in the next chapter.

Many individuals in the first and third categories, that is, participants who were significantly involved in Judaism after Livnot but became less so over time, and those whose Jewish involvement changed very little as a result of Livnot, describe their current attitude toward Jewish observance as one of "not yet." Many felt that while their lives and situations do not currently support the level of Jewish observance they might want, Judaism is attractive and meaningful to them. As such, increased religious observance or community participation is an element that many feel they would pursue in the future, particularly after establishing families of their own.

While the general patterns that I have outlined above are useful for the articulation of larger trends, the Jewish lives of Livnot past participants are extremely diverse and resistant to easy classification. Beyond these general patterns lie the complex and idiosyncratic realities of participants' Jewish choices and decisions. Life after Livnot is truly a riot of voices describing different experiences, emotions, plans, and hopes. While commonalities in the experiences of alumni do exist, the most salient theme is, I believe, diversity. Whether *sheitel*-wearing or church-going, residing in the West Bank, the Upper West Side, or the West Coast, meditating or *mishnah*-quoting (and sometimes both), past *chevre* embody radically different priorities and feelings about what it means to be Jewish. This chapter describes and analyses some of the most common Jewish experiences of participants after Livnot, without overlooking the fact that those experiences are just as multiple, varied, and difficult to categorize as any other part of social life.

As we have seen in the previous chapters, Livnot offers a vision of "traditional" Judaism that is choice-oriented, partial, and designed to appeal to its audience of young North American participants. But participants do not tend to leave Livnot prepared to accept a simple, ready-made construction of Judaism. Rather than passively accepting a homogeneous, static, or monolithic construction of Jewish culture, participants create and negotiate multiple, creative, personal Judaisms. Most past *chevre* approach their Judaism as processual and negotiable, a cultural edifice that is constantly under construction rather than completed, fixed, or unvarying. The range of their Judaisms is wide, and the significance that participants ascribe to their Livnot experiences is deeply felt. More than any other factors, the common threads that run through participants' post-Livnot experiences, negotiations, and sense-makings are diversity and creative blendings between realities once believed incompatible. In the search for a simple label, we might call these post-Livnot Judasims "postmodern" in the sense that they comprise self-directed, nontraditional borrowings and combinations that consciously reflect a desire to locate a personally workable Judaism.

What follows are the coming-home, life-after-Livnot stories of four past participants, chosen to illustrate the general patterns, range of diversity, and dynamic hybridities mentioned above.

TAMARA SAPIR

A twenty-year-old woman attending college in New Mexico, Tamara was interviewed ten months after she completed Livnot. After her return to North America, she lived for a brief period at her parents' home in California. Here, she was, as she explained, "really trying to, not keep *shabbat*, but keep awareness of it." Soon after she moved to a nearby city where she lived with two other Jewish women, one of whom was also a Livnot past participant. Because it was important to her, and because observance was now significantly more feasible than in her parents' home, Tamara began to observe *shabbat* and some degree of the dietary laws, in addition to praying regularly: "Because it was easy [to keep *shabbat*]. It was walkable, I could go out to [*shabbat*] dinner [at someone's house] and then go home to my bed rather than having to always crash at someone else's place ... I wasn't keeping kosher but I was pretty much keeping vegetarian and only eating *kosher* meat ... At that point, I was still and had been since Israel, *davening* [praying] every night. I was *davening maariv* [the evening service]."

When Tamara first returned home, her friends were very understanding of the changes she had undergone during her time in Israel, and supportive of her religious choices, feeling it was "rad" (radical) that she was investigating her own culture and spirituality. But over time, Tamara's new Jewish commitments, particularly *shabbat* observance, resulted in increasing tensions with her close friends. Tamara also found to her surprise that it was her Jewish interests that were particularly problematic for her Jewish friends, who tended to become defensive about their own levels of Jewish observance: "Weirdnesses sprung up. Like, 'Well why can't you come over Friday night? I'm having a party.' Little things. Like, 'If we want to do something on Saturday, why do I always have to come over to your place and then we can walk? It seems unreasonable' ... What wound up happening was that my Jewish friends started feeling alienated from me. In the sense that, 'Well, if I don't keep *shabbat*, are you looking down on me? And what do you think about me then, that I don't keep it, and what does that say about me?'"

As a young woman with a deep commitment to pluralism, Tamara was surprised to learn that she inspired such defensiveness in her friends, who seemed to expect her to be judgmental and intolerant of their choices: "That is what hurt me the most. Because I really believe whatever path you walk in is kind of just whatever makes you love [others] more and [be] more peaceful. So I wouldn't hold anyone else to any stringency level of anything that makes myself more peaceful. But you can say that to someone, and they can believe what they want."

Approximately eight months after her return from Israel, as Tamara explains, she "stopped observing *shabbat* so strictly," and although she continues to light candles on Friday nights, she no longer engages in regular daily prayer. Her Judaism has more recently taken a different focus, one with which she expresses a deep contentment. It is a Judaism that is "non-observant" by any traditional standards, but it is a Judaism grounded in Tamara's personal commitment to ethics and the ideal of *tikkun olam*, or repairing the world. She explains that she feels

> really like there's no point in being in this world if you're not going to make a difference in it ... I feel like that's directly inspired by Livnot, directly inspired from my feeling about what it means for me to be a good Jew. But then it gets weird. So, I'm on the search and rescue team, which is a volunteer position, where we go into the mountains and you rescue people who've been stranded. But they meet on Saturdays. But that feels okay to me. Right now, that feels okay to me to be hiking on Saturday, looking for someone who might be injured, or just hiking and learning rescue skills. And when it stops feeling okay then maybe I will start keeping *shabbat* again. But for me, keeping *shabbat* when I'm grumbling about it to myself, isn't going to purify me for the week ahead. So what I've been doing is I've been going Friday

afternoons ... [a friend] and I cook for *shabbat*, and I come over
and have *shabbes* dinner with them on Friday nights. That kind of
is my fix right now. It feels really great ... In general, what I'm
doing is what feels good to me. I'm doing the volunteer stuff and
I'm doing the Friday night stuff and the holidays. I'm going to
build a *sukkah* [a temporary, outdoor booth for the festival of
Sukkot] in my backyard. And I'm meditating in the mornings,
which for me is steps for getting back into official prayer again.

Tamara is clearly in the process of forging a Jewish life for herself,
one that is meaningful and workable for her. Hers is a Judaism directly
influenced by Livnot, one that is both mixed with and expressed
through her love of nature, her feelings of social responsibility, and her
interest in meditation. Tamara experiences no painful contradictions
between enjoying more conventional *shabbat* activities on Friday night,
and doing less traditional volunteer work on Saturdays. Tamara's
Judaism is extremely important to her, a fundamental part of her self-
understanding and how she envisions her relationship to the world:

I'm really feeling I'm in a place right now where it [Judaism] is
starting to be mine, which is a really good place for me. I'm in a
place right now where I'm really happy for the first time in a
really long time. As long as I can remember. I think that's because
I'm kind of doing what feels right to me, in all aspects of my life,
at the pace that it feels right to me. I'm not feeling pushed into it
[Jewish observance] by anyone or anything ... Making it [Judaism]
mine is what keeps *shabbes* in mind for me. On Saturdays that's
hiking. And what keeps *shabbes* in mind for me on Fridays is
cooking and having *shabbes* dinner. That's where it fits into my
place. And knowing, I mean I have the intention that I'm going to
be *kosher* at some point. Maybe even this summer ... Keeping
shabbat is an intention that I have in life. But I know that I'm not
at a place where I can do that now ... when I can really handle it
with a pure spirit, where I wouldn't alienate other people, and
I won't alienate myself. That's really huge.

Tamara's story illustrates a pattern that is common among Livnot
past participants. For many alumni, like Tamara, life after Livnot
includes making conscious, extensive, creative accommodations and
modifications to normative Judaism in order to construct a meaningful
and workable Jewish life for oneself.

ANNE BRAUN

Anne, married and in her early thirties, spoke with me just over two years after she had completed Livnot. Following the program, she had remained in Israel for another five months to study in a more intensive Jewish learning program in Jerusalem, and over time she became increasingly observant. After completing her second program of study, Anne travelled for a period through Europe and India, and finally became engaged to a Jewish man of Orthodox background from England. Soon after their marriage, they moved to Israel together, where our interview took place in their kitchen.

Anne came to Livnot in the mode of a classical spiritual seeker, with a long, serious involvement in an Eastern religious tradition and a commitment to one particular teacher in India. Livnot showed her an alternative to the Judaism she had experienced growing up, in which, she explained, "I didn't learn anything about Judaism that felt to me to be spiritual, as a child." Anne described how the experience of Livnot gave her a deeper, more meaningful sense of what Judaism had to offer spiritually, and also provided her with a level of basic knowledge about Jewish tradition and the culture that her ancestors had shared:

> They [Livnot] are basically trying to give you a deeper sense of Judaism and maybe what your grandparents were doing. There was a big part of me that grieved, I think, after Livnot, and during. Like, "Gosh, I never knew this." I was like, "Did my grandparents really light candles on *shabbat*? Was this the way of life of my ancestors?" I literally had no idea. Livnot gave me the chance to really learn a lot, in an environment that wasn't pushing me to be any specific way ... There was an aspect of irritation towards that aspect of my upbringing, because there was a wealth, a sea of beauty that I never was told about. I just thought this was the way it is to be Jewish. And now I see that that is not really the only way of being Jewish. But it was the only way that I knew. I had no idea that some people don't drive on *shabbat*! I don't think I even knew what *shabbat* was.

Generally, Anne's family was supportive of her growing observance and interest in Judaism. Anne's religious involvement was bolstered by her mother's own interest in Judaism, and by her father's active dislike for Anne's interest in other religious traditions. However, Anne recounts that her grandparents and some of her friends felt threatened by the paths that Anne was choosing to pursue in her life. While she observes *shabbat* and *kashrut* according to normative Orthodox standards, in addition to other traditional Jewish practices such as *taharat hamishpacha*, Anne is herself unsure of how to label her level of religious observance:

> I would say to Simon [my husband], "What are we?" We don't really like to consider ourselves Orthodox. We're Jewish, we keep the sabbath, and we don't really know. We don't really feel like we want to call ourselves anything ... In one sense, there's a comfort in being labelled. But there's also a lot of irritation for me. I think that, thank God, we have a group of friends ... very amazing people, who are Orthodox, but then, that's the question: What is Orthodox? Maybe because I have a very open mind, I might say something different than the guy next door who's got *payos* and a black hat and twelve children. So to that extent, maybe we're not Orthodox. To my friends in America I'm very religious. Even that I would cover my hair going to *shul* is very religious, even though I don't cover my hair always. So on the whole I don't like to be pegged into any particular group. I just prefer to be a human being and people can see my inner self, rather than have to associate me to anything. It's difficult, because in some ways I don't fit in anywhere.

Staying true to her understanding of herself, and recognizing her personal interests and paths, in *addition* to living an observant Jewish life, is important to Anne. She remains committed to her teacher in India, to her own meditation practice, and to her interests in alternative healing. Her quest is, as she put it, "to find a balance between Anne and the creative aspect of me, and Judaism." Livnot, she feels, has encouraged her to develop a more balanced, personal, individual kind of relationship with Jewish tradition than she might have discovered elsewhere. She contrasted her own experience at Livnot with the experience of other people she knew where she studied following Livnot, and who became observant:

> I find that a lot of the people that I went, not to Livnot with, but the second place that I learnt, a lot of my friends had become very religious, and I can't even relate to them. I don't think a lot of them really understand me so much. They more strived to associate themselves to some sort of group of Judaism. Some kind of

Chassidic group, or, you know, their husband wears this kind of *kipah* or that kind of *kipah* ... I think that the reality is that once you actually step into life in an Orthodox community, I don't know how open an Orthodox community is, realistically, to pick and choose. But I do pick and choose. I don't know if that came from Livnot or if that came from my sense of autonomy. I think Livnot played a part in it. I think also because you get a very broad perspective [at Livnot], so I was exposed to a lot. As opposed to just being exposed to a very little bit, and then having only a little bit to choose from.

Anne has chosen to live her life as an observant Jew, in part owing to her experiences at Livnot. At the same time, she also feels free to explore other facets of herself, her interests, and spiritual experience, enjoying a combination of Jewish tradition and personal freedom also encouraged by Livnot. She strives constantly to locate a deeper, more personal spiritual meaning in her Jewish practice and to integrate her Judaism into her life. This path of developing a personal accommodation to Judaism can be a lonely one, and the individual may find little in the way of general support from the community. During a short return visit to America, Anne found her experience of the Jewish community to be deeply alienating. Involved with the Orthodox community in a city in the southwest United States, she found that "They're all pretty religious in a certain way. I wanted my Judaism to be a bit more creative." Musing on the attempt to live her own Judaism in a religious community in Israel, Anne commented: "I struggle with it [creating my own Judaism]. I think that ultimately that's what I strive to do with my life now. There are aspects in which I feel defeated. Sometimes I feel like is there a place? Is there the ability for openness here? Is there the ability for me to rise above the confines of what appears to be Jewish in Tzfat, let's say, because this is where we're living and it's a very religious community. How can I be strong enough amongst the pressure? ... I struggle with it."

Together with her husband, Anne dreams of a committed, creative Jewish future and praxis, combined with teaching others to locate and create their own kinds of Jewish meaning:

Simon [my husband] and I have this vision, this inspiration, to start a Jewish retreat centre, a healing centre. That's a big part of me, and who I am and who I was. It's very creative. It's needed.

I think that it's a struggle, but it's a beautiful striving, a beautiful struggle, to make Judaism personal and to bring in that aspect of how can we teach to others and how can we actually live an inspired Jewish life that doesn't end up being just ordinary ... How can I derive more meaning from the holidays and make it more creative? ... Meditation and doing Jewish meditation. Looking at the *Kabbalah* as more appealing, which isn't something that I've been deep into, but in small ways. Taking different *psukim* [verses] from the Torah and doing chanting.

However observant, Anne emerged from Livnot eager to integrate her own interests and spirituality with traditional Judaism. Her story is very different from those of some past *chevre*, but remarkably similar to the experiences of other alumni. Like other Livnot participants, Anne did not emerge from the program as a "cookie-cutter" Jew, but rather as one articulation of a vibrantly diverse, hybrid, creative set of Judaisms. For Anne, Livnot was part of a foundation from which she felt able to develop and expand Jewishly. As she explained, "I think that without your roots, it's very difficult to actually grow. That's what Livnot gave me: a chance to learn about my roots so that I could grow."

YAKOV COHEN

I interviewed Yakov at his home on a large West Bank settlement, in the caravan area reserved for *yeshiva* students. Together with his wife and two young children, Yakov lives an obviously observant religious life. Their living room is crowded with religious books, and Yakov himself sports the conventional yeshiva look of white shirt, black suit, and black hat. Once upon a time, he was called Jake, but he began using his Hebrew name shortly after doing the Livnot program in 1992. Yakov's story, like Anne's, exemplifies the general pattern of increasing religious observance. I have included it because his particular articulation of Judaism is more normative, and less obviously creative than is Anne's.

It is a little disconcerting to reconcile Yakov's ambivalent path to Livnot with his current lifestyle. Of his Jewish background, he explained that

I really didn't think about my Jewish identity or about Jewish identity at all. I wasn't really interested. I didn't come to Israel because of any Zionist or religious interest. I came because

I majored in Russian in college, and I wanted, in a different way, to continue that. I worked in the Jewish Federation in the States, and had a positive experience there working with Russian immigrants, and people there had spent time in Israel and had a really good time when they were younger. So it was through them I got the idea to come to Israel ... I've totally changed my life since then. I'm totally involved in different things, different identity ... I wasn't interested in religion. I wasn't looking for it, I didn't want it. When it was first offered to me, I rejected it ... So Livnot provided me with something that I didn't even know was up my alley at all. I was kind of blindsided by the whole thing. I wasn't a seeker, I wasn't Mr Spiritual. I wasn't always into it. I never took a religion course, I never thought about religion, I never thought about Jewish identity.

Yakov described poignantly the Judaism he encountered while growing up, which was focused primarily on the need for Jewish survival. This kind of Judaism emphasized the Holocaust as a threat to Jewish survival and taught a powerful taboo on intermarriage as a way to ensure Jewish survival. Looking back on this Judaism, Yakov feels that it was lacking in any positive, meaningful, or active Jewish content. While Yakov did not perceive such a lack while he was growing up, participating in an alternative formulation of Judaism at Livnot surprised him in a positive manner:

It [Livnot] gives people a much more positive sense of themselves as Jews. My Judaism [growing up] was very much focused on how you can't marry someone who's not Jewish. Not to do that. There was always this incredible focus on the Holocaust and everything that happened, all the horror and negativity of that. So it was a wonderful change for me, for people to be focused on Judaism as a focus on life, on building something positive ... a Judaism focusing on something which is full of life, and a lifestyle, a way of life. Instead of my Jewish identity being tied to "I'm part of that nation which was in the Holocaust," which is a very negative identity. I think it definitely didn't encourage me to want to get Jewish.

After completing Livnot, Yakov acted as *madrich* for the following program in Tzfat. It was during this second period at Livnot that he began taking on certain religious, ritual obligations. He then pursued further learning at a "beginner" *yeshiva* in Jerusalem, an experience that he found to be extremely different from Livnot. The *yeshiva* curriculum focused on questions about God and theology to a much greater degree than did the Livnot program. Realizing a desire to pursue more extensive, serious Jewish study, Yakov sought out a more intensive traditional *yeshiva* environment. Yet he also specifically sought out a *yeshiva* that would allow for a certain degree of pluralism and diversity in ideas and lifestyles within the framework of Jewish observance. As Yakov explained:

> I wanted to come to a place of learning which was not oppressively *hashkafic* [wedded to a particular outlook]. Where they didn't dress differently or talk differently. So this is a very non-threatening *yeshiva*. It's very mainstream. There's no desire to belittle any other *yeshivot* or any other ways of doing things. It's very open. That's exactly what I was looking for. It was easy for me to come here, and I was able to go from one place to another of places which are very open and places which didn't have a picture of exactly who they wanted to create. They didn't want you to walk out dressing this way, talking this way, acting this way and having been given this set of ideas. They're interested in you getting whatever you needed and getting wherever you should go. If you went this way or that way or this way or that way, there wasn't really a problem. The thing they were interested in was your getting something positive out of the experience and doing something positive with it.

Yakov's desire for a tolerant, open learning environment was, he observed, directly influenced by his experiences at Livnot. In making the choice to attend this particular *yeshiva*, where he ultimately received rabbinic ordination, he sought the advice of Livnot staff members, who actively supported his decision:

> I think that he [a staff member] knew they were a *yeshiva* where I was not going to end up being exclusionary toward most of the Jewish world. It's not so much an issue of being *haredi* [ultra-Orthodox] or not being *haredi*, being a Zionist or not being a Zionist, but just not one of those people who think they have an exclusive lock on what is the right way to be Jewish, and lock everyone else out. Because that's anti-Livnot. Livnot is opening

everyone up and giving everyone the wonderful experience that they can take to warm themselves up to their Jewish identity. I think that definitely he [the staff member] sent me here, and Nachum [another staff member] also liked it, because they felt like this was a place where there was a lot of positive Jewish identity available, with a minimum of exclusionary attitude. It [Livnot] definitely affected my choice in coming here.

While Yakov expresses deep respect and gratitude toward Livnot and particularly toward certain staff members with whom he has an ongoing relationship, he does not return to Tzfat to visit the program anymore. The choices that he has made for himself and his own priorities and Jewish needs make such an encounter uncomfortable. The Livnot environment presents particular issues and challenges for Yakov as a highly observant Jew that make him less inclined to spend time there:

As I became more religious, it became weirder and weirder to go back to Livnot. Because Livnot is not openly religious. I felt it became harder and harder to come and expose myself to the programs there and to be around those people because it was [for current participants] like, "Oh, you went over the deep end" … Going back [to Livnot], they're not as focused on the ritual observance as people in a *yeshiva* community are. Certainly, they're observant and they are very concerned about their observance. But there are things that after being in a *yeshiva* for a long time, you're just less comfortable with. Also, in order to do Livnot, you have to be willing to be exposed to scantily clad women and people whose attitudes are coming out of the big frat party which is college, and you have to put yourself into that. And *kol hakavod* [all my respect] to people who are willing to do that, but I'm in a very sheltered environment, especially before I was married, when I was just learning all the time, with young men all the time and rabbis, and I'd go back to Livnot and it was bizarro land. To have a long conversation with a female would have been just bizarre for me, because I wasn't around it at all. So it was very strange.

For Yakov, life after Livnot was one of increasing religious observance and study in a traditional environment. He returned to North America only for very short periods of time. His story represents another facet of the many experiences participants pursue following the program. Yakov's own desire for a creative Judaism, encouraged by Livnot, is particularly apparent in his choice of a learning environment that was "not oppressively *hashkafic*." Within the framework of normative religious tradition, Yakov sought a place to study that, rather than seeking to create a certain model of Orthodox Jews, encouraged pluralism, autonomy, and creativity.

KEVIN NEILSON

Sitting in a Manhattan café, Kevin described his Livnot experience to me four years after he participated in the program. He lives in New York City, works in a bank, and looks like any other young, single, North American urbanite. Kevin's background was one of nominal Conservative Judaism. His childhood and adolescence were spent in a comfortable suburban Jewish neighbourhood, where he neither questioned religion actively, nor knew much about it. Only when he moved to New York City did Kevin realize that there was a broader non-Jewish world that knew little or nothing about the culture he had taken for granted:

> I grew up, basically, in a Conservative Jewish family. We weren't extremely religious, but we followed all the holidays, *bar mitzvah*, all the traditional things. Growing up around mostly Jewish people, I took Judaism for granted a little bit. All of my friends that I grew up with were Jewish. Everyone I went to school with was Jewish. But I didn't know much about the religion, to be honest. Because I never had any reason to know anything. Nobody ever asked. Nobody seemed too concerned. Just a Conservative, average, middle-class upbringing in a pretty Jewish area. I found myself working in a bank in Manhattan ... I started realizing there is a world, even in New York City, that isn't all Jewish. People found out I was Jewish, and they were very interested in the religion ... People would ask me a million questions ... I guess I wanted to learn a little bit more.

Even while growing up in a highly Jewish environment, Kevin still felt the dominance of non-Jewish society and norms. There were times as a child, Kevin explains, when he felt embarrassed to be Jewish, and he was confused by the pressure of cultural difference, exacerbated by a lack of Jewish knowledge. It is precisely that knowledge about Judaism and Israel which Kevin gained at Livnot that makes him feel proud of his cultural tradition:

> I've been more proud to be a Jew since I went [to Livnot]. There was times in my life, when I was a young child, that I was a little bit ashamed to be Jewish. I grew up in a Jewish area and I was with mostly Jewish people ... but even as a youngster I had a group of friends that weren't Jewish, and I remember lying to them and telling them, "Oh yeah, we have a Christmas tree at home. I'm not Jewish." Then there was times when I didn't care about the religion. I just didn't understand it. Like, why are we different than any other religion? Why don't we celebrate Christmas? Why do we celebrate *Rosh Hashana* and *Yom Kippur*? Why is Israel a Jewish state? And a lot of those questions were answered for me when I went there [to Livnot]. I found that I'm really proud to be Jewish and I learned a lot about the history that I didn't know a lot about, with the exception of seeing *The Ten Commandments* a couple of times. It was enlightening.

Livnot, Kevin explains, was an extremely significant experience in his life, both for personal growth and Jewish learning. Unlike Tamara, Anne, or Yakov, however, Kevin remains what some people call a "twice-a-year Jew," attending synagogue on the High Holidays, perhaps participating in a Passover *seder*, yet doing little more in terms of traditional Jewish observance. Kevin is no more obviously observant of Jewish tradition and practice four years after Livnot than he was prior to attending the program:

> I learned a lot about my religion ... so when I did come back, I had more of a view of what I wanted to become as a Jew. I realized that as much as I loved *shabbat* dinners and I loved a lot of the religious aspects, like going to synagogue on a weekly basis and not using any kinds of electrical appliances on weekends [*shabbat*], being *kosher* pretty much the whole time, I realized that that's something that I wouldn't want to do in my life. Before that I had a lot of questions. Maybe I'm missing out. Maybe I should do that. My grandfather was a religious man ... I thought to myself, maybe I'm missing something. But I realized that I'm glad I experienced it for the time I did, but I wouldn't want to be religious.

In part, Kevin feels free to make this choice to be non-observant because Livnot did not force religious tradition on participants, nor did staff members expect him to conform to their priorities and lifestyles. Moreover, while Kevin chose to put very little in his Livnot "shopping cart" in terms of religious observance or participation in traditional Jewish culture, it is the cultural knowledge made accessible by Livnot that, Kevin feels, makes him a better Jew. Simply the possession of information empowers him and makes his choices Jewish, regardless of the level of Jewish practice in which he engages:

> [Through Livnot] I learned a lot more about the religion, which was my main goal. I can answer peoples' questions. And honestly, I can answer my *own* questions. I know a lot about things I had no idea about ... Even coming from a kind of Conservative family, I was a Jewish, almost illiterate in the religion ... So yeah, I am in the same boat [as before I went to Livnot], I'll be honest with you, as far as religious beliefs. But I feel that I'm a better, more knowledgeable Jew than I was. Definitely better. Because knowledge is power ... No, I didn't become more religious. But I feel like I'm a better Jew than I was. I'm a more knowledgeable Jew.

While a number of Livnot alumni create a Judaism that is blended with other religious traditions and cultural practices, as will be discussed below, many others create a Judaism that involves re-visioning the tradition from the inside. Modifications of normative religious observance allow these former *chevre* to participate in traditional Judaism in ways that they find comfortable, palatable, or realistic. This inevitably requires a meeting of worlds. Many participants are mixing basic Jewish observance with the "realities" of North American culture in an effort to create a workable blend that appeals to both their Jewish and contemporary Western identities.

Many Livnot alumni discussed the ways in the which they have developed personal understandings of core Jewish practices, like *kashrut* or *shabbat*. Adam, for example, adjusted the normative rules of *kashrut* for practical reasons that included avoiding parental conflict. Part of his dietary regimen was grounded in a concept of consciousness based on knowledge:

> The dietary laws – that was a big thing for me. So I tried to modify my diet to where I wasn't necessarily *kosher*, but it was

more that I would try not to mix milk and meat. I didn't deal with any of the plates stuff, like separate plates, because that involved not being able to eat in my parents' kitchen ... A lot of times I either tried to keep things vegetarian, in which case I just didn't have to deal with it, or consciously, when I ate meat, to not have milk around. Or when I knew that I was eating something that was not *kosher*, like calamari, I would consciously realize that I was eating something non-*kosher*, whereas before it was like yeah, whatever, never phased me one way or another.

Rebecca too, has chosen to follow her own, highly individual, modified understanding of traditional dietary laws. It is significant that even though she came to Livnot as unaware as her peers of both *kashrut* theory and practice, ten months after the program she can choose a particular, idiosyncratic form of observance and justify it using arguments from Jewish law:

The one big thing that I've tried to keep, sort of, is *kosher*-ish ... I do kind of bend the rules, in that I don't separate chicken and milk. That's mostly ideological for me. Because you know what? Poultry had nothing to do with milk. Nothing. I know, who am I to be Rav [Rabbi] Rebecca and interpreting the Torah. But it just seems like kind of a really, really stupid rule to me ... if you said chicken and eggs together, don't do it, I would say fine. But no one says anything about chicken and eggs, it's only milk and meat. And that whole line about boiling a kid in its mother's milk, it's so personal. Like there's this baby and you're killing it in something that came from it's mother. I could see where the greed would come from. But chickens don't know from milk. And Eliyahu was saying ... they [the rabbis] had this big debate. And one group was saying what I was saying, which is that chickens and milk have nothing to do with each other. And the other group was saying chickens are meat, people are going to get confused, people are going to think they're sinning, so just group it all together. Which to me is ridiculous. So any time someone questions me about it, like "That isn't really *kosher*, is it?," I give them the full explanation ... It makes me feel better. Because even when I'm leading the most secular of lives, I'm still not getting a cheeseburger. And I'm still stopping to think about it, which I think is important ...
I liked what we learned about how keeping *kosher* isn't just a set

of health rules, it's also a learning to pay attention. Because it *does* make you stop and think, "Can I have that?"

In a similar fashion, and like many other Jews, Livnot past participants develop personal understandings of *shabbat*. These range from viewing the sabbath as a conscious day out from a high-powered, workaholic lifestyle to practicing more conventional Jewish traditions of family meals, synagogue attendance, and observance of extensive *shabbat* prohibitions. Many past *chevre*, however, locate themselves somewhere between these two extremes, choosing a *shabbat*, perhaps irregularly, that is both high in Jewish content and adapted to their lifestyles, values, and priorities. Susan, a college student in California, for example, was eager to arrange a *shabbat* dinner on her return to North America, but was aware of her own needs and limits, as well as those of her friends:

We decided to have a *shabbat* dinner and invited a few of our Jewish friends. But it turned out to be a bigger thing than that. There were about fifty people there, maybe a third of whom were Jewish. Kate and I went through the whole traditional thing; hand washing, lighting candles, not talking until you have a piece of bread, baked *challah*, had some traditional foods, sang – did kind of the whole deal and taught everybody about it as we went along … a lot of people had questions, and we had our particular way of explaining things, that were very Livnot derived, but also had commentary about how it really works into our own lives. It felt really good. It felt very Jewish and very observant. But also very realistic. Realistic in terms that I could share it with my non-Jewish friends, and it was interesting to them. And realistic in terms of we did a lot, and it felt very Jewishly rich as an experience, but it wasn't using Kleenex [to avoid ripping toilet paper] in the bathroom, and I drove over to her house and I drove home. Yet because I had experienced the intensity of what *shabbat* can be, by doing it at Livnot … Having experienced that I could do it [*shabbat*] to a lesser degree, and thus more realistic, while still breathing the full life of it.

Susan happily describes one *Simchat Torah* holiday spent in a predominately gay and lesbian congregation in Berkeley, and her joy at associating with educated, enthusiastic Jews whose Judaism fits into their chosen lifestyles. The experience inspired her to offer the following message of experimentalism and audacity to other past participants who seek a personally meaningful, workable Judaism: "To search those things out and try on a half a dozen different jackets, to see which one feels the best. Because people, when they first go to Livnot they've come from one background, and Livnot provides you with a whole different thing. And there's a zillion shades of gray in between, and it's going to be one of those shades of gray that fits. It's a trial and error thing, so be adventurous."

For some past *chevre*, particularly those who are religious seekers and who have been involved with other religions, Judaism is a tradition that they interpret and often practice in tandem with other religious traditions. Like Anne's pursuit of Jewish religious observance alongside spiritual practices learned from a Sikh teacher in India, Sam combines serious *yeshiva* study and an active observant lifestyle with his prior interest in and love for Buddhism.[1] A well-travelled Canadian with a deep interest in religion, Sam views his creation of a personal, individual Judaism to be a kind of religious responsibility, a goal for which he provides theological justification:

My creative Judaism involves what I've learned in Buddhism. It means that I understand certain concepts in what would be considered a Buddhist way, in terms of ego and freedom, liberation, enlightenment, and even God in a certain sense of ultimate reality, of being present, of understanding prayer as meditation not as supplication or as request ... My inner attitude of always trying to question it and prod myself to always go further with my spiritual awareness and closeness to God ... I feel as being made in the image of God, that image is ultimately one of creator. So my responsibility as a Jew is to be creative, and to always be creating Judaism. Creating it anew. Each time I open a *siddur* [prayer-book], to experience something new and something different. To experience God and his reality in a new way. And with that underlying intention, the whole religious life becomes something of a palette. I just have to create.

While Sharon, for example, might not consider herself in any way actually a Taoist, she is deeply interested in Eastern philosophies and reads regularly from the Tao te Ching, a practice she feels does not conflict with, and often complements her own Jewish beliefs and practices: "I do try and read a chapter [of the Tao te Ching] ... every night.

I think I got started on it before I went to Livnot the first time [as a participant]. I just wanted something to bring me a little bit of peace, and some way to become a little bit more aware of things and think about things. Have a little more serenity. So I started doing it for that. And it works really well with Judaism ... 'The Tao is return.' Like, that's perfect. So I do that at night, and when I remember, I say the *Shma*. And when I wake up every morning, I say the *Modeh Ani*. Because I want Jewish in there too. It's not just about the Tao."

TENSIONS AND CONFLICTS

The extensive diversity in the Judaisms of past participants is not the result of a lack of knowledge: participants are aware of basic, normative, traditional practices. Participants have actively lived in a community that most Jews would accept as observant. Rather than combining diverse practices as a result of ignorance, past *chevre* interpret and choose from the Judaism they have encountered, which is undeniably limited and selective, to construct a practice and lifestyle that "works" for them. This process is not always easy or without conflict. Participants rarely feel radically free to fashion Judaism in a completely unconstrained manner. Sharon feels that at Livnot, she experienced what some alumni call "the right way," that is, the "authentic," "traditional" form of observance. Owing to the knowledge she gained of normative standards of Jewish observance, Sharon does feel some tensions about recreating Judaism according to her tastes. There are, as she puts it, "voices in her head" that remind her of Jewish tradition, and that she actively tries to ignore:

I choose what I want to do. And I still wrestle with that. I still wrestle with some of the voices in my head going, "Well if you do that, why don't you do this?" If you're eating off of glass plates or something like that to try and keep *kosher*, well eating un-*kosher* meat off a *kosher* plate, what does that mean?[2] But I'm doing it for me. I'm doing it for the tribe, I guess, for the upkeep of the tribe, too. But I can't do it to their specifications. And I don't feel that Livnot had specifications. I think they just showed us, you know, that whole shopping cart thing. It's what is important to me. Sometimes I wonder even if it's the Jewish thing or if these are concepts that happen to be in Judaism that I think are cool, so I'm doing them. Like saying *brachot* [blessings] over food. I started saying them because ... I just wanted to be aware and conscious and grateful of things in my life. I think that's what it is. I shape it, and I don't really care if somebody tells me it's not the right way. For me, it's the right way now.

While making blessings over food that is not *kosher* would be anathema to most observant Jews, and simply illogical to others, for Sharon it is emblematic of her spiritual consciousness and her need to make a Judaism that is her own. At the same time, creativity and its appropriate limits remain difficult issues for her, and one with which she struggles.

In a similar fashion, Anne felt tension about her own hybrid Judaism, which she resolved by consulting a rabbi about her continued attachment to a spiritual teacher to ensure that she was not in violation of Jewish law. Wendy's situation illustrates an even more acute conflict about the limits of mixing traditions and the boundaries of Judaism, perhaps because the tradition she is practicing alongside Judaism is not an abstract, philosophical system like Buddhism or Taoism, but rather neo-Paganism, whose polytheism seems to contradict the core, foundational monotheism of Judaism:

I've really been struggling with what I want. I'm still searching. I love Judaism, but I've also found a different spirituality path that has really pulled me in. I have been attending a women's group. They're pagan, but it's not like a very forcing environment. It's more like a group of women who just get together and drum and talk and do some kind of ritual with candle lighting ... I don't feel like I worship anything. I just acknowledge Mother Earth and the feminine spirit, and I really like saying Goddess instead of God, because I feel like it's genderized. I'm really into this whole gender thing. I wanted to escape from this thing that when I say the word God, that I see a man, like we talked about in one of our classes ... I needed to get away from that stereotype, and to have abso-lutely nothing behind the name. Because when I say the word Goddess I just think of beauty and nature and creation and earth and sky. There's no faith to it. That's really important to me ... In fact, this Friday, I'm going to be with my Goddess group, so we're going to light *shabbat* candles at the Goddess group ... In a way, I feel like I'm shaping my own Judaism. It's been a struggle because I wanted to fit in within a certain community, and I wanted to be something concrete. But I realized that I am

something concrete, and I'm going to flow where I need to flow.
So I feel like I'm almost recreating things ... I feel like I'm creating
my own rules, almost. I like that better because I don't feel as
though I need to fit into a specific role or stereotype.

As a lesbian who is newly aware of her sexual preferences, Ruth has
been plagued by even greater conflict. While she returned from Israel
deeply committed to practicing an observant Jewish lifestyle, it was only
several years later that she could look back and refer to her Orthodox
period "as a last-ditch attempt to avoid coming out." Ruth's final realization of her sexual preferences and acceptance of being a lesbian wreaked
havoc on her Jewish involvement and religious life. Wondering how she
could find a spiritual connection to traditional Judaism if that tradition
could not include her sexual orientation, Ruth painfully abandoned
Jewish life to explore issues around her lesbianism. It is by a radical
modification of traditional Judaism that she feels the possibility of creatively negotiating both her queer and Jewish identities and commitments: "I felt like, once I knew this is the way it's supposed to go according
to Judaism, [then] not doing it, making up anything on my own or
creating anything on my own, is less than that, somehow. And that's
something I'm just going to need to get over. Because what I'm titling
'the right way' is *not* the right way for me. It's *not* right for me ... I'm
in the process now of trying to reconcile it and trying to find some way
that I can have both [Judaism and lesbianism]. But it's not been pretty."

Many past participants blend their new Jewish interests and identities
with American popular culture and the values with which they were
raised, often consciously and sometimes less so. Working in the Jewish
community establishment in San Francisco, and deeply involved in
Jewish activities, Gail spoke extensively about the "contradictions" she
felt in her lifestyle. After we had talked together for several hours, I
suggested she might use the word "hybrid" in place of "contradiction."
Gail became very excited and used the term to describe her own situation. Theoretically astute, she noted that "it's a hybrid when you're
viewing the glass as half full, and it's a contradiction when you're viewing it as half empty." Describing her own, sometimes tension-filled combination of Judaism and the elements of American youth culture she
enjoys, Gail explained:

My hybrid [self] includes going dancing at gay clubs. Sometimes
that feels like it's a hybrid with being a nice Jewish girl. My hybrid

includes being interested in meditation and other kinds of spirituality. But not very seriously and often in a Jewish context. My hybrid includes drinking lots of Diet Coke and occasionally smoking cigarettes ... I'm a nice Jewish girl but I have lots of tight black clothes. It always comes back to these sex, drugs, and rock and roll things that somehow feel like they got left out of being a nice Jewish girl. But actually, I feel like I definitely do all of those things that are tempered and balanced and mostly healthy ... But it's taken me five years of working through that stuff to feel like I get to be all of those things at once. I really thought that in order to be a Jew I somehow had to look like Rebecca [the sister of a friend]. She's beautiful, physically, and also in her life. I love her life. And I don't want her life. I don't want it. She's a day school teacher, she's married to a doctor, she's religious ... and I'm totally not Rebecca. It feels like some of the things I really, really love are so non-Jewish. And I don't know who defines those things as Jewish or how I understand them to be non-Jewish ... I am starting to relax ... into feeling very Jewish and very lots of other things.

While participants' Jewish lives after Livnot are best characterized by diversity and hybridity, it is clearly neither smooth nor unproblematic. Implicit in the notion of hybridity is a degree of tension and ambivalence that arises from being "betwixt and between" social or cultural categories.[3] From Lévi-Strauss's work on the ambiguity of tricksters who mediate oppositions, to Victor Turner's study of liminality and the revitalizing potential of anti-structure, and Mary Douglas's consideration of the danger and power inherent in anomalies that crosscut distinct categories, anthropologists have recognized cross-culturally the strength and terror of mixing the unmixable, and of states and phenomena that fall between stable classifications.[4] From the perspective of highly classified modernity, the hybrid is an ambiguous, dangerous, uncomfortable monster that challenges given structures and rests outside of normal social groupings.

Individual Livnot alumni fashion their own fusions of Judaism with everything from American popular culture to queer politics, or from Buddhism to environmental activism. On a continuum, some of these expressions are closer to the pole of normative, "traditional" Judaism, while others locate themselves closer to the pole that represents the other cultural expression with which their Judaism is blended. The vast majority of past participants find an accommodation for themselves somewhere between the two extremes. For those people, hybridity can be a particularly lonely space. Many past *chevre* describe feeling misunderstood by family and friends, who began to view the individual as somehow "too Jewish": conversely, past *chevre* often reject the Judaism of their North American relatives and peers as too superficial, meaningless, or unconscious. Nor do they often find an easy niche for themselves in the traditional Jewish community, which might see former Livnot participants as excessively liberal, idealistic, or creative. Alumni sometimes describe the Judaism of the traditional community as uninspiring, narrow-minded, or restrictive. In many ways, the social and religious positions of Livnot past participants are, at least initially, uncomfortable, ambivalent, and often isolated.

As both Tamara and Anne mentioned, participants commonly experience difficulty relating to friends and family. Many alumni describe a significant degree of tension in their relationships following Livnot, as a result of several factors. First, the choice to observe certain fundamental Jewish ritual practices tends to affect basic family functioning and social relationships. *Kashrut*, for example, significantly limits the option of eating with those who do not observe the practice, and *shabbat* restricts weekend leisure time. Second, the decision to pursue greater religious observance sometimes threatens family members and peers, who fear becoming unable to relate to the individual, or who are concerned that a cult-like mind-control has been brought to bear on the participant. Even those participants who simply become more involved in the Jewish community or seek further Jewish learning can meet with incomprehension from their families for whom Judaism might be found less meaningful or less actively interesting. The family members and friends of Livnot alumni are usually much like participants before going to Livnot: possessing little respect for Orthodoxy and having many stereotypes and myths about religious Jews. Thus, family and friends often respond to the more observant or Jewishly interested individual with a marked lack of support or even derision.

As Laura recalls, when she initially came home following Livnot, she wanted to keep parts of the dietary regulations and observe some *shabbat* rituals. Her family was amused by this decision and teased her about it:

When I first came home, I tried doing the *kosher* thing. And everybody made fun of me, at first. They really did. Everything

I was trying to do, people made fun of me. But I didn't care ...
"Aw, what are you, a rabbi now?" Just little things, they made fun
of me a little bit, my family. I came back and I went to my mom's
house ... I was trying to do the *shabbat* thing and just little things
I was trying to do. And they were making fun of me ... They just
teased me a little bit ... I got mad at them. Like, my whole life
you're trying to get me to do more Jewish things, and now I'm
doing it and you're making fun of me. Yeah, it bothered me.

Similar family tensions mark the situation of Larry, who took part
in Livnot several years after his sister Ilana had done the program. Ilana
had continued her Jewish studies at a Jerusalem *yeshiva* and became
traditionally observant following Livnot. As a result, their other sibling
was particularly concerned that Larry too would become religious in
Israel. Larry's brother greeted his stories and Jewish enthusiasm with
unrelenting opposition and antagonism, a tension that Larry found both
surprising and painful:

He [Larry's brother] was not willing to look at my experience, and
look at what I was doing in Israel, open-mindedly, and say, "Oh,
Larry is doing something to grow and to expand his life in a positive way, and to explore, and I'm just going to be supportive of
that and see what it's all about, and be cool." Rather than that,
he was clearly antagonistic towards it. When I spoke to him once
or twice prior to coming home, he seemed more concerned that
I might be becoming observant, or more religious, and that was
obviously a negative thing in his mind. He was much more
concerned with that, than with how I might be simply exploring
or growing. Which I thought was sort of narrow-minded on his
part. So I got home and there was actually a couple of really bad
incidents – that also surprised me.

Some parents, nervous that their children might have become increasingly religious in Israel, attempt to test a past participant's level of
observance in surreptitious ways, hoping for reassurance that their child
has not changed. When Warren returned from Livnot, his parents tried
roundabout ways to determine his level of Jewish commitment: "I spoke
to my parents, and the first time we got together [after coming home
from Israel], we were making plans and it was like, 'Let's go out and
we'll get a big lobster.' I couldn't believe what I heard on the phone!

Just because they definitely wanted to hear my reaction. It came out more directly later. I said, 'Well, okay, if you want to go to a lobster place, that's fine. Whatever.' They were like, 'So you're not *kosher*?' ... They were very scared and nervous about how I'd come back."

Conflict can also arise for past participants concerning the Jewish choices of other family members. Feeling newly committed to and interested in their identity as Jews, Livnot alumni often experience situations involving intermarried, highly assimilated, or Jewishly uninterested siblings as sites of intense family conflict. Barb describes her experience:

The first Friday I was home I wanted to make a really nice *shabbat* dinner and invite my family. My sister-in-law is Catholic and my niece is baptized. My brother and sister-in-law and my niece came over for dinner and I made chicken and potatoes and all that stuff. It was nice, we did some prayers, I did the washing of the hands, and my sister-in-law looked at me funny. Then after the dinner she wanted to give my niece milk at the table and I just flipped. I said, "No you can't do that," and she said, "Why not?" So I explained to her that "I don't mix milk and meat anymore, and I just made a chicken dinner, so I would prefer it if you didn't serve it." And my mom was like, "Oh, what's the problem?" And my sister in law was like, "Oh, what's the problem?" And it was a very big conflict for a while with my mother trying to appease the whole situation with my sister-in-law not being Jewish. I felt she was taking it out on me, being more religious than I had been beforehand and more Jewish identified on a daily basis. I felt really pushed away in a lot of ways from my family. My sister told me later that she was worried that I was coming home as a religious freak, and my best friend said the same thing as well. And it was very hard. I felt extremely culture-shocked not only from the travelling but from the whole idea that I was different. My family wasn't understanding as much as I would have liked.

Finally, conflict can arise with family when past participants seek a Jewish experience they feel to be "authentic," that is, similar to events they enjoyed at Livnot, with comparable enthusiasm, spirituality, and intensity. While it is rarely a surprise, the realization that family simply do not understand or appreciate the positive Jewish experience that was so significant to the Livnot participant is often frustrating and isolating.

Rebecca poignantly describes this kind of tension with her family during Jewish holidays:

> The High Holidays were rough ... I knew it wasn't going to be that great ... I don't know. You know how it is at Livnot, when you do it for real, with the no switching the lights [on and off], you're dressed up, you're doing this and you're doing that. [I had to deal with] my brother complaining about having to go to services, having to drive to the services, and you know, the lights on and off. I tried not to do it myself, but you can only fool yourself so much. Then coming home from services and they're watching TV, and trying not to do it, but then finally giving up, because I couldn't stand it. And no one wanting to talk, like not even wanting to bring up the topic, because I knew the reception was going to be, "Uh oh, here comes Rebecca with the Jewish stuff she learned." So not even wanting to bring up the topic of why that time of year was so important. I just got really depressed when I went to their services. So that kind of sucked ... It was like that for Passover too. Very depressing.

Many participants told me stories of family tension resulting from their Jewish experiences at Livnot, with similar disappointment. However, increased levels of observance or Jewish involvement do not necessarily lead to alienation. Depending on their internal family dynamics and the manner in which individuals presented their Livnot experiences and Jewish interests, some families were more supportive of past participants' choices. Moreover, some participants explained that their families participated in their new Jewish commitments when the observance was family-oriented, presented without pressure, and low on ritual requirements or prohibitions, such as weekly *challah* baking and *shabbat* dinners.

In addition to familial tensions, many participants also had trouble relating to their previous network of friends following Livnot. Ascribing new importance to Judaism, and having recently taken part in an earnest, deep thinking community for three months, Livnot alumni often feel misunderstood by their peers, or simply less interested in those priorities they once shared in common. Spending time in a country as politically tempestuous and acutely tense as Israel can also alter participants' views about what is truly important or serious. Television shows, clothes, career moves, and sports can appear empty or facile to participants who have become used to a more intellectually, spiritually, and emotionally challenging environment. David is a part-time actor who emigrated to Israel several years ago. Directly after Livnot, he returned to the United States to complete his drama program at university:

> When I came back [from Israel], I was filled with loathing for being back ... It was hard for me being back with my friends because I had a totally new set of things that were important to me in my life. They [my friends] were still worried about all the acting things. All of a sudden I had Israel to worry about, and keeping abreast of Israel and what's going on and caring about it. I had just spent the summer helping out people who were worse off than me, painting their houses and making a little contribution to society. And here I was back in this group of people that were just basically concentrating on themselves ... That was hard, going back to that. I felt like I was up in the sky [at Livnot] and now I'm coming back down to, what? ... It was just really hard getting back into the swing of things. One of the hardest things that I had to deal with was the first day of classes ... What we do at the very beginning of the day is we warm up: we lie on the floor with our knees bent and our backs flat on the ground and breathe and vocalize and do voice warm-ups and body warm-ups ... Afterwards we got around in a circle and discussed how the vocal sounds affected us, the vowel sounds we were working on. It was serious stuff, but it was just so ridiculous to me. To accentuate it, one of the girls in my class said, very seriously, completely straight-faced – this was her life – she said, "I felt the 'oo' in my bloodstream." I just wanted to laugh in her face and run screaming back to Israel.

Although many participants experience tensions with friends and family after Livnot, many past *chevre* also find themselves in an uncomfortable position vis-à-vis the Jewish community. After their return from what might be termed a unique Jewish environment, participants are often eager to become involved in the Jewish community, only to find that it does not meet their expectations. Significant dissonance can result from the difference some alumni perceive between the spiritual, joyful, questioning Judaism experienced at Livnot, and the Judaism of the mainstream community in North America. It is often a painful surprise for past *chevre* to realize that some of the most attractive elements of the Judaism experienced at Livnot are not always espoused by the normative Orthodox community. After Livnot, Hannah spent a few weeks learning at a *yeshiva* for women in Jerusalem, and was criticized there for her pick-and-choose approach to Judaism:

Livnot has a shopping cart feel, or a shopping cart view. But no other Jewish place has that. If you go somewhere, no other Orthodox place, the *shuls* or the *yeshivas*, they're not about taking what you want ... It is not okay to pick what you want to take out of Judaism. I've already had that experience, and it was pretty upsetting ... I think it was at the *yeshiva*, but I just remember someone saying ... about how you can't just take part of God, that Judaism wasn't just take what you want, because that's not what it's about. I don't remember what it was, but I just remember that I was really upset with Livnot ... I don't think they [Livnot] were feeding me a line. I think that [shopping cart analogy] makes sense, and I'm still going to feel that way. Because for me, I believe in God and I have God in my life. And I think that God would rather me take something than nothing ... it [the shopping cart] really leaves you with nowhere to go, or with no one who really understands what you're talking about because they think that you're this idealistic person. We basically have an unrealistic view. I mean, I would love to be a Jew Livnot-style, where men and women basically dance and sing together. Not touching, but in the same spot. Where in reality, that's not going to happen, if you're in a really religious area.

Some participants find it extremely painful to realize that the joy and growth that they experienced living in a community of young Jews who shared similar liberal values and priorities could not be replicated in their North American Jewish community. Wendy recounts that she

didn't find it [the Jewish community] very open. I tried. Oh, I tried. I went to synagogue, and there's no one there your age ... I just wanted to find someone on my level. We just didn't click. I felt people very patronizing. Also, I recognized a lot of prejudice among almost everyone I met. Prejudice against people who aren't Jewish. I'm hypersensitive to that ... So I found I was getting really frustrated because people just kept talking about other

people, and that's what their social life existed on ... I'm like, you
know, I'm sick of this. I tried before I went, I tried again [after
Livnot]. Why am I constantly around these people that are insensi-
tive, are degrading, and have no right to have any kind of prejudice? I got frustrated and I was like, forget it. I'm not trying
anymore. It was really hard. It really threw me. I'm like, wow,
I've had these amazing relationships with Jews, and where are they
in my community? Where are they? So that kind of crushed things
... I guess I came back with high hopes.

As discussed in chapter 4, many participants found their stereotypes
about Orthodox Jews challenged by the experience of Livnot, and
replaced them with a greater sensitivity and empathy toward observant
lifestyle choices. However, extensive contact with a small, select group
of Orthodox Jews who are particularly committed to ethical behaviour,
spirituality, non-judgmental attitudes, and tolerance for others can also
foster unrealistic ideals about all observant Jews. Felice describes her
discovery that not all Orthodox Jews are as kind, helpful, or ethical as
the observant people she met at Livnot, and that not all observant Jews
follow Livnot's kind of Judaism:

I have a lot more negative feelings now than I used to the further
I get away from my experience [at Livnot]. Because I just think
that there's a lot of hypocrisy ... just all those acts of lovingkind-
ness, and that whole thing. I just feel like it's bullshit when you
see a lot of Orthodox Jews. And there could be a method to why
they're doing that, but it never comes off as kind. That's never the
sense I get from really religious people. Not to be rude, but a lot
of ultra-Orthodox in this city, like the ones who were showing me
apartments in Williamsberg, they were assholes! They had attitudes ... That's what makes me think it's hypocritical. I just don't
feel like a lot of ultra-Orthodox Jews practice what they preach.
I just don't think that, you know, that whole Livnot thing [about
how] you can't just study and not be a good person, and you can't
just be a good person and not study, you have to have both – I
feel like one end of that is lacking [among ultra-Orthodox], and
that they're concentrating so much on following God's law. My
friend Linda was telling me that ... after *shabbat*, they were trying
to drive back to the city and they were getting lost, she and her
friend. And they stopped two teenage religious boys in the street

and tried to ask directions, and no one would give them
directions. No one would even look at them ... I just feel like,
once you get out in the real world, not everyone is like that [the
way people were at Livnot]. Things like that, like what I just
described to you, happen a lot ... That's why a lot of people have
nervous breakdowns and freak out after Livnot. Because they think
that the world is this safe environment. But it [Livnot] is not real
life. It's not. Even if you stay in Israel. It's like as close as going
back to the womb as a lot of people are going to get in terms of
Judaism ... I think that [Livnot] was the ideal. Unfortunately,
it's not the norm.

Similarly, Ruth observed that she had developed high expectations of
religious Jews, and believed optimistically that their behaviour would
be consistent with the principles and lifestyle they seemed to espouse.
Ruth reflected on a particularly disappointing encounter with one
Orthodox Jew:

It was more like my expectations of them [religious people] were
higher now that I knew more about the religion. I felt like you
were supposed to know better, because you learned this and you're
supposed to know better. So my standards in judging their morals
were higher than for your average person who didn't know about
Judaism. So in that sense, I was let down. Because I was finding
people that were just as human as me, and was not really willing
to let them be just as human as me. I had one experience with
somebody ... he's Orthodox, and he was here [visiting the US].
It was all like "My wife, my kids," so dedicated to family and he's
from a moshav. It was like this whole sense. So he came out here
to do his little tour-around-lecture singing thing ... So he was here
and he was at a friend's house of mine, and giving over Torah and
singing and stuff. And two of my friends were giving him a
massage at the same time. And I just looked over I was like
"Yech." One was massaging his hands and one was massaging his
neck. I looked over and I was like, "How's your wife, back in
Israel, taking care of your nine kids, slaving away while you're
here in California getting massaged by two young women?" Like,
"How's your wife doing?" So I was really let down ... I was really
angry about that. The moshav too was like, supposed to be the
highest of the high and the deepest of the deep and the place

where you could be the most spiritually connected ... and here's this guy being a total asshole.

Finally, many past participants express bitter disappointment about trying to get involved with organized Jewish ritual life, often finding it dry, unenthusiastic, rigid, uninspiring, unfriendly, boring, or materialistic. Some past *chevre* complain with resignation that, no matter what the mainstream community has to offer, it simply "isn't like Livnot." This dissonance between the Judaism learned and experienced at Livnot and the Judaism found outside of the program is a common difficulty for past participants. It is also a situation to which participants adjust. Over time, the problem of dissonance becomes less acute. Alumni come to recognize the idealism of the Livnot environment, and eventually seek a Judaism and Jewish community that works well enough for them, rather than one that is exactly like Livnot.

CONCLUSION: MULTIPLE JUDAISMS

Life for participants following the time they spend at Livnot U'Lehibanot is clearly no monolithic or homogeneous experience. What emerges is a picture of personal accommodation and modification of the normative tradition in ways that make it work for individuals. This process can involve the hybridization of Judaism with another religious tradition, a fusion of observance with personal ideals and interests, creative variation of Jewish law, or the choice of relative non-observance. The basic information, support, non-judgmentalism, and non-coercion of the Livnot program allow for and encourage the emergence of such diversity in past participants' Jewish lives.

It must be understood that Livnot participants are not alone in this transformation of tradition. All Jews, no matter how "mainstream" or "traditional," are busily creating, negotiating, and hybridizing Judaism in some sense. All variants of contemporary Jewish practice, from Orthodox to Reform, and Renewal to Conservative Judaism involve some modification of the way Judaism was practiced in the past. Ultimately, it becomes impossible to talk cogently about traditional Judaism, forcing us to speak rather of "traditions" and "Judaisms." While some of these articulations may be more or less obviously in line with Jewish law as it has been traditionally conceived, and more or less accommodating of modernity and non-Jewish society, all Judaisms are fluid, emergent, and invented. All Jews are picking and choosing, to different degrees. While the Judaisms of Livnot past participants are often creative and colourful in the extreme, they remain, nonetheless, variations on familiar Jewish themes. As hybrid articulations that rarely sit comfortably within one community or another, these Judaisms also represent sources of tension and conflict for past participants.

7

The Power to Choose

Past *chevre* emphasize that the central significance of Livnot for their Judaism is that the experience offered them a key which unlocked the possibility of Jewish participation. As many alumni explain, Livnot allowed them entrance into the Jewish world by providing them with the basic knowledge, confidence, and interest to explore Jewish life more seriously. When we discussed the notion of empowerment together, Sam spoke of how he came to acquire a feeling of entitlement through Livnot, and of his realization that he too possessed a role and a voice in the Jewish community: "[I learned] that ultimately we're equal. That no matter what somebody knows, everyone has a point to make and a challenge to make. The empowerment was ... being able to stand up for yourself. I felt like I could go into any Jewish environment afterwards, whether very Orthodox or Reform or Conservative, and feel like I'm a Jew and I have a place here, and nobody can tell me no. And whether they know more knowledge or whatever, spiritually we're equal. I can challenge the status quo if I want, because I'm a Jew and I have a say in this religion."

Similarly, Kelly expresses the view that Livnot provided her with the basic tools required to discuss, argue, and participate in both Jewish life and discourse. Like many individuals with whom I talked after Livnot, Kelly insists that she was neither able to engage in serious conversation about Jewish issues before Livnot, nor had she any particular interest in doing so. Reflecting with some embarrassment on her understanding of Judaism before Livnot, Kelly explained what the program brought her: "Livnot introduced the idea that there was more [to Judaism] ... We never would have been having this conversation a year ago. I didn't have the vocabulary. I didn't have all the cards. Maybe that's why it hits a nerve with me, the idea of not having all the cards. Because I realize that I could have lived my whole life that way with this opinion about Judaism. But now I know how limited that was. Because I didn't actually know what I was talking about [before Livnot]."

As already discussed above, the acquisition of more Jewish knowledge, interest, and options is not an uncomplicated development at the social and familial levels. Ruth wryly credits Livnot with making Judaism not only a significant issue for her, but also an active point of tension and conflict in her life: "I didn't know anything about Judaism before Israel. I didn't care. I didn't care at all. Going to Israel made me care. And now it's a struggle." But while that struggle is one that creates significant anxiety for Ruth, especially as a lesbian, she does not regret the experience.

In a similar fashion, Sharon describes how Livnot made involvement in Judaism an acute concern for her, an issue about which she cares deeply, and thus a potential locus for conflict. Like Ruth, Sharon had experienced little tension with Judaism before Livnot because she rarely thought about it. In some ways, Sharon explains, she feels that the knowledge she gained at Livnot only added to her confusion:

I have understanding for the way things are done [traditionally]. I'm not sure that I necessarily agree with them. I fight it. I fight with it. Because on the one hand I think, "Yeah, we have to keep the traditions the way they are, because how else will Judaism survive?" But on the other hand, I'm like, "But Judaism is not going to survive if we can't adapt it to the way we are now" ... [Before Livnot] it [this question] was never there. I never had to fight for it, because I was never doing anything with it. So it didn't make a difference to me ... The only reason that I have this tension now is because I'm actively thinking about these things. Before I never had the knowledge and I never had the want to think about things in that way. They were just not something that came up in my mind. Now it always is ... It just wouldn't have come up for me. It just wouldn't have been a topic of conversation ... I'm less confused because I have a sense of where I want to go and what's important to me. I'm more confused because I have these battles now going on in my mind on exactly how do I want to get there.

Robert also expresses a feeling of confusion, but like Sharon, he perceives that confusion to be grounded in and a result of increased knowledge. Referring to a *shabbat* discussion he had with a rabbi during Livnot, Robert proudly describes his acquisition of self-assurance in his opinions, and a new degree of comfort engaging in Jewish discussion, as a result of feeling more informed about Judaism: "My confusion now is informed confusion. I definitely have something to base some of my judgments on ... like at the settlement, I talked to a rabbi and I disagreed with him. He got pissed off and I kept disagreeing with him. I wouldn't have done that before I came. I would have been like, 'I don't know anything about any of this' ... I wasn't accepting what he said, whereas before I didn't think I had the authority to say that, or even the authority to feel that."

This feeling of "informed confusion" of which Robert speaks is shared by many past participants. The confusion stems from Livnot's emphasis on information that is not simply abstract, factual, or academic, but rather aims to be Jewish learning that is personally relevant and challenging. Confusion arises when participants take up the task of working out for themselves what kind of Judaism they want, need, or can accept. Participants are "informed" by Livnot's provision of both knowledge and a positive experience of Judaism, leaving them more able to make Jewish choices for themselves and more inclined to do so.

The ability to make informed personal decisions, however agonizing these might sometimes be, is one that Tamara describes using terms that contrast a self-directed Judaism with an other-directed Judaism. Tamara believes that Livnot encouraged her to take responsibility for her own Jewish choices in a way that is consistent with her aspirations and needs, rather than coerce her into adopting a religious lifestyle as defined by others. Having briefly, as she puts it, "slipped" into a *yeshiva* before coming to Livnot, Tamara expresses gratitude for the chance to develop a Judaism of her own making:[1]

Livnot is giving me a step back and saying why don't you see where you are thinking of going, why don't you see where you are going and how you can even just integrate that into where you are [currently]. That it doesn't have to be a whole leap from the ground up into the air. It can just be you're on the ground and you'll jump up and you'll come back down. You'll just learn a lighter way to walk. Or a way to dance. Or a way to make it be you doing it rather than somebody else in your body ... This is me trying to direct myself more and to direct the extent that I want Judaism to have control over my life or integrated into my life.

This same notion of self-direction is expressed by Fern through themes of adulthood and responsibility. In contrast to the kind of Judaism she explored and developed at Livnot, Fern feels that her prior Jewish involvement was more "childish," an element in her life for which she took no personal responsibility and left to the direction of her parents: "I see myself [now] as an adult person of the Jewish people, not as a child of the Jewish people. Until now, I have not taken my place in the Jewish world because I've just reacted to my upbringing. I've still been a child. Almost to the point that what I do doesn't really matter, I'm not quite as responsible as everybody else ... Whereas now I have an adult's mentality. Which is, I know certain things that I'm supposed to do as an adult, or certain Jewish values that are for me to live by, not my parents. For *me* to live by. So I feel much more a part of the adult Jewish community."

For most participants, this kind of Jewish "adulthood" or the development of a sense of responsibility for their own Jewish choices is made possible through the attainment of some basis for making those choices. As the following statements make clear, Livnot is perceived by participants to offer precisely that basis for informed decision-making that has empowered them to construct their own Jewish lives:

Livnot is giving to me a basis for how I choose to live Jewishly in my adult life. From the standpoint of what that actually means, Livnot is giving me the ability to make a choice. FERN

I have more of a basis for knowledge [since Livnot]. I definitely know a thousand times more about Judaism and about Israel, and I have more of an ability to make informed decisions about those things than I did. And I'm definitely more attracted to Judaism than I would have been. LEANNE

Regardless of what anyone does after doing a Livnot program, in terms of being more or less observant, more or less actively involved in Judaism, the learning and understanding that can be gained from it can be invaluable ... The people who I shared experiences with and learned from by the examples of their lives, knowledge of the history of Judaism, and knowledge of the religion itself is very valuable – regardless of what I do with it. Regardless of my degree of observance, it's important to be informed, to be informed about it – so that whatever decision you make is an informed decision. LARRY

I feel I'm empowered to make my own decisions [about Judaism], and no one has the right to judge me or to question my hypocrisy, if I can call it that ... Now they're educated decisions. It's not just, "Oh, so and so is doing that and maybe I should do that too." They're really educated decisions I make. DIANE

A lot of my stuff [that I wanted to achieve at Livnot] was about being knowledgeable about Judaism, so I could make educated, informed decisions about it. I grew up Reform, and I just didn't get a lot of the meaning behind things. I went through, I had a *bat mitzvah* and everything. And I had no understanding of what it meant or any spiritual reasoning or thought behind any of it. Livnot filled in those blanks, and I call that knowledge. Now I can make much more informed decisions. MARNI

I was *bar mitzvah*-ed and confirmed[2] and went to Israel, and I didn't know anything. Literally ... I don't see how any Reform Jew would have tools [to make Jewish choices]. Then there's just so many people that even if they did have the tools, they've never had any kind of ecstatic, passionate experience with Judaism. I could point to maybe twenty-five ecstatic, passionate interactions with Judaism [that I had at Livnot] that kind of feed me, and that will last a long time. I mean, I'm hoping those weren't my only and last. It's not like the last hurrah. But in the US you're certainly not coming across those opportunities very often ... But at least you've had a taste of it [at Livnot]. You know what it's like, and you know what it can be like. And you can hopefully find it, or create it for yourself ... I think that's the hardest challenge, is infusing deli-identity[3] with some tools that can help you grow your own identity and build it. BARRY

These feelings of possessing the power to make informed choices are the result of achieving fundamental knowledge about, and an experience of, the normative Jewish tradition, both of which they did not have previously. Many past participants described the importance of acquiring access to a "traditional," "Orthodox," "authentic" Jewish model from which they could pick and choose. This "blueprint," "right way," "menu," or "rules for playing the game" offers past *chevre* a stable basis from which they can create their own Judaisms:

It [Livnot] has to offer a sense of the blueprint. The blueprint that's out there that you can make your own. You can make your own house. It's the basic blueprint for a house. You can turn it into whatever you want ... it allows you to internalize the point as you want it. So I have no doubt that if my sister did Livnot, she would get a very different sense of it than I did. She's a very different person ... But you can take from the same blueprint your own recipe, and spice it up how you need to. Or ignore it altogether. But it's in you somewhere. TAMARA

We were doing it [Judaism at Livnot], I guess, almost the "right" way. We had our breaks and freedom, but they still tried to instill in us that this is the way that they had decided is the correct way to do it, or as far as the *halacha* was written, this is what is halachically written. That's what you had your choices from. It was good to learn those things, because without it I wouldn't be able to tell myself, "You can do this, and you can think about that." Based on the knowledge that I have, I can make the choices that are right for me. ROSE

I definitely feel more knowledgeable ... that I have the tools. Absolutely that I have the tools. And I have a little bit more of an understanding of what there is to be done and what the rules are. Even if I'm not doing something the right way. I'll go, "I know that it could be done this way, and this is the way it's really supposed to be done." Then I'll say to myself that it's okay if I don't do it now like that, because I can't take it all on at once. So I definitely have the menu to order from, let's say. I have the list of all the products in the store. SHARON

I learned so much about Judaism that I never knew. I got a really good base ... [and the chance] to learn about Orthodoxy and then you know the foundation. Then you can develop what you want out of it. I can't develop my own sense if I don't know what the rules are. You can't play the game unless you know the rules kind of thing. I wouldn't have known how I want to celebrate *shabbat* unless I knew how to celebrate *shabbat*, or what does it say about what is *shabbat*. What's the essence of it. I don't think it was a waste of time at all [even though I'm not observant]. I got a great Jewish education. MELISSA

Similarly, Gail views Livnot as having provided her with the opportunity to learn about and take part in one particular, rich, traditional Jewish way of life. She feels she can now approach Livnot as a resource, something that she can draw upon and that she can "take pieces of" in forming a Jewish lifestyle that is personally meaningful and plausible:

Livnot helped me define my Judaism by showing me what my options were. Or showing me another option. Or showing me *an* option, I should say, even. That one way to be a Jew is to be a religious Jew, and live in Israel and to marry some nice guy and cover your head and have lots of babies, and to have a really meaningful life ... that was rich with tradition and beauty and purpose ... That's what Livnot showed me. What that did for my Judaism, after I figured it out, is that I could take pieces of that life, and be that, and still be myself in so many other ways. That in the moments when I pursued that feeling of the meaningful, depth, rich, connection-to-God stuff, that I can fully be there and that I can take myself seriously. It's not cheesy, it's not a joke. It's very connected and it's me. And that the only way to access that is *not* by moving to Meah She'arim[4] and covering my head. That actually, back to the whole contradiction thing, I feel very real and present doing that [Jewish life] *and* doing a whole bunch of other things that reflect a twenty-seven-year-old's life in Berkeley, California.

This sense of empowerment to make informed choices about the contours and content of one's own Jewish commitments and observance is also expressed by individuals who have very little Jewish involvement or interest after Livnot. Those participants whose Judaism after Livnot is not quantitatively different from the Jewish lives they led prior to Livnot have also undergone a significant change in terms of their abilities to make Jewish decisions. Since they now possess the ability to make a choice, their lack of Jewish observance or involvement is no longer as constrained by lack of information or experience as it once was.

Taking part in Livnot has enabled these participants, like others who have pursued a more active Jewish life, to make informed choices about their Judaisms:

> [Before Livnot] I didn't care. I didn't know. So it's like [now], okay, I'm not doing all the rituals and I'm not following all the *mitzvot*. But I wasn't doing that before I went to Israel, either. Now I'm not doing it, and I know more. So I have more guilt, I think ... Now I don't do it, and it's not like I'm just not doing it because I don't know and I don't think about it and I don't care. I'm *consciously* not doing it. RUTH

Marni's situation represents what some might see as a particularly challenging case of developing the freedom and responsibility to make Jewish choices. Engaged to a practicing, committed Catholic, very interested in pursuing spiritual growth, and having explored Christianity because of her partner's beliefs, Marni was once seriously considering converting from Judaism to Roman Catholicism. But Marni realized that she did not have adequate knowledge about her own cultural heritage to decide categorically against Judaism, and went to Livnot to learn more: "I could have become a Christian in the past year. I was really close but I couldn't do it. Because I had to understand where I came from. I had to have this piece [Livnot] and come from *this* place of knowledge and sense of wholeness stepping into a decision like that. I couldn't do it responsibly. It would have just been filling a void irresponsibly if I had stepped into it then."

But there is no triumphant, uncomplicated, post-Livnot conclusion of Jewish cultural preservation to Marni's story. While she has, following her experiences at Livnot, decided that she considers herself to be Jewish and that she will not convert to Catholicism, Marni still attends both church and a Reform temple regularly with her fiancé, and does not deny the possibility that she will raise her children as Catholics. The experience of Livnot, Marni feels, enabled her choices to be real ones – choices made with her eyes open, knowledgeable about her cultural heritage, and able to responsibly assess what she wants for herself in terms of Judaism.

This option has not always been available to Jews, a group whose power to choose how to articulate its culture has historically been restricted by both physical coercion and more subtle, homogenizing forces of assimilation, including the values of Christian universalism, the Enlightenment, liberalism, modernity, and the anglo-conformist ethos of melting-pot America. Livnot functions as part of a corrective to the effects of coercive culture loss, however benign such effects might appear. The program offers a measure of empowerment by providing information about Judaism and a positive experience of the culture to North American Jews who have had little of either. That empowerment, grounded in knowledge and perceiving value in Judaism, is a fundamental prerequisite for participants' ability to create a Judaism for themselves, of whatever contours they choose. While past participants choose Judaisms that range from Orthodox variations to very little obvious Jewish involvement, all consciously fashion some kind of personally defined mixture of Jewish tradition and American culture. The experience of Livnot provides them with at least the basic tools to construct their own Judaisms. It is this kind of ability that permits seeing transformation where once there was only a lament of assimilation, and active hybridity in what once was solely culture loss.

In post-colonial studies, a similar recognition of hybridity can validate the capacity of subordinate peoples to create their own emergent cultures from a fusion of Western and native elements. However, it is imperative to be aware that this capacity can diminish over time. We can, with anthropologist James Clifford, recognize the creative abilities of peoples like the New Guinea Wahgi who hybridize tradition and modernity.[5] Nonetheless, it is also crucial to realistically consider what tools, particularly traditional ones, will be available for future generations to draw upon for their own cultural inventions. While the parents or grandparents of Livnot participants might have been able to make more informed choices about the kinds of Judaism they wanted for themselves, that ability has become radically diluted as many second or third generation immigrants to North America grew up with little serious Jewish background.[6]

It was precisely this haunting concern that was expressed by Melissa, who works in the Manhattan Jewish community:

When I was in the phase of being very bowled over [by Judaism], I was starting to question so many things about how I was brought up. I think I remember the day I realized that I had no idea if my parents believed in God or not. I was floored. I was like, "I don't even know how my parents feel about God. That's so weird. I can't believe we've never had this discussion." ...
Then I became sort of resentful that they didn't bring me up with

stronger values, and they didn't bring me up with more tradition. Why didn't they care? Why *aren't* they connected? The other thing that kills me is my grandmother grew up in an Orthodox household. This is two generations later, and I knew *nothing*. Where does it go? How does that happen? She grew up in an Orthodox house! I couldn't get over that ... I couldn't even understand how that happens. That was really powerful for me, in terms of how easily things get lost.

As quoted in chapter 6, Anne was similarly saddened to realize the scope of tradition that had been lost in her family, and surprised by the magnitude of her ignorance about the culture practiced by her grandparents: "There was a big part of me that grieved, I think, after Livnot, and during. Like, 'Gosh, I never knew this.' I was like, 'Did my grandparents really light candles on *shabbat*? Was this the way of life of my ancestors?' I literally had no idea."

This kind of reaction is not at all uncommon among Jews who grew up in North America, who often do not even realize how little they actually know about the culture of their grandparents. Even anthropologists are not immune from such "rootlessness," as anthropologist Ruth Behar shows, in writing about learning of her grandfather's death:

I wanted to say the mourner's *Kaddish*, to perform some sort of ritual for Zayde, but the truth was I was totally ignorant of Jewish death customs (later, I learned that the *Kaddish* is not recited alone, nor is it recited for grandparents) ... My paternal grandfather had died six years before ... I had hurried to the flower shop in Léon, wiring a fancy bouquet to New York, forgetting that this was the wrong tradition, that in Jewish tradition flowers are not given at death ... That summer my [maternal] grandfather died, I asked myself, in grief and rage, what bizarre accidents of education, ambition and stupidity had led me to know how to recite a rosary instead of a basic Hebrew prayer ... Together with the pain of having lost him, there was the pain of having lost so much of the culture and the history that had been part of his lived reality and that had not been passed on to me.[7]

Livnot U'Lehibanot provides participants with precisely what they and staff members say it does: a menu from which to choose, a possible blueprint, the rules of the game as it has traditionally been played, a vocabulary that enables participation in the ongoing dialogue that is Jewish life. The Livnot program is unique in the Orthodox world, and uniquely powerful in the fact that it *encourages* precisely the processes of hybridization and choosing that, scholars suggest, happens anyway. Livnot is not a case of simple nativism, ethnic activism, or an attempt at return to some romantic, pre-modern Judaism. Staff neither expect nor desire participants to leave the program living observant Jewish lives, although certainly some former *chevre* do choose that route. The experience of Livnot gives participants the ability to choose and encourages them to exercise this ability. With the basics of knowledge needed to make informed choices, and a positive experience of "traditional" Judaism that challenges their preconceptions, *chevre* are given the tools and support that help them to begin building their own Judaisms.

It is one thing not to observe *shabbat*, for example, because one has never done so before, does not know what it entails, or believes that it is primitive, stultifying, or meaningless. It is quite another to choose non-observance of *shabbat*, having experienced it in a positive, joyful context, and possessing knowledge of its origin, meaning, and practice. The first is a passive decision, born of ignorance and stereotypes, the result of growing up in an environment which disdains Jewish tradition and learning, and exerts subtle pressures on its members to "be American," and to avoid "excessive" ethnic or religious difference. The second form of non-observance is a significantly more active, responsible, adult choice based on information and experience. And while they might both have the same outcomes of non-observance, it seems indisputable that the latter choice is superior to the former in that the decision is an informed one. Such a choice, grounded in greater knowledge and experience, is also one that remains open to the possibility of change later in life, as the information and experience remain tools at the individual's disposal.

Perhaps even more important than the power to choose, is that Livnot offers unaffiliated, modern, North American Jews something plentiful from which to choose. Post-Enlightenment Jewish life has indeed been labelled "ambivalent" by a number of observers.[8] Rather than resolving the ambivalence of North American Jewish life, Livnot in fact sharpens that ambivalence, at least initially. Participants arrive at Livnot feeling little of the conflict between Jewish and American values that have been chronicled in previous studies. For Livnot *chevre*, popular American values are by far more prominent, and those values or activities thought of as Jewish are barely distinguishable from them.

The possibility of choosing between multiple plausible options, a situation that often causes ambivalence, is obviously a pre-condition for exercising the power to choose. Livnot gives participants something new to choose from – based on an appealing exposure to "traditional" Judaism – and thus offers them the ability to make more informed choices for themselves, rather than defaulting to American values. It also makes their choices more difficult, their lives more complicated, and their relationships to Judaism more ambivalent. As chronicled throughout this work, the "traditional" Judaism presented to participants is one that is designed to appeal to contemporary North American values of individualism and moralism. But this is done, and done effectively, in the words of Eliyahu Levy "in order that people even hear." Livnot thus offers a challenge, however necessarily gentle, to participants' Americanized Judaism with a Judaism that, however deeply Western, modern, and "untraditional" is much more Jewishly grounded than the Judaism with which they arrived.

It is not my intention to suggest that Livnot provides complete agency to choose, should such a thing even exist. Rather, it *contributes* to that ability. Livnot helps participants become active "choosers" (however confused or ambivalent) in their Jewish identification, instead of remaining passive "victims" of their parents' Jewish choices and the effects of living in a society derived from a Christian matrix. For Jews who possess poor Jewish educations, scathingly negative views of Judaism, and unflattering stereotypes about other Jews, the options for creating a viable, hybrid Jewish identity are severely curtailed. Clearly, there can be little cultural imagining of the future without some familiarity with the past, however that (imagined) past may be understood. To mistake a lack of Jewish knowledge and tools for real, active choice is misguided, opening the door to a view of cultural transformation as naive as a persistent belief in primitivism. The hopeful story of cultural hybridity is, as Clifford admits, darkened and troubled by shadows.[9] And one of these shadows is cast by the realization that cultural destruction can occur to such an extent that no future can be imagined or built. Livnot offers participants a Jewish "toolbox" to which they previously did not have access, owing to the particular historical and political pressures that have been brought to bear on Jews in the West. The Livnot toolbox, clearly, is constructed. It is also presented to participants as a continuous, authentic, and pure tradition. Yet it is only through gaining access to that toolbox that a resilient, transformative, future-oriented, emergent Judaism can be built by each individual. Livnot's emphasis on non-coercion, selectivity, and multiple interpretations, emphases which are unusual in the world of Orthodox Jewish outreach, encourages precisely such a hybrid building process.

Rather than looking at inventions such as Livnot and focusing on the loss of an authentic tradition or, alternatively, hoping for the rebirth of such a tradition through cultural transmission, one can instead view such programs as providing the opportunity to look simultaneously backward and forward, into the past for tools that can be used to build identities, and toward a future in which these tools can be used creatively. Constructions of tradition like that offered by Livnot offer social scientists a two-fold message that acknowledges both culture loss and the possibility of resilience. For participants, Livnot U'Lehibanot facilitates an awakening of the agency they need if they are to make informed Jewish lifestyle choices. And it is through the acquisition of such agency by individuals that culture change progresses beyond assimilation to become creative and dynamic transformation.

AN ETHNOGRAPHER TRANSFORMED:
FALLING IN LOVE WITH THE NATIVE WITHIN

Throughout the period of collecting this data, I was, obviously, seriously interested in Judaism. But I pursued this interest holding tenaciously to my identity as an academic. For some reason that I do not recall, I believed firmly that "academic" and "religious" were incompatible, particularly for scholars of religion. I would sneak up to the park each *shabbat*, laptop and cigarettes in hand, to catch up on my work. Livnot was not my journey. It was my job to "see through it," not to be affected by it.

It would be an obvious simplification, however tempting, to suggest that I began my research as an academic, and finished it as a Jew. Of course, I was deeply implicated in these two worlds both before I began this project, and after its completion. But it was through this research that I realized the Other whom I studied was also part of me, and worthy of some serious thinking. And as much as I tried to keep things separate, this interest and attention to questions of my own Judaism affected how I thought about my research, and what sense I made of it. Some Livnot staff members have remarked, only half-joking that I had to do the program four times for it to stick.

While losing sleep and shedding tears over fieldwork and ethnographic writing is a common part of the process, some of my concerns were exacerbated by the presence of this "inner other." My research field had also become a personal site of exploration, struggle, and learning. Me and my "native within" got to know each other, and became increasingly more comfortable together.

It was during the writing of this work that I moved to a larger city in order to seriously explore Orthodox Judaism. Somehow I found a *shul*, a community, and a Jewish environment that nurtured my growing observance. Soon enough I would also meet a man whose love of Judaism and the academy were similar to mine. Our Jerusalem wedding would be filled with the exuberant dancing and singing of Livnot staff members and participants.

Once an academic who happened to be a Jew, I became a noticeably Jewish academic. I fell in love with my self as Jew, my Jewish self, and in so doing I came to love the Jews and all who struggle with their Judaism, and the Jewish tradition that they work with and against. This, I believe, makes me a better researcher – open to nuance, caring deeply, and eager to tell the truth.

While writing this work, and peeking out from this new (to me, then) "Jewish" vantage point, I had to wonder if what is good for individual Jews is necessarily congruent with what is good for the Jewish people. I found myself caring about the future of the Jewish people, where before I would have only argued about the fictional, constructed nature of "peoplehood." I began to think that an abundance of hybridized, creative Judaisms might sound a dangerous note for the future of American Judaism. Were these personal Judaisms "good for the Jews?" The fact that I even cared at all was radically new for me. Where once I would have appreciated and encouraged any individual expression of Judaism, I found myself increasingly worried about *the* group, *the* tradition, *the* community – a trio that I knew was imaginary, but one to which I nonetheless felt a growing intellectual and personal responsibility.

IS IT GOOD FOR THE JEWS?

The value of Livnot for the Jewish people and its future is an issue that I cannot help but wonder about, as both a social scientist and an involved, committed member of the community. Clearly, at a fundamental level, Livnot is good for the Jews, providing knowledge and a positive experience of Jewish culture. The situation of participants who come to the program tells a sorry tale about many of American Jewry's adult children: one rife with religious meaninglessness, rootlessness, and alienation.

Participants know shockingly little of their cultural heritage, and often care about it even less. If nothing else, the fact of Livnot's appeal to participants points to a deep-seated problem with the practice and transmission of North American Judaism. Community leaders who worry about assimilation and intermarriage must ask themselves the obvious question: If there is nothing in Judaism that appeals to Jewish youth, that speaks to them and their situations, why should they feel compelled to participate in and transmit the tradition? Why *not* intermarry? Why not practice Zen Buddhism?

While the community focuses on ensuring physical, numeric survival, the lack of accessible, relevant, meaningful Jewish education and experience beyond childhood both harms the possibility of effective cultural survival and contributes to physical loss through assimilation, intermarriage, and low birthrates. North American Jewry's striking lack of familiarity with Jewish ritual, literature, language, and history and the effect of such extensive cultural ignorance are poignantly described by Alan Dershowitz, and worth quoting at length:

In light of this long commitment to teaching and learning, it is sadly remarkable that no group in America is less knowledgeable about its traditions, less literate in its language, less familiar with its own library than the Jews. We are the most ignorant, uneducated, illiterate Americans when it comes to knowledge of the Bible, the history of our people, Jewish philosophy, religious rituals, and traditions. More Jews can tell you the name of Jesus' mother than Abraham's father. More Christians than Jews can recite the Ten Commandments. More Muslims than Jews know the story of Abraham. American Jews, who are the most highly educated group in this country when it comes to general knowledge, are the least educated group when it comes to knowledge of their own heritage. We get our history from *Fiddler on the Roof*, our traditions from canned gefilte fish, our Bible stories from television, our culture from Jackie Mason, and our Jewish morality from the once-a-year synagogue sermon most of us sleep through. The typical non-Orthodox Jew today has no idea what is contained in the Jewish library beyond a children's-storybook summary of the Bible, has little familiarity with Jewish history before the Holocaust and the establishment of Israel, and has virtually no knowledge about the diversity of Jewish tradition. The famed Yiddisher cup – the Jewish mind – is only half full:

it is overflowing with general knowledge, but it is almost completely empty when it comes to Jewish knowledge. It is this ignorance as much as assimilation, intermarriage and low birthrates that threatens the survival of Jewish life in America today.[10]

The Israel, Jews, and Judaism on display at Livnot are not representative of the "whole" truth, nor do they offer an accurate portrait of what they do present. The Jewish options offered at Livnot are selective, restricted, and idealized. Some might find the careful packaging and marketing of Judaism to be somehow distasteful, even deceitful. But as R. Laurence Moore explains in *Selling God: American Religion in the Marketplace of Culture*, what Livnot is doing is neither new, nor unique: "Once churches began to do something other than tending the faithful, once they started beating the bushes in search of new members, once they took on the holy mission of converting the world, they were in the business of selling ... The religious proselytizing generated by free markets and competition will always in someone's opinion be huckster-ism. Those who cry 'hucksterism' with respect to someone else's religion are usually no less engaged in selling. They only imagine that their selling is more professional, more tasteful."[11]

While Livnot, and Jews more generally, does not normally engage in seeking converts from among non-Jews, the proselytism that does occur is aimed at those who *are* Jewish, with the aim of presenting them with a particular articulation or vision of Judaism.

For all the Jewish choices that Livnot seems to offer or support, many are withheld and ignored. Not everything can be had at the Livnot supermarket. Participants are encouraged to seek a workable, personal Judaism, but they are encouraged to do so using the ingredients of "traditional" Judaism. I would argue that however idealized and lim-ited, the Livnot portrait of Judaism is at least one that is both grounded in Jewish tradition and one that resonates, to greater and lesser degrees, with participants. Livnot encourages the development of a desire, and perhaps even ability, to make choices about Judaism, rooted in some knowledge of and appreciation for a cultural heritage. Whatever those choices are, however they are made, and whatever manifestations of Judaism they come to underlie for participants, they are significantly more real, effective, and informed Jewish choices than participants were able to make before the program. Through Livnot and a positive encounter with traditional Judaism, participants are empowered to become "Jews by choice" rather than "Jews by accident." While Livnot is not the answer to the problems faced by American Jewry, it is part of an answer – one that allows participants to rise above the choices that were made for them by their parents, the forces of assimilation, and the experience of living in a non-Jewish society.

Obviously what is good for individual Jews is not necessarily congruent with what is good for the Jews as a group. Thomas Luckmann concludes his seminal work *The Invisible Religion: The Problem of Religion in Modern Society* facing a similar issue, one which he leaves unanswered: "How is one to decide whether the new social form of religion is 'good' or 'bad?' It is a radically subjective form of 'religiosity' that is characterized by a weakly coherent and nonobligatory sacred cosmos ... [it] represents a historically unprecedented opportunity for the autonomy of personal life for 'everybody.' It also contains a serious danger – of motivating mass withdrawal into the 'private sphere' while 'Rome burns.'"[12]

The religious sphere is but one, albeit core, arena in which privatism, individualism, and institutional withdrawal are the order of the day. In his recent book *Bowling Alone: The Collapse and Revival of American Community*, Robert Putnam explores civic disengagement in contemporary American society. He examines a vast array of communal institutions and social values, including religion, to demonstrate a precarious, and ultimately harmful decline in "social capital."

Concern about the implications of the increasing privatization of religion is as old as recognition of the phenomenon itself. There is, no doubt, a profound tension inherent in the respective values of individualism and community, between liberty and fraternity. Jewish tradition was itself aware of this dynamic, as illustrated by this brief yet forceful metaphor from a seventh-century text: "'Shall one man sin' – Rabbi Shimon bar Yochai taught: It is to be compared to people who were in a boat, and one of them took a drill and began to drill a hole beneath himself. His companions said to him: Why are you doing this? He replied: What concern is it of yours? Am I not drilling under myself? They replied: But you will flood the boat for us all."[13]

The "informed assimilation" chosen by some Livnot participants remains assimilation, however empowered or more freely chosen on the basis of increased Jewish knowledge and experience. The veneration of free, informed, individual choice is obviously the product of the Enlightenment and modern individualism – hardly Jewish sources. Equally, the line between a personal Judaism and one that is conflicted, confused, or absurd can be a fine one. As a social scientist, I am able to accept and find value in almost any articulation of Judaism, however untraditional. As a Jew who is increasingly concerned about the future of Judaism, however, I am forced to wonder if perhaps all these individualized Judaisms are not potentially destructive.

Individualized religion has, not surprisingly, long been decried by religious institutions themselves as being both self-serving and superficial. Sociologists, however, are not confident in asserting what this tendency implies long-term. Whether privatization adds weight to the secularization thesis, pointing to a decline of religion, or whether it suggests instead a transformation and revival of religion, is still under debate. Similarly, some scholars of contemporary Jewish life in North America see assimilation and decline where others see revitalization. But even those more optimistic analysts such as Cohen and Eisen, who envision change rather than loss, are aware that disengagement from public, institutional Judaism does not bode well for the future of Jewish life.

In their recent book, Susser and Liebman strongly assert that the kind of individual, creative Judaisisms enjoyed by past participants of Livnot are not good for the survival of the Jews:

> what can be said about the privatized syndrome that cannot be equally said of dozens of other garden-variety forms of modern consciousness? What are its differentia? That Judaism and Jewishness are more flexible, more given to protean reinterpretations, less wedded to any particular symbol or theological system, less obligating or judgmental, more modern and au courant, more relevant, more sensitive to trends as they develop, that is, more chameleon-like than any other religious community? That it simulates a kind of Unitarianism ornamented with Jewish peculiarities? It hardly needs saying that all of this does not add up to a recipe for success.[14]

Susser and Liebman suggest that the real problem of religious privatism is that such a choice is rarely an *educated* one. Rather, they suggest, it is more often an option grounded in a lack of Jewish content and knowledge: "To incorporate American values [into Judaism], however, it is obviously necessary for there to be a Jewish corpus into which they can be synthesized. Confrontation between cultures requires two cultures. Dialogue involves relating and withstanding simultaneously. For those lacking Jewish cultural content, the ability to confront and withstand is forfeited. What remains for them is only an American monologue.

Widespread Jewish illiteracy means that the vast majority of American Jews are adept at only one cultural language: American."[15]

While almost all Jews in North America must come to some kind of creative accommodation with modernity and non-Jewish society, it seems obvious that there is a radical difference between a Jew whose accommodation is, for example, the pursuit of secular education *in addition* to religious education, and one who chooses to express her Judaism in Sufi dance because she knows no Hebrew and cannot relate to the standardized prayerbook. While the latter might be, after Livnot, a more informed decision than it would have been without the program, and thus one expressing deeper personal agency, it remains a very "un-Jewish" choice that might contribute little to the good of the Jewish people as a whole. The issues here are complex and potentially painful, weighing the needs of the individual against the needs of the community, in a manner that easily develops into attempts to determine the boundaries of what constitutes "Jewish" – a task for which this faint of heart social scientist finds little taste.

Livnot helps to ensure that the spiritual marketplace in which participants shop is not one that is entirely unregulated. It offers young people seeking to create their own, personal articulations of spirituality, a blueprint, a menu, some resources that might help guide their way. Livnot helps ground the fluidity of religious experimentation in the form of Jewish tradition. While there are no guarantees of how, or even if, participants will actually use this Jewish toolbox in the construction of their own identities, simply having access to it serves to anchor the individual search for a meaningful religious identity in the historical, communal experience of Jewish texts and observances. As such, Livnot offers a balance, however imperfect, between the individual and the communal.

Doubtless, the Livnot experience is no real remedy for the serious challenges and dilemmas of being Jewish in contemporary North America. But it does point most effectively to both the contours and nuances of those challenges, and to some preliminary routes and potential pitfalls on the way to addressing them.

Notes

1 This is a translation of the fifth verse of the Friday evening prayer *Lecha Dodi*, composed in sixteenth-century Tzfat by Rabbi Shlomo Alkabetz. Prayers at Livnot are conducted in Hebrew. This translation is from *The Complete Artscroll Siddur/Siddur Ahavat Shalom*.

2 Transliteration of Hebrew words follows popular usage and is the system used at Livnot itself.

3 Introduction to Reimer 1997, xviii.

4 Sixty-eight per cent of respondents agreed with the statement, while 19 per cent disagreed, and 14 per cent were not sure. See S. Cohen 1988, 116.

5 See Luckmann 1967.

6 See Laurie Goodstein, "To Bind the Faith, Free Trips to Israel for Diaspora Youth," *New York Times,* 16 November 1998, A7. It is not clear that this number is limited to those taking part in organized Israel programs.

7 See S. Cohen, n.d.

8 Geffen 1993, 69.

9 In 2000 the Council of Jewish Federations came together with United Jewish Appeal and United Israel Appeal to form United Jewish Communities.

10 Goodstein, "To Bind the Faith."

11 The *havurah* movement is one of small, traditional, egalitarian prayer and study groups. See Prell 1989 and Weissler 1989. Jewish renewal is a melding of Judaism with techniques of mysticism, meditation, and a "new age" ethos. See Lerner 1994. The *ba'al teshuvah* movement is one

of individuals who were raised in liberal or secular homes, who have become religiously observant as adults.

12 Roof 1999, 10.

13 Ibid., 35.

14 Barack Fishman 2000, 10.

15 Cohen and Eisen 2000, 184.

16 Roof 1999, 37.

17 See, for example, Wertheimer 1993; Phillips 1991; and S. Cohen 1991.

18 The term "past participant" suggests an experiential focus to the program, whereas "alumni" is more associated with a formal, learning environment. Because Livnot consciously tries to emphasize both experience and study, I use the terms interchangeably.

19 In my own experience and from what Livnot staff members have told me, women consistently and noticeably outnumber men in the program. The sex breakdown of my sample reflects this phenomenon.

20 See Shapiro 2003a.

21 On native anthropologists, see Kondo 1986 and Narayan 1993. Noting a similar phenomenon, Abu-Lughod (1991) uses the term "halfie" to connote "people whose national or cultural identity is mixed by virtue of migration, overseas education or parentage" (137).

22 Behar 1996, 177.

23 Boyarin 1992, 21.

CHAPTER TWO

1 In 1993, Livnot acquired a building in the Katamon neighbourhood of Jerusalem. The Jerusalem campus has been used to operate condensed, three-week versions of Livnot for participants unable to commit to a three-month long program. Both the Tzfat and Jerusalem programs visit each other's campus.

2 See Jerusalem Talmud, Rosh Hashana 2:1. While there is mention of a city called Tzfat in Judges 1:17, and the valley of Tzfata in 2 Chronicles 14:9, neither corresponds geographically with Tzfat of the Upper Galilee.

3 This corresponds to the first two centuries of the common era. The most important teacher or *tanna* traditionally thought to be buried near Tzfat is Shimon bar Yochai.

4 The name of the city is spelled many different ways in English, most commonly Safed or Tzfat.

5 Quoted in Ben-Sasson 1985, 635.

6 Called "Lurianic" after the creator of this system, Rabbi Isaac Luria, who is more commonly known as the Ari.

7 In the Middle Ages, the name *Sepharadi* was applied to the Jews of Spain (*Sepharad*). Following the expulsion from Spain, their descendants settled in North Africa, Italy, Syria, and the central provinces of the Turkish Empire. Today, the term *Sepharadi* is commonly and loosely used to designate all members of the oriental Jewish communities, in contrast to *Ashkenazim*. Jews from communities in North Africa and the Middle East are also referred to as *Mizrachi* (Oriental) Jews.

8 When I was a *madricha* for the program in 1993, I was told that the beds had to be made up before participants arrived at Livnot so that they would not be faced with the decrepit state of the mattresses until laundry day.

9 Many physical changes have occurred at Livnot since I was first there in 1992, as a result of new construction and the sale of some buildings.

10 For reasons of *kashrut*, certain products, especially grains, need to be checked for evidence of bugs. Finding *chevre* up late at night sifting through oatmeal for the next morning's breakfast is not uncommon.

11 For example, the schedule during the fall program of 1997 was disrupted by major Jewish holidays falling on *shabbat*, which Livnot did not want participants to have free. In order to fit in the free time, one of the free periods was held during the week rather than over *shabbat*.

12 The operation of electricity is prohibited on *shabbat* according to the modern application of traditional Jewish law which forbids the lighting and extinguishing of fire on *shabbat*.

13 Men lead the prayer services at Livnot. This is owing to various *halachic* prohibitions, and because Livnot is next door to a *yeshiva* whose students would most certainly be offended by overhearing a woman lead a prayer service.

14 It is traditional to refrain from speaking between the ritual handwashing and making the blessing over bread and eating it.

15 The names of all participants and staff members have been changed.

16 A *shofar* is a hollowed ram's horn which is blown to produce a loud sound.

17 National service (*sherut le'am*) is a program for young religious women who perform community work as an alternative to regular military service. While women can be completely exempted from army service on religious grounds, many modern Orthodox women with strong nationalist feelings tend to choose this alternative for serving the country. Ultra-

Orthodox girls, on the other hand, participate in neither national service nor the military.

18   In my experience at Livnot, I have come across only one regular teacher in the program who is not "obviously" religious, that is, he does not wear a *kipah*.

19   *Tzitzit* are the ritual fringes attached to a four-cornered garment worn by observant men. The practice is based on the biblical commandment of Num.15:37–40. Some men wear these fringes tucked inside their clothing, while others choose to wear them hanging outside to make them visible. Leaving *tzitzit* visible is commonly perceived to be "more religious," as is wearing a beard.

20   Staff members have changed since my first encounter with Livnot in 1992. The individuals that I describe here are the staff members from the summer of 1997. Some staff members have changed between my fieldwork and this writing.

21   The application screening process is quite rigorous. Staff concerns about a potential participant being "too positive" toward observant Judaism or having "too much background" are common. Naturally, participants are screened more strictly when there is a large number of potential *chevre*, and less so when numbers are down, as was the case during my fieldwork.

22   Because tearing is prohibited on *shabbat*, many observant individuals will use pre-torn toilet paper or tissues in the bathroom.

23   A boy becomes *bar mitzvah* at the age of thirteen, and marks his reaching the age of adult religious responsibilities. A girl traditionally becomes *bat mitzvah* at the age of twelve. The Reform movement, however, celebrates a girl's *bat mitzvah* at thirteen, hence the discrepant ages mentioned by some Livnot participants.

24   Wendy is referring to a Reform temple.

25   The actual term is *haftarah*, which means "departure" and refers to the additional portion of the Bible, taken from prophets or writings, that is read in synagogue on Shabbat after the Torah portion. *Ashkenazi* pronunciation renders this "*haftorah*," which this informant mistakenly thinks is actually "half Torah."

26   The principle of "*kiruv rechokim*" is derived from a combination of several Jewish concepts, including the biblical injunction to "admonish your neighbour" (Leviticus 19:7) and the notion of Jewish mutual responsibility.

27   In discussing Livnot, I have found that many people are suspicious about the possibility that Livnot might possess a hidden agenda involving

encouraging participants to adopt Jewish observance. I, too, was deeply dubious about the claims of staff members, and asked many questions in an attempt to discover anything resembling a desire for participants to become observant. I discussed the question of participant success and failure extensively with staff members, but found no covert strategies to motivate religious observance, nor even a strong desire for participants to become religious after Livnot. However, some staff members did admit to feeling a certain, almost parental joy when participants did end up becoming religious, simply because these individuals had made choices similar to those that the staff members had made for themselves.

28 One resident of Tzfat who runs a *yeshiva* was critical of the fact that Livnot was "too anti-*kiruv*" and perceived the program to be missing a great opportunity to bring its participants to religious observance.

29 Schoem 1989, 54.

30 Ibid., 92.

31 In Reimer 1997, vii.

32 Dershowitz 1997, 294.

33 Schoem 1989, 98.

34 I am indebted to Clifford for this extremely useful play on "routes"and "roots" (1994, 308).

CHAPTER THREE

1 Of eighteen interviewees at Livnot in 1997, I found only two people who had been to Israel for extended trips. These individuals had already developed more complex understandings of Israel and felt themselves to have a more personal relationship with the country than did other participants. These more extensive Israel experiences of some participants should not be thought to imply that their attitudes toward Israel were unaffected by Livnot but simply that some individuals had a more nuanced sense of Israel already in place.

2 A bombing occurred in the Ben-Yehuda pedestrian mall of Jerusalem on 4 September 1997, just days after a group of participants arrived in Israel for the fall Livnot program.

3 Two participants said "beautiful," while three participants associated Israel with "home."

4 See S. Cohen 1991.

5 E. Cohen 1992, 58.

6 See E. Cohen 1979 and E. Cohen, Ben-Yehuda, and Aviad 1987. Erik Cohen asserts that the difference between the existential tourist and the

pilgrim is that the pilgrim approaches a centre that is already sacralized within her own culture, whereas the existential tourist goes outside her own society to locate an alternative, elective centre (1992, 55). This definition, however, relies excessively on a bounded, singular, homogeneous understanding of culture. Have Livnot participants gone outside of their own, presumably "North American" culture, in order to seek out an elective centre, or are they rather participating in the sacralization of *eretz yisrael* that occurs in the Jewish tradition that is also their culture through ancestry? It is precisely through the experience of Livnot, and through the encounter with Israel as part of the Livnot program, that the notion of here and there, centre and periphery, "my" culture and that of "others" becomes problematized for participants.

7 E. Cohen 1979, 191.

8 The "new city" of West Jerusalem is not denigrated or restricted in any way to participants, and Livnot's Jerusalem campus, where participants stay, is in the West Jerusalem neighbourhood of Katamon. The "new city" is simply deemed irrelevant. Arab East Jerusalem is even more radically ignored, an area whose existence is not even mentioned by the program.

9 See Katriel 1995. These Zionist ideas eerily mirror the early political thrust in the *Wandervogel* movement, of which Laqueur writes: "Rambling was an art, they said; it had to be purposeful, those who engaged in it had to learn to be observant, to become more familiar with the Fatherland and its people. This education by rambling was to produce a new German, who had a better, more rounded picture of his country, and whose identification with and love of that country was deeply rooted in his personal experience" (1962, 7).

10 See Ben-David 1997.

11 See Katriel 1995. This is illustrated most recently in the aborted 2005 hikes to Gush Katif to protest the planned Israeli withdrawal from Gaza.

12 Participants, like most North American Jews, remain wholly unaware of the intense struggle against nature in Israel, waged by the Zionist movement in the early part of the century in order to drain swamps, build roads, and "make the desert bloom."

13 There is ethnographic evidence pointing to this practice among other cultures. See Geertz 1983, 134–7 on the extensive travelling across territory by Moroccan kings in the eighteenth and nineteenth century to demonstrate sovereignty.

14 Babylonian Talmud, Bava Batra 100a.

15 Babylonian Talmud, Ketubot 111a.

16 Clearly, this quotation offers more than just a portrait of the land of
   Israel. Daniel's repeated use of an inclusive "we" presents participants
   with a strong sense of Jewish peoplehood and history, as will be
   discussed in the next chapter.

17 This message is actually very politically contentious. The question of
   whether the modern, political state of Israel fulfills religious yearning for
   the return to Israel that Jewish tradition believes will accompany the
   redemption is one that carries profound implications. While religious
   Zionists believe the modern Israeli state to signal "the beginning of our
   redemption," religious non-Zionists or anti-Zionists see the state as
   pre-empting God's work of redemption.

18 Many elements of Livnot's approach to Israel possess clear echoes of the
   philosophy of Rabbi A.I. Kook (1865–1935), the first *Ashkenazi* chief
   rabbi of Palestine. His merging of religious Orthodoxy and Zionism was
   revolutionary, and formed the basis for the national-religious movement. While Livnot is not officially identified with Rav Kook, he and his
   work are held in high esteem by many individual staff members, the
   vast majority of whom are religious Zionists.

19 The poem reads:
   My brothers the heroes of Golan
   I wanted to write to you, my brothers
   With beards and sooty faces and all the other marks
   I wanted to write to you – you who stood alone
   Facing enemy tanks from front and flank.
   You whose clanking tracks set a land trembling,
   You who proved that armor is iron but man is steel,
   To you, who gave a shoulder and extended a hand
   And destroyed them in their masses one by one
   I wanted to write you a hymn if only one
   For each of the few who stood against the many.
   I stand here on the ramps and count them by their scores
   Sooty hulks and abandoned tanks and cold corpses
   And I remember how you worked alone and in pairs
   One turning on a light while the other struck from close,
   And I looked on towards the bloody path and Mazrat Beit Jan
   And the night of move to ambush at America-Yair crossing
   And the artillery that pounded at dawn,
   And I remember the hundred and twenty-seven
   And the gang on tanks, and their joy
   when they heard and felt cease-fire coming.

I look back and see the faces of heroes,
Who will not come back with us, nor tell their exploits,
Those who saw the oncoming monster and fired till it stopped,
Who loaded another shell and another belt till they paid with
   their blood.
I remember all of them – Yair, Ami and Amir and Zelig Bluman
   and all the others who fought like lions till morning dawned.
I stand here alone and my heart is filled with a silent prayer:
Let there be no more war...

October 1973

KOBI

20 Leaving a stone marker on the headstone is a common practice at
   Jewish cemeteries.

21 David Ben-Gurion was the first prime minister of Israel and instrumental
   in the creation of the state. Awareness of his identity constitutes
   extremely basic knowledge about Israel.

22 The name *Livnot U'Lehibanot* itself comes from a pioneering song,
   whose English lyrics are "We came to the land to build and to be built
   by it."

23 See Malkki 1997 for an exploration of scholarly and nationalist rhetoric
   of territorial rootedness.

24 Gupta and Ferguson 1997a, 40.

25 For example, on borderlands, see Anzaldua 1987; on diaspora, see Lavie
   and Swedenburg 1996 and Clifford 1994; on transnationalism, see
   Hannerz 1996.

26 Gupta and Ferguson 1997b, 6.

27 Malkki 1997, 59.

28 Lowenthal 1996, 183.

29 Malkki 1997, 60.

30 The safety and privilege experienced by many Jews in North America
   also ensure that they are proportionally less inclined to emigrate to
   Israel. As Liebman and Cohen explain, "they [North Americans] reject
   the Israeli image of Jewish life outside Israel (in the diaspora) as
   precarious, distorted, and incomplete, and the Israeli claim that Israel
   offers a genuine home to the Jew, who can lead a full Jewish life there
   without fear of alienation from the larger society" (1990, 93). This
   means that many North American Jews tend to reject certain basic
   propositions of classical Zionism, most notably the mass resettlement of
   all Jews in Israel.

31 Eisen 1986b, 289.

32 This once-assumed financial and political support for Israel has recently become more open to question. Concerns in recent years about the pace of the Middle East peace process and conflict over the status of Reform and Conservative Judaism in Israel have widened the division between North American Jewry and Israel.

33 See S. Cohen 1991.

34 Ibid., 124.

35 Comparing Israeli and American understandings of Israel, Liebman and Cohen note that "ties to land, people, and religion among Israeli Jews are all correlated. In sharp contrast, the vast majority of American Jews have little appreciation for the centrality of the land of Israel in Jewish tradition, nor do they appreciate the extent to which Israelis, even secular Israelis, have invested land with a sacredness all its own. It is fair to say that to most American Jews, even those with strong interests in Jewish life and Israeli matters, land constitutes an instrument of Israeli security; to the Israeli, it is often an end in itself" (1990, 74). Moreover, these researchers claim that "Israelis both secular and religious, from the political left as well as the right, feel a special tie to the land of Israel, with implications for their core identities as people, as Jews, and as Israelis. Hardly any American Jews even realize that the land of Israel played an important role in traditional Judaism, in part because many lack a strong interest in the fine points of Jewish tradition. And few American Jews appreciate the land's special meaning for Israelis beyond its instrumental functions" (ibid., 94). While possibly over-idealizing Israeli attitudes toward the land, the distinction made by these authors is, in my experience, generally correct.

36 The racial component involved in thinking that someone else's practice, even a physical ancestor's, is somehow one's own, that is, in what sense we could possibly call this a *re*-territorialization rather than just a territorialization, is powerfully engaged by Walter Benn Michaels 1992. See Boyarin and Boyarin 1993 for a challenging response.

37 Religious tradition suggests that the physical city of Jerusalem is an imperfect, "lower" or "earthly" expression of an ideal, "heavenly," or "upper" Jerusalem. See Babylonian Talmud, Ta'anit 5a, Hagigah 12b.

38 The centrality of the Land of Israel is displayed even in language. The Hebrew expression *ha'aretz* translates as "the land," but is used exclusively for the land of Israel. Thus, the expression *chutz la'aretz* means "outside of the land" and refers to anywhere outside of Israel.

CHAPTER FOUR

1 See Zerubavel 1995. Also, discussing a similar case of linking two unrelated episodes in Jewish history, Zerubavel explores the Israeli comparison between the radically different events of Masada and the Holocaust. In the past, she explains, Israeli culture emphasized the contrast between the two events, presenting the former as a case of heroic death for a greater cause and the latter as a passive and worthless loss of life. A radical transformation in Israeli attitudes toward the Holocaust since the 1960s encouraged the development of a new narrative which constructs the two events as similar tragedies. Zerubavel writes that "the new commemorative narrative thus establishes a continuity between Masada, the Holocaust, and the State of Israel" (1994, 88). She attributes this to the Israeli perception of constituting an entity under siege, or one facing potential catastrophe, similar to the Jews at Masada and during the Holocaust.

2 See Zerubavel 1995.

3 The ninth day of the Jewish month of Av is a day of fasting and mourning in remembrance of the destruction of the Second Temple, as well as other historical Jewish tragedies.

4 Of course, Jewish collective memory is neither monolithic nor unchanging, and takes different forms according to community, period, and purpose.

5 Lowenthal 1996, 112, 119.

6 Ibid., 147.

7 Tamar Katriel (1997) examined the construction of pre-state history presented at Israeli settlement museums. Similar to Livnot's attitude toward its teaching of Jewish heritage, she quotes one museum guide as asserting, "History they can learn at school ... Here they come for the experience" (23).

8 The disproportionate number of staff members from North America is not a matter of any official Livnot policy, however useful a common background might be. Rather, as one staff member explained to me, Livnot simply does not make sense to most non-American Israelis. Ultra-Orthodox Israelis disagree with the program's lack of effort to promote observance, while Israeli secularists usually do not have the positive view of traditional Judaism that Livnot tries to foster. *Sephardim,* as one staff member explained to me, simply do not understand American Jews and their identity issues. These factors tend to make Israelis who did

not immigrate from North America or Western Europe less inclined to want to teach at Livnot.

9 *Tzitzit* are the ritual fringes and *payos* are the sidelocks worn by observant Jewish men.

10 *Chabad-Lubavitch* is a Chassidic sect which, while perhaps the most liberal of Chassidic groups in terms of their participation in mainstream culture and contact with less observant Jews, is perceived by many non-Orthodox Jews as extreme in orientation.

11 Numerous studies of diverse religious communities have noted the important role that an emphasis on family life plays for potential converts (see Ammerman 1987; Danzger 1989; Neitz 1987; and Aviad 1983). Like the situation of Livnot participants, the attraction of religious families for newly-observant Jewish women, and the centrality of the women's desire to create their own families, is clearly articulated by Davidman's informants (1991, ch5).

12 Synagogue membership or sending Hebrew School tuition can be significant expenses for families.

13 The popular term JAP is an acronym for Jewish American Princess. It is used as a shorthand for materialism, privilege, sexual frigidity, and superficiality.

14 See Turner 1969. Referring in particular to the transition phase, Turner has defined the concept of liminality as a marginal state, the cultural realm with few or no attributes of the past or future position of the individual who is "betwixt and between" social states. Turner also distinguishes between the "structure" of society, as a differentiated and hierarchical system based on political-legal-economic positions serving to separate people in terms of status, power, or property, and "communitas," the unstructured community of equal individuals that recognizes a fundamental human bond. "Communitas" is the prime attribute of the transitional or liminal stage, and is characterized by simplicity, unselfishness, humility, feelings of comradeship and egalitarianism, and the absence of rank (1969). It is the quality of release from the normal social structures and hierarchies that distinguish individuals from each other. While not a "rite of passage" in a classical sense, Livnot too is marked by the three phases of separation, liminality, and aggregation.

15 See Woocher 1986.

16 Liebman and Cohen 1990, 26. This North American Jewish ambivalence between universalism and particularism comes out most often around issues of intermarriage. In a recent newspaper essay, a

reader lamented that "they [our parents] sent us out into the world as children, backpacks full of love and acceptance slung over our shoulders, and now they want to drag us back inside and lock us in our rooms until we see only black and white. Or should I say Jew and non-Jew?" Dana Bookman, "My Cousin, Her Boyfriend and the Marriage Dilemma," *The Globe and Mail,* 18 March 1999, A24.

CHAPTER FIVE

1 See Liebman and Cohen 1990.
2 Ibid., 138.
3 The Hebrew phrase for God's command to Abram in Genesis 12:1 "to go" is *lech lecha*, which can be translated as "go to yourself."
4 Presumably, Robert is referring to the tendency of some Christians to quote John 3:16.
5 A *sheitel* is a wig that some observant women wear to cover their own hair in public.
6 See Luckmann 1967, 98–9. This choice-oriented approach to Jewish tradition, both characteristic of Livnot and pervading contemporary North American Jewry, was articulated within modern Jewish philosophy in the early twentieth century. Franz Rosenzweig in particular "shifted the authority of observance from a commanding God to the individual self who hears the commandment" (Eisen 1998, 208) and did so within a general framework of encouraging Jewish practice. See Eisen 1998, ch7. Rosenzweig's approach to observance based on personal authenticity is more explicitly accepted by liberal Jewish traditions in North America than it is by orthodoxy.
7 Numbers Rabbah (Naso) 13:15. There are many other *Midrashim* which point to the possibilities of multiple and indeterminate readings of scripture. See Handelman 1982 and Gorenberg 1996.
8 At Livnot there is little need to address questions of the ultimate boundaries of participants' Judaism, since the overwhelming majority of participants come to the program identifying clearly as Jews. They are simply not sure about what that identification means for them.
9 On Friday nights, however, there is a *Kabbalat Shabbat* service, and grace after meals is recited together after *shabbat* meals.
10 As Mary Douglas notes, "Ritual has become a bad word signifying empty conformity" (1973, 19), and "The move away from ritual is accompanied by a strong movement towards greater ethical sensitivity" (41).

11 Here Daniel refers to the opening line of a core Jewish prayer called the "*Sh'ma*," made up of passages from Numbers and Deuteronomy. It is recited several times daily, and begins, "Hear O Israel, Hashem is our God, Hashem, the one and only" (translation from *The Complete Artscroll Siddur/ Siddur Ahavat Shalom*).

12 The class was based on a discussion of Pirkei Avot 4:1.

13 Clearly, this egalitarian portrait of Judaism could be readily challenged by reference to the unequal ritual situation of women in Orthodox tradition. However, since prayer and synagogue are peripheral at Livnot, it becomes easy to elide some of the most obvious gender inequalities that exist in the tradition that would be unpalatable to participants. Issues of women in Judaism are discussed below.

14 These laws are based on a biblical prohibition. See Lev. 15:19, 18:19, 20:18. The laws of family purity prohibit all physical contact between husband and wife during her menstrual period, and for seven days after. The couple is permitted to resume physical contact following the woman's immersion in a ritual bath.

15 This benefit of *taharat hamishpacha* is also cited in traditional Jewish sources. See Babylonian Talmud, Niddah 31b.

16 Unfortunately, the male viewpoint was less easily available to me in this part of the research. Most classes dealing with sexuality and gender are held separately for men and women. This ensured that I heard women's issues, concerns, and opinions in far greater detail. Also, there are often significantly more women than men on any individual Livnot program, allowing women's voices to sometimes be heard as more representative than they might actually be. A (male) staff member explained to me that Family Week is much more significant for women than for men, because women discuss these intimate issues in a more personal, detailed manner than men do.

17 Equally, observant married individuals do not normally touch members of the opposite sex except their spouses, and rarely touch their spouses in public.

18 See Stacey 1987. Stacey (1983) also argues that it is possible to discern a radical-feminist ancestry in some new, conservative feminist thought.

19 See Davidman 1991 and Kaufman 1991.

20 Men and women do stand separately. According to Livnot staff, this is because the prayers welcoming the *sabbath* (*Kabbalat Shabbat*) are simply custom and have a lesser status than other kinds of prayer.

21 The exception to this is on *Rosh Hashana and Yom Kippur*, when participants are required to attend synagogue services.

22 Deuteronomy 8:8 praises the land of Israel as "a land of wheat and barley, of vines and fig trees and pomegranates, a land of olive trees and honey." These products (with honey commonly understood as dates) make up the seven species, after whose consumption a special blessing is required.

23 According to Jewish dietary laws, meat and dairy must be kept separate and require separate utensils. Participants were thus at fault for using dairy knives for cutting vegetables, but meat cutting boards and pots. The real problem, however, was that the vegetables included onions, which are considered, like heat, to transfer the quality (dairy or meat) from utensils or pots to each other.

24 In the North American Jewish community, the comparison between intermarriage and the Holocaust as tragedies threatening the survival of the Jewish people is not uncommon. I recall being warned as a child that intermarriage grants Hitler a posthumous victory.

25 When asked to specify what the "one or two things" are that Livnot tries to make participants do, he clarified that reducing intermarriage is really the only issue.

26 This also reflects Israeli culture which views Orthodox tradition as normative, whether accepted or rejected. The term "Orthodoxy" is almost non-existent in Israel since other formulations of Judaism, such as Conservative and Reform, are still considered deviant.

27 The ritualized holiday meal. Here Ariela refers to an actual *halachic* discussion concerning the required size of a piece of unleavened bread that must be eaten to fulfill one's ritual obligation.

28 While Orthodox rabbinical opinions differ about the *halacha* on this matter, it is not common Orthodox practice to allow women to dance with Torah scrolls. I was not present at this event, as it occurred before my fieldwork. The attack was publicly denounced by the chief rabbi of Tzfat.

29 Sollors 1986, 6.

30 On issues of "descent" versus "consent" in religious and ethnic identification among Jews, see Sharot 1998.

31 See Schoem 1989 and Woocher 1986.

CHAPTER SIX

1 Sam is part of a phenomenon of Jewish Buddhists, popularly known as "Ju-Bu's." While largely undocumented, the over-representation of Jews practicing Buddhism is large enough to be noticed. See Boorstein 1997; Kamenetz 1994.

2 Because it is considered non-porous, glass plates are easily switched between being used for meat and being used for dairy foods. While it has greater pliability than many other materials, and is thus quite useful for traditional *kashrut* observance, glass is not open to the kind of radically flexible use to which Sharon puts it, as she is uncomfortably aware.

3 "Hybridity," while an increasingly useful analytical category in anthropology and post-colonial theory, is at the same time "one of the most widely employed and most disputed terms in post-colonial theory" (Ashcroft 1998, 118). The concept is drawn from the biological sciences, in which a "hybrid" refers to the new species that results when two existing species are crossbred, cross-pollinated, or grafted together. In post-colonial thought, "hybridity" describes the result of culture contact: the cultural exchange and creolization that occurs between colonizer and colonized, between Western and traditional cultures, between centre and margin, between dominant and subordinate powers. Alternative terms, including "transculturation," "syncretism," "creolisation," "trans-ethnicity," and "hyphenated identities" are also used to describe similar processes.

4 See Lévi-Strauss 1963; Turner 1969; and Douglas 1966.

CHAPTER SEVEN

1 While *yeshiva* study is not common for participants prior to Livnot, many *yeshivot* in Israel actively seek out young, secular tourists and encourage them to visit for classes.

2 Confirmation is a Reform and Conservative Jewish ceremony held during an individual's teenage years. It signifies an ongoing commitment to Jewish learning following *bar/bat mitzvah*.

3 "Deli-identity" refers, like the common expression "bagels and lox Judaism," to a Jewish identity perceived by many to be superficial, centred as it is on certain cultural features like food, but lacking in actual religious content.

4 A well-known ultra-Orthodox neighbourhood in Jerusalem.

5 See Clifford 1995.

6 This is not to say that those earlier generations possessed some radical freedom to choose and create Jewish (or other) identities, but rather that their agency was constrained in different ways.

7 Behar 1996, 69–71.

8 See, for example, Bauman 1991; Furman 1987; Liebman 1973; and Schoenfeld 1998.

9 Clifford 1997, 187.
10 Dershowitz 1997, 292–3.
11 Moore 1995, 264.
12 Luckmann 1967, 117.
13 Midrash Rabbah, Leviticus 4:6.
14 Susser and Liebman 1999, 87. I do not believe that Susser and Liebman are referring to actual Unitarianism here, but rather use the term as a cipher for a multitude of liberal, universalist ideas. I suspect that "Unitarianism with Jewish particularities" would be extremely successful in contemporary North American Jewry, but significantly less so over generations – why maintain the particularities?
15 Ibid., 88.

Bibliography

Abu-Lughod, Lila. 1991. "Writing against Culture." In *Recapturing Anthropology: Working in the Present*, ed. Richard Fox, 137–62. Santa Fe: School of American Research Press.

Ammerman, Nancy. 1987. *Bible Believers: Fundamentalists in the Modern World*. New Jersey: Rutgers University.

Anzaldua, Gloria. 1987. *Borderlands/La Frontera: The New Mestiza*. San Francisco: spinsters/aunt lute.

Ashcroft, Bill et al. 1998. *Key Concepts in Post-Colonial Studies*. London and New York: Routledge.

Aviad, Janet. 1983. *Return to Judaism: Religious Renewal in Israel*. Chicago: University of Chicago Press.

Badone, Ellen and Sharon Roseman, eds. 2004. *Intersecting Journeys: The Anthropology of Pilgrimage and Tourism*. Urbana and Champaign: University of Illinois.

Barack Fishman, Sylvia. 2000. *Jewish Life and American Culture*. Albany: SUNY Press.

Bauman, Zygmunt. 1991. *Modernity and Ambivalence*. Oxford: Polity Press.

Behar, Ruth. 1996. *The Vulnerable Observer: Anthropology That Breaks Your Heart*. Boston: Beacon Press.

Bellah, Robert et al. 1985. *Habits of the Heart: Individualism and Commitment in American Life*. Berkeley: University of California Press.

Ben-David, Orit. 1997. "*Tiyul* (Hike) as an Act of Consecration of Space." In *Grasping Land: Space and Place in Contemporary Israeli Discourse and Experience*, ed. Eyal Ben-Ari and Yoram Bilu, 129–45. Albany: SUNY Press.

Ben-Sasson, Hayyim, ed. 1985. *A History of the Jewish People*. Cambridge: Harvard University Press.

Berger, Peter. 1967. *The Sacred Canopy: Elements of a Sociological Theory of Religion*. Garden City, New York: Doubleday.

– 1979. *The Heretical Imperative: Contemporary Possibilities of Religious Affirmation*. New York: Anchor Press.

Berger, Peter, Brigitte Berger, and Hansfried Kellner. 1973. *The Homeless Mind: Modernization and Consciousness*. New York: Random House.

Berger, Peter and Thomas Luckmann. 1967. *The Social Construction of Reality: A Treatise in the Sociology of Knowledge*. New York: Doubleday.

Bibby, Reginald 1987. *Fragmented Gods: The Poverty and Potential of Religion in Canada*. Toronto: Stoddart.

Boorstein, Sylvia. 1997. *That's Funny, You Don't Look Buddhist: On Being a Faithful Jew and a Passionate Buddhist*. New York: Harper San Francisco.

Boyarin, Daniel and Jonathan Boyarin. 1993. "Diaspora: Generation and the Ground of Jewish Identity." *Critical Inquiry* 19: 693–725.

Boyarin, Jonathan. 1992. *Storm from Paradise: The Politics of Jewish Memory*. Minneapolis: University of Minnesota.

Breakstone, David. 1995. "Holy Land or Disneyland? A Cautionary Guide to the Israel Experience." *Moment* 20 (6): 58–61.

Chazan, Barry. 1994. "The Israel Trip: A New Form of Jewish Education." In *Youth Trips to Israel: Rationale and Realization*. New York: Jewish Education Service of North America.

Clifford, James. 1983. "On Ethnographic Authority." *Representations* 1 (2): 118–46.

– 1986. "Introduction: Partial Truths." In *Writing Culture: The Poetics and Politics of Ethnography*, ed. James Clifford and George Marcus, 1–26. Berkeley: University of California Press.

– 1988. *The Predicament of Culture: Twentieth Century Ethnography, Literature and Art*. Cambridge and London: Harvard University Press.

– 1994. "Diasporas." *Cultural Anthropology* 9 (3): 302–38.

– 1995. "Paradise." *Visual Anthropology Review* 11 (1): 92–117.

– 1997. *Routes: Travel and Translation in the Late Twentieth Century*. Cambridge: Harvard University.

Clifford, James and George Marcus, eds. 1986. *Writing Culture: The Poetics and Politics of Ethnography*. Berkeley: University of California Press.

Cohen, Erik. 1979. "A Phenomenology of Tourist Experiences." *Sociology* 13 (2): 179–201.

– 1984. "The Sociology of Tourism: Approaches, Issues, and Findings." *Annual Review of Sociology* 10: 373–92.

– 1985. "Tourism as Play." *Religion* 15: 291–304.

– 1992. "Pilgrimage and Tourism: Convergence and Divergence." In *Sacred Journeys: The Anthropology of Pilgrimage*, ed. Alan Morinis, 47–61. Westport: Greenwood Press.

Cohen, E., N. Ben-Yehuda, and J. Aviad. 1987. "Recentering the World: The Quest for 'Elective' Centres in a Secularised Universe." *Sociological Review* 35 (2): 320–436.

Cohen, Steven. 1983. *American Modernity and Jewish Identity*. New York and London: Tavistock.

– 1986. *Jewish Travel to Israel: Incentives and Inhibitions among American and Canadian Teenagers and Young Adults*. Jerusalem: Jewish Education Committee of the Jewish Agency.

– 1988. *American Assimilation or Jewish Revival?* Bloomington: Indiana University Press.

– 1991. "Israel in the Jewish Identity of American Jews: A Study in Dualities and Contrasts." In *Jewish Identity in America*, ed. David Gordis and Yoav Ben-Horin, 119–36. Los Angeles: Wilstein Institute.

– 1995a. "The Impact of Varieties of Jewish Education upon Jewish Identity: An Inter-Generational Perspective." *Contemporary Jewry* 16: 68–96.

– 1995b. "Jewish Continuity over Judaic Content: The Moderately Affiliated American Jew." In *The Americanization of the Jews*, ed. Robert Seltzer and Norman Cohen, 395–416. New York: New York University Press.

– n.d. "Introduction: The Ethnography of the Israel Experience." Melton Center for Jewish Education in the Diaspora, Hebrew University, Jerusalem.

Cohen, Steven and Arnold Eisen. 2000. *The Jew Within: Self, Family and Community in America*. Indianapolis: Indiana University Press.

Cohen, Steven and Leonard Fine. 1985. "From Integration to Survival: American Jewish Anxieties in Transition." *Annals* (July): 75–88.

Cohen, Steven and Susan Wall. 1994. "Excellence in Youth Trips to Israel." In *Youth Trips to Israel: Rationale and Realization*. New York: Jewish Education Service of North America.

Danzger, Herbert. 1989. *Returning to Tradition: The Contemporary Revival of Orthodox Judaism*. New Haven: Yale University.

Davidman, Lynn. 1991. *Tradition in a Rootless World: Women Turn to Orthodox Judaism*. Berkeley: University of California.

Dershowitz, Alan. 1997. *The Vanishing American Jew: In Search of Jewish Identity for the Next Century*. Boston: Little, Brown and Company.

Dominguez, Virginia. 1993. "Questioning Jews." *American Ethnologist* 20 (3): 618–24.

Douglas, Mary. 1966. *Purity and Danger: An Analysis of Concepts of Pollution and Taboo*. London: Routledge and Kegan Paul.

– 1973. *Natural Symbols: Explorations in Cosmology*. New York: Penguin Books.

Eade, John and Michael Sallnow. 1991. *Contesting the Sacred: The Anthropology of Christian Pilgrimage*. London: Routledge.

Eisen, Arnold. 1986a. *Galut: Modern Jewish Reflection on Homelessness and Homecoming.* Loomington and Indianapolis: Indiana University.

– 1986b. "Off Center: The Concept of the Land of Israel in Modern Jewish Thought." In *The Land of Israel: Jewish Perspectives,* ed. Lawrence Hoffman, 263–97. Notre Dame: University of Notre Dame Press.

– 1998. *Rethinking Modern Judaism: Ritual, Commandment Community.* Chicago: University of Chicago.

Fein, Leonard. 1988. *Where Are We? The Inner Life of America's Jews.* New York: Harper and Row.

Frank, Gelya. 1997. "Jews, Multiculturalism, and Boasian Anthropology." *American Anthropologist* 99 (4): 731–45.

Frank, Naava. 1996. *Adolescent Constructions of Jewishness: The Nesiya 1988 Summer Trip to Israel.* Unpublished doctoral thesis. Graduate School of Education, Harvard University.

Frey, Nancy. 1998. *Pilgrim Stories: On and off the Road to Santiago.* Berkeley and Los Angeles: University of California Press.

Furman, Frida. 1987. *Beyond Yiddishkeit: The Struggle for Jewish Identity in a Reform Synagogue.* Albany: SUNY Press.

Geertz, Clifford. 1983. *Local Knowledge: Further Essays in Interpretive Anthropology.* New York: Basic Books.

– 1973. *The Interpretation of Cultures.* New York: Basic Books.

Geffen, Peter. 1993. "The Israel Experience." *Moment* 18 (6): 68–70.

Glazer, Nathan. 1987. "New Perspectives in American Jewish Sociology." *American Jewish Year Book* 87: 3–19.

Goldberg, David and Michael Krausz, eds. 1993. *Jewish Identity.* Philadelphia: Temple University Press.

Goldberg, Harvey, ed. 1972. *Cave Dwellers and Citrus Growers: A Jewish Community in Libya and Israel.* Cambridge: Cambridge University Press.

– 1987. *Judaism Viewed from within and from without: Anthropological Studies.* Albany: SUNY Press.

– n.d. "A Summer on a NFTY Safari (1994): An Ethnographic Perspective." Department of Sociology and Anthropology, Hebrew University, Jerusalem.

Goldenberg, Robert. 1989. "Is There an 'Essence of Judaism' After All?" *Judaism* 38 (1): 21–7.

Goldscheider, Calvin. 1986. *Jewish Continuity and Change: Emerging Patterns in America.* Bloomington: Indiana University Press.

Goldscheider, Calvin and Alan Zuckerman. 1984. *The Transformation of the Jews.* Chicago: University of Chicago Press.

Gorenberg, Gershom. 1996. "Introduction." In *Seventy Facets: A Commentary on the Torah from the Pages of the Jerusalem Report.* Northvale and London: Jason Aronson.

Gupta, Akhil and James Ferguson. 1997a. "Beyond Culture: Space, Identity and the Politics of Difference." In *Culture, Power, Place: Explorations in Critical Anthropology*, 33–51. Durham and London: Duke University Press.

– 1997b. "Culture, Power, Place: Ethnography at the End of an Era." In *Culture, Power, Place: Explorations in Critical Anthropology*, 1–29. Durham and London: Duke University Press.

Handelman, Susan. 1982. *Slayers of Moses: The Emergence of Rabbinic Interpretation in Modern Literary Theory*. Albany: SUNY Press.

Hannerz, Ulf. 1996. *Transnational Connections: Culture, People, Places*. London: Routledge.

Heilman, Samuel. 1982. "The Sociology of American Jews: The Last Ten Years." *Annual Review of Sociology* 8: 135–60.

– 1989. *Cosmopolitans and Parochials: Modern Orthodox Jews in America*. Chicago: University of Chicago Press.

– 1992. *Defenders of the Faith: Inside Ultra-Orthodox Jewry*. New York: Schocken Books.

– 1995. *Portrait of American Jews: The Last Half of the 20th Century*. Seattle and London: University of Washington Press.

– n.d. "Young Judea Israel Discovery Tour: The View From Inside." Department of Sociology, Queens College, City University of New York.

Herberg, Will. 1955. *Protestant, Catholic, Jew*. New York: Doubleday.

Herman, Simon. 1970. *American Students in Israel*. New York: Cornell University Press.

Hochstein, Annette. 1986. *The Israel Experience: Educational Programs in Israel*. Jerusalem: Jewish Education Committee of the Jewish Agency.

Hoffman, Lawrence, ed. 1986. *The Land of Israel: Jewish Perspectives*. Notre Dame: University of Notre Dame Press.

Kamenetz, Rodger. 1994. *The Jew in the Lotus: A Poet's Rediscovery of Jewish Identity in Buddhist India*. San Francisco: Harper San Francisco.

Katriel, Tamar. 1991. *Communal Webs: Communication and Culture in Contemporary Israel*. Albany: SUNY Press.

– 1995. "Touring the Land: Trips and Hiking as Secular Pilgrimages in Israeli Culture." *Jewish Folklore and Ethnology Review* 17 (1–2): 6–13.

– 1997. *Performing the Past: A Study of Israeli Settlement Museums*. New Jersey: Lawrence Erlbaum Associates.

Katz, Shaul. 1985. "The Israeli Teacher-Guide: The Emergence and Perpetuation of a Role." *Annals of Tourism Research* 12: 49–72.

Kaufman, Debra. 1991. *Rachel's Daughters: Newly Orthodox Jewish Women*. New Brunswick, NJ: Rutgers University Press.

Klausner, Samuel. 1987. "What Is Conceptually Special about a Sociology of Jewry." *Contemporary Jewry* 8: 74–89.

Kondo, Dorinne. 1986. "Dissolution and Reconstitution of Self: Implications for Anthropological Epistemology." *Cultural Anthropology* 1: 74–88.

Krasz, Ernest and Gitta Tulea, eds. 1998. *Jewish Survival: The Identity Problem at the Close of the Twentieth Century.* New Brunswick, NJ: Transaction Books.

Kugelmass, Jack, ed. 1988. *Between Two Worlds: Ethnographic Essays on American Jewry.* New York: Cornell University Press.

Laqueur, Walter. 1962. *Young Germany: A History of the German Youth Movement.* London: Routledge and Kegan Paul.

Lavie, Smadar and Ted Swedenburg, eds. 1996. *Displacement, Diaspora, and Geographies of Identity.* Durham and London: Duke University Press.

Lavie, Smadar, Kirin Narayan, and Renato Rosaldo, eds. 1993. *Creativity/ Anthropology.* Ithaca: Cornell University Press.

Lerner, Michael. 1994. *Jewish Renewal: A Path to Healing and Transformation.* New York: G.P. Putnam's Sons.

Lévi-Strauss, Claude. 1963. *Structural Anthropology.* New York: Basic Books.

Liebman, Charles. 1973. *The Ambivalent American Jew: Politics, Religion and Family in American Jewish Life.* Philadelphia: Jewish Publication Society.

– 1988. *Deceptive Images: Toward a Redefinition of American Judaism.* New Brunswick, NJ: Transaction Books.

Liebman, Charles and Eliezer Don-Yehiya. 1983. *Civil Religion in Israel: Traditional Judaism and Political Culture in the Jewish State.* Berkeley: University of California Press.

Liebman, Charles and Steven Cohen. 1990. *Two Worlds of Judaism: The Israeli and American Experiences.* New Haven: Yale University Press.

Lipset, Seymour and Earl Raab. 1995. *Jews and the New American Scene.* Cambridge: Harvard University Press.

Lowenthal, David. 1996. *The Heritage Crusade and the Spoils of History.* London: Viking Press.

Luckmann, Thomas. 1967. *Invisible Religion: The Problem of Religion in Modern Society.* New York: MacMillan.

Malinowski, Bronislaw. 1967. *A Diary in the Strict Sense of the Term.* New York: Harcourt, Brace and World.

Malkki, Liisa. 1997. "National Geographic: The Rooting of Peoples and the Territorialization of National Identity among Scholars and Refugees." In *Culture, Power, Place: Explorations in Critical Anthropology,* ed. A. Gupta and J. Ferguson, 52–74. Durham and London: Duke University Press.

Michaels, Walter Benn. 1992. "Race into Culture: A Critical Genealogy of Cultural Identity." *Critical Inquiry* 18 (Summer): 679–80.

– 1995. *Our America: Nativism, Modernism and Pluralism.* Durham: Duke University Press.

Mittleberg, David. 1988. *Strangers in Paradise*. New Brunswick, NJ: Transaction Books.

Mittleberg, David and Lilach Lev Ari. 1995. "Jewish Identity, Jewish Education and Experience of the Kibbutz in Israel." *Journal of Moral Education* 24 (3): 327–44.

Moore, Laurence R. 1995. *Selling God: American Religion in the Marketplace of Culture*. New York: Oxford University Press.

Morgan, Edward. 1991. *The 60s Experience: Hard Lessons about Modern America*. Philadelphia: Temple University Press.

Morinis, Alan. 1992. "Introduction: The Territory of the Anthropology of Pilgrimage." In *Sacred Journeys: The Anthropology of Pilgrimage*, 1–28. Westport: Greenwood Press.

Narayan, Kirin. 1989. *Storytellers, Saints, and Scoundrels: Folk Narrative in Hindu Religious Teaching*. Philadelphia: University of Pennsylvania Press.

– 1993. "How Native Is a 'Native' Anthropologist?" *American Anthropologist* 95 (3): 671–86.

Neitz, Mary Jo. 1987. *Charisma and Community: A Study of Religious Commitment within the Charismatic Renewal*. New Brunswick, NJ: Transaction Books.

Phillips, Bruce. 1991. "Sociological Analysis of Jewish Identity." In *Jewish Identity in America*, ed. David Gordis and Yoav Ben-Horin, 3–26. Los Angeles: Wilstein Institute.

Prell, Riv-Ellen. 1989. *Prayer and Community: The Havurah in American Judaism*. Detroit: Wayne State University.

Putnam, Robert. 2000. *Bowling Alone: The Collapse and Revival of American Community*. New York: Simon and Schuster.

Rabinow, Paul. 1977. *Reflections on Fieldwork in Morocco*. Berkeley: University of California.

Reimer, Joseph. 1997. *Succeeding at Jewish Education: How One Synagogue Made It Work*. Philadelphia: Jewish Publication Society.

Roof, Wade Clark. 1999. *Spiritual Marketplace: Baby Boomers and the Remaking of American Religion*. Princeton: Princeton University Press.

Rosaldo, Renato. 1986. "From the Door of His Tent: The Fieldworker and the Inquisitor." In *Writing Culture: The Poetics and Politics of Ethnography*, ed.. James Clifford and George Marcus, 77–97. Berkeley: University of California.

– 1989. *Culture and Truth: The Remaking of Social Analysis*. Boston: Beacon Press.

Schiffman, Lisa. 1999. *Generation J*. San Francisco: Harper.

Schoem, David. 1989. *Ethnic Survival in America: An Ethnography of a Jewish Afternoon School*. Atlanta: Scholars Press.

Schoenfeld, Stuart. 1998. "On Theory and Methods in the Study of Jewish Identity." In *Jewish Survival: The Identity Problem at the Close of the Twentieth Century*, ed. Ernest Krasz and Gitta Tulea, 107–19. New Brunswick, NJ: Transaction Books.

Shaffir, William. 1983. "The Recruitment of 'Baalei Teshuvah' in a Jerusalem Yeshiva." *Jewish Journal of Sociology* 25 (1): 33–46.

Shapiro, Faydra. 2001. "Learning to Be a Diaspora Jew through the Israel Experience." *Studies in Religion* 30, (1): 23–34.

– 2003a. "Autobiography and Ethnography: Falling in Love with the Inner Other." *Method and Theory in the Study of Religion* 15 (2): 187–202.

– 2003b. "Making It Personal: Teaching Judaism to North American Jewish Youth in Israel." *Journal of Jewish Education* 69 (1): 46–56.

Sharot, Stephen. 1998. "Judaism and Jewish Ethnicity: Changing Interrelationships and Differentiations in the Diaspora and Israel." In *Jewish Survival: The Identity Problem at the Close of the Twentieth Century*, ed. Ernest Krasz and Gitta Tulea, 87–105. New Brunswick, NJ: Transaction Books.

Smith, Valene, ed. 1977. *Hosts and Guests: The Anthropology of Tourism*. Philadelphia: University of Pennsylvania Press.

Sollors, Werner. 1986. *Beyond Ethnicity: Consent and Descent in American Culture*. New York: Oxford University Press.

Stacey, Judith. 1983. "The New Conservative Feminism." *Feminist Studies* 9 (3): 559–83.

– 1987. "Sexism by a Subtler Name? Post-industrial Conditions and Postfeminist Consciousness in the Silicon Valley." *Socialist Review* 96 (November–December): 7–28.

Susser, Bernard and Charles Liebman. 1999. *Choosing Survival: Strategies for a Jewish Future*. New York: Oxford University Press.

Tipton, Steven. 1982. *Getting Saved from the Sixties: Moral Meaning in Conversion and Cultural Change*. Berkeley: University of California Press.

Tipton, Steven and Mary Douglas, eds. 1983. *Religion and American Spiritual Life in a Secular Age*. Boston: Beacon Press.

Turner, Victor. 1969. *The Ritual Process: Structure and Anti-Structure*. New York: Cornell University Press.

– 1974. *Dramas, Fields and Metaphors: Symbolic Action in Human Society*. Ithaca: Cornell University Press.

– 1985. "Liminality, Kabbalah, and the Media." *Religion* 15 (July): 205–17.

Turner, Victor and Edith Turner. 1978. *Image and Pilgrimage in Christian Culture*. New York: Columbia Press.

Turner, Victor and Edward Bruner, eds. 1986. *The Anthropology of Experience*. Urbana: University of Illinois Press.

Waxman, Charles. 1981. "The Fourth Generation Grows Up: The Contemporary American Jewish Community." *Annals of the American Academy of Political and Social Science* 454: 70–85.

– 1983. *America's Jews in Transition*. Philadelphia: Temple University.

Weissler, Chava. 1989. *Making Judaism Meaningful: Ambivalence and Tradition in a Havurah Community*. New York: AMS Press.

Werbner, Pnina and Tariq Modood, eds. 1997. *Debating Cultural Hybridity: Multi-Cultural Identities and the Politics of Anti-Racism*. London: Zed Books.

Wertheimer, Jack, ed. 1993. *The Uses of Tradition: Jewish Continuity in the Modern Era*. New York: Jewish Theological Seminary of America.

– 1997. "Politics and Jewish Giving." *Commentary* 104 (6): 32–6.

Wertheimer, Jack, Charles Liebman, and Steven Cohen. 1996. "How to Save American Jews." *Commentary* (January): 47–51.

Woocher, Jonathan. 1986. *Sacred Survival: The Civil Religion of American Jews*. Bloomington: Indiana University Press.

– 1994. *Toward a "Unified Field Theory" of Jewish Continuity*. New York: Jewish Education Service of North America.

Wuthnow, Robert. 1998. *After Heaven: Spirituality in America Since the 1950s*. Berkeley: University of California Press.

Wyschogrod, Michael. 1971. "Faith and the Holocaust: A Review Essay of Emil Fackenheim's *God's Presence in History*." *Judaism* 20 (3): 286–94.

Zenner, Walter, ed. 1988. *Persistence and Flexibility: Anthropological Perspectives on the American Jewish Experience*. Albany: SUNY Press.

Zerubavel, Yael. 1994. "The Death of Memory and the Memory of Death: Masada and the Holocaust as Historical Metaphors." *Representations* 45 (Winter): 72–100.

– 1995. *Recovered Roots: Collective Memory and the Making of Israeli National Tradition*. Chicago: University of Chicago Press.

Zisenwine, David and David Schers, eds. 1997. *Making a Difference: Jewish Identity and Education*. Israel: Tel Aviv University School of Education.

Index